THE DISCOVERING YOUR ESSENCE PATH SERIES

Timeline Collapse
& Universal Ascension

The Future of Third Dimensional Earth and Fifth Dimensional Terra

E. M. Nicolay and H. L. Jang

A Handbook to Higher Levels of Spiritual Guidance

Forethought Publishing
Bernville, Pennsylvania

Forethought Publishing
Post Office Box 576
Bernville, PA 19506

Copyright © 2015 by E. M. Nicolay and H.L. Jang
Cover design by FTC Group
Text design by FTC Group

All rights reserved. This book may not be reproduced in whole or in part without written permission from the publisher, except by a reviewer who may quote brief passages in a review; nor may any part of this book be reproduced, stored in a retrieval system, or transmitted in any form or by any means electronic, mechanical, photocopying, recording, or other, without written permission form the publisher.

Contents

Introduction   i

Part One   **The Probable Future of the Third Universal Dimension and Planet Earth**   2

Chapter 1   Ascension and the Collapse of Current Third Dimensional Space-Time   4

Chapter 2   A Third Universal Dimension Future   29

Chapter 3   The East to West Passage of Energetic Flow and the Beginning of Our Narrative on the Future of the Third Dimensional Timeline   45

Chapter 4   The Unraveling of North America and Failure of the United States on the Continuing Third Dimensional Timeline   58

Chapter 5   The Emergence of the Eurasian Enlightenment   73

Chapter 6   More About the Unraveling of America on the Third Dimensional Timeline   86

Chapter 7   A Timeline in Turmoil and Beyond   96

Chapter 8   The Weaponization of Nature Leading to Catastrophic Earth Changes and Occurrences   116

Contents

Part Two	**The Future of the Fifth Universal Dimension and Planet Terra**	**152**
Chapter 9	The Non-Linear Movement of Time and Space	154
Chapter 10	The Ascension Mechanics of a Universal Dimension	163
Chapter 11	Terra: Earth at a Higher Oscillation in a Fifth Dimensional Time-Space Wave	177
Chapter 12	The Tertiary Pole Structure of Fifth Dimensional Terra	183
Chapter 13	Reality Manifestation on Fifth Dimensional Terra and Terran Societal Structure	193
Chapter 14	The Evolving Characteristics of Terran Human Angelic Incarnations	225
Chapter 15	The Current and Future Direction of Terran Civilization	246
Chapter 16	The Multidimensional Karmic Influence on the Future of Terra	262
Chapter 17	A Parting Word About Possible and Probable Futures	308

Contents

Appendix Abbreviated Third Universal Dimensional Earth Timeline   320

Other Essence Path Books   328

Book Three of The Essence Path Series:
"The System Lord and the Twelve Dimensions: New Revelations Concerning the Dimensional Shift of 2012-2250 and the Evolution of Human Angelics" Summary   329

Book Two of The Essence Path Series:
"Fear, Faith & Physical Reality" Summary   330

Book One of The Essence Path Series:
"Your Essencepath Path and Other Quintessential Phenomena" Summary   331

 **INTRODUCTION**

What is the future? Is it a predetermined logistic, a place set in time and space where everyone arrives at some predestined point? Is it a specific perspective that people discover along the way while focused in a present moment? Is it a coordinate that each is headed towards and will someday pass through? Or is the future something that is malleable, permeable and changeable depending upon the current space, time and dimension where you find yourself. These are questions that everyone might do well to explore, and this is particularly true at a moment when the actual time and dimension in which you have existed for millennia is collapsing, or more aptly put, evolving, as the current time and dimension reaches a new vibrational definition. It is there in that new vibrational frequency that the coming world, a new dimension and, consequently, a new timeline await you.

In this book, we would like to explore with you the notion of where you are headed within the context of newly emerging timelines. More specifically, we wish to explore with you the events of two probable future time-space scenarios, projected outward and based on the movement and frequency of the current dimensional timeline's collapse and regeneration.

The period you are in could be said to be a true fork in the road for both you and your reality. One direction, or timeline if you please, will provide for a continued Third Dimensional reality, one that is actually the evolution of the Second Universal Dimension as it merges with and becomes the current Third Dimensional space-time you now know. The other timeline and future will follow the evolution of the current Third Dimensional timeline as much of what it contains raises its oscillation and vibrational quality to become the continuation of a Fifth Dimensional reality.

The direction, or timeline, that each of you will follow shall depend in large part on your own Soul matrix association, your present level of growth and consciousness and your ability to hold higher dimensional frequencies - light energy - when in physical incarnation. As we have said in the past, Ascension on the part of entities and their associated Soul matrix is a matter of individual effort and choice, and is not usually accidental.

True time, not the unit of measurement but the space wave it represents, is a spiral wave of photon energy that could be compared to a groove or wormhole, which forms the dimensional space that surrounds you and, for the most part, the Solar System (and sometimes even the Galaxy) of which you are a part. Within it you incarnate and life is generated. You know this as physical reality. As one universal dimension or wave collapses, it evolves by merging with and becoming the continuation of the next universal dimension. In the case of a universal dimension, the process is one where an evolving space-time wave raises (or lowers as the case may be) its resonance to the point of merging with another space-time wave. In doing so, one Universal dimension becomes the continuation of the next, and so on and so forth through the universal structure. Generally, this is known as Ascension.

Those entities that have Ascended in conjunction with this space-time wave, the former inhabitants (incarnates) of the prior space-time dimensional wave, are now potentially able to incarnate within the new, higher dimension. This process ensures the evolution of the entities by allowing further and more expansive opportunities for growth and higher consciousness as they proceed on their long journey through dimensional incarnations making the way back to "Source." But it's important to remember that this is not a universal path, and the process remains a highly individualized evolution. Those whose Soul matrices are not able to incarnate at the higher dimensional resonance, or more precisely, those whose consciousness is not sufficient to animate incarnations within physical bodies that now exist at a much higher frequency (in a much higher space-time wave motion), remain within incarnations in the prior space-time wave coordinate.

Of course, to be clear, this prior space-time wave coordinate is not truly the same one that existed before the universal dimension's Ascension and even though the individual entity has not Ascended and finds everything unchanged, in an unperceived manner the dimension itself has actually evolved. Thus those same entities are now incarnating in a newly formed *version* of third universal density that appears similar but actually is the Ascended Second Universal Dimension, which is now resonating at Third Dimensional oscillation. Even so, for the most part the entities that do not raise their consciousness sufficiently to Ascend will continue their learning experiences blissfully ignorant of the fact that Universal Ascension has taken place. To them, for all intent and purpose, they are simply continuing incarnations in the same (albeit newly formed) Third Universal Dimension.

What we have come to discuss with you then is what you may expect ahead on either the road that is the continuation of Third Dimensional existence, for those of you remaining within the same space-time wave coordinate of Third Dimensional Earth, or, for those who Ascend into a higher level of vibrational existence, what you may expect within the new, higher dimensional reality that you will find in incarnations on Fifth Dimensional Terra. For those who have not followed our prior explorations with you concerning universal multi-dimensional overlap, be aware that Earth, or different versions of the entity known to you as Earth, exist at various overlapping dimensional levels and though you currently find yourselves focused and tuned into the Third Universal Dimension where the planet is known as Earth, it is no less real or unreal than its Fifth Dimensional counterpart, which is known as Terra, or its seventh dimensional overlay, the planet Gaia. Each of these dimensional versions of Earth, as well as accompanying versions found throughout all twelve of the known Universal dimensions, has its own physics, oscillation, motion, spin, space-time wave and physical form of reality, and while there is substantial sharing and overlap amongst them, they exist independently as well as uniformly within the universal structure.

We do not exaggerate when we say that the two space-time outlooks that are the subject of this book, the probable timeline of Third Dimensional Earth on the one hand and Fifth Dimensional Terra on the other, are vastly different. In fact, following one you will find a continuation and even a worsening of the fears and devastation being perpetuated in your modern world today. Following the other, a higher vibrational resonance heralds what those before you have called the Golden Age of Humans, and in fact we would go as far as to say that the period of enlightenment prophesized through the ages by your seers is predominantly a glimpse of life on Fifth Dimensional Terra. The majority of Human Angelic incarnations on Earth today will Ascend to new cycles of incarnation on Terra, the Fifth Dimensional version of Earth, as part of their continuing process of consciousness growth. Moreover, the period being experienced both on Third Dimensional Earth and Fifth Dimensional Terra can be said to open up a new era for all Human Angelics.

Is the future monolithic and static as so many think? Is it carved in stone or preordained by an Anthropomorphic God-like Being, as many others are led to believe? To both these questions we would firmly answer, "No." But we would add the caveat that there is in fact a potential for determining probable futures based upon the current choices perpetuated within the present moment, your *Now*. These probable future courses, which tend to be the result of the merging of possible and parallel future timelines into one lead timeline, are the futures that those who are termed psychic or intuitive are usually able to discern. However, such discernment should not be confused with the belief that this means the future is permanently fixed within this or that probability. Nor does it mean that it has been pre-determined for or by you and certainly not by some elusive superior or higher Being. It simply implies that the *probability* (the future) is being reshaped constantly based on the "*Now*" in concert with the impact of possible and parallel futures. The *probable* future is constantly in the process of shifting, changing and reverberating backwards and forwards (in the time wave).

That said, what we would like to explore with you here the *probable* future events that will befall an Earth remaining within Third Dimensional vibration, where you are currently incarnated. In addition, we will take a look with you at the *probable* future events of Fifth Dimensional Terra, Earth at a higher dimensional resonance within its own space-time wave and following its own timeline. Part One of this book provides you with a brief description of the Ascension process (found in more detail in our former book, "The System Lords and the Twelve Dimensions"), which is currently underway and will ultimately merge second dimensional Earth so that it becomes Third Dimensional Earth and becomes the continuation of the current space-timeline you know

now. It will also provide you with specific coming world events over the course of the next several hundred year history on the Third Dimensional timeline, providing particular truths concerning an emerging (and much prophesized) coming world conflict and the geo-political changes that will result on Earth.

Part Two of our book will provide you with some insight into the probable future (based on choices and karma reflected through the dimensions and coming out of the "Now") of the Fifth Dimensional space timeline for "Terra." We will provide you with what to expect as you begin your potential future incarnations in a Fifth Dimensional reality once you have *Ascended* your consciousness and vibrational signature, a prerequisite for maintaining physical incarnations in the Fifth Dimension. In all cases, please understand that what we shall provide you with here is not specific information related to the personal and private incarnations of each entity, but the mass consciousness, vibrational make-up and physical properties of the new Fifth Dimensional space-time line, as well as the creative forces that will be available and prevalent within that probable future destiny.

Regardless of the time-line or universal dimension we will discuss, we do so in order to assist you to understand the vastly important choices before you today with respect to the on-going Ascension process, the Ascension of Human Angelic Soul matrices and your own physical incarnations.

As you shall discover in Part One of our book, the destiny of Third Dimensional Earth, permeable and changeable as it may be, is problematic at best and potentially will prove the most challenging period in the Modern Era (defined by your historians as beginning in approximately 10,000 BCE), a short segment within Earth's long Third Dimensional history. Preferable to this destiny, as many will no doubt agree, is the information contained in Part Two of our book, which will detail the awakening of human consciousness and the wondrous incarnations awaiting Angelic Human Souls on Fifth Dimensional Terra (an independent galactic reality not to be confused with the notion of "heaven" or paradise currently found in your religious and esoteric philosophies).

We will make every attempt to describe for you the related learning, growth, political, social and cultural structures and probable events in each of these time-space realms. In doing so, particularly with regard to the current and emerging Third Dimensional timeline, we will provide you with more revelations related to the symbolism and work of the universal "System Lords," specifically the real life incarnations and work of the ninth dimensional Masters we have termed the "Physical System Lords" and the "Spiritual System Lords." This will include details of those Masters' struggle to guide Third Dimensional human consciousness through what has been termed by Prophets in the past as the coming "Armageddon," an imminent and poignant time destined to effect all of Third Dimensional Earth, changing the nature of your current world.

We do not however, wish to imply that we are randomly making prophesies, or merely providing you with predictions common to your mythologies, for this is not the case and, indeed, from a free-will perspective not truly accurate and, thus, not really possible. We wish only to demonstrate the *probable* space-time line trajectory that is relevant based on the current position and space-time wave coordinates. We will do so by exploring Third Dimensional Earth's current vibrational quality, its mass consciousness backdrop and the choices being made daily by each and every one of you, as well as the quantum group energies existing around you within the "Now."

In every case, these things are subject to change based on innumerable possibilities, choices, parallel futures and energetic influences. Additionally, there is a matter of specific dates and times relevant to your current time measurement that we might use, which could be said to be problematic at best. Many intuitive predictors of your future, even those with genuine abilities, are widely admonished when what they see transpiring at a given point does not happen at the actual measured moment it is anticipated, even when the event is accurate but it occurs years before or years later than expected. This is generally so because actual space-time is in a constant state of flux and change, despite the fact that your measurement of time is for the most part on an inadequate and linear calculation based on what you perceive as fixed points. However, the workings of the Universe, celestial and planetary rotations and the motion that measured time is based upon are not as fixed as your science or even your astrology leads you to believe.

What happens when those rotations and movements are naturally or energetically altered in spite of your measurement? Well, space-time changes even though the linear measurements you use do not. In such a case what was May on your calendar two hundred years ago might, as an example, be closer to July today even though you are still using a month of May designation. Likewise, what was the year 2035 on the time continuum of ten years ago might today have shifted to a point closer to the measurement you would now identify as 2056 or 2075, though it is still considered to be 2035 by your measures. Therefore, what was "predicted" for 2035 might not occur now until your year 2075 (40 years later), and similarly what was expected in 2075, altered by the dynamic interface of choice, karma, free will and the spiraling of space-time, could as easily occur closer to the linear time measurement of say 2056. Any attempt to designate when the event would occur using the established measurements therefore, would inevitably prove to be wrong or seem by your measure to be incorrect. For the most part, in the analysis of probable events seen on the timeline substance rather than time period measurement is generally the more important consideration.

Similarly, as we have attempted to explain to you previously, there are always events, both within the scope of a Soul's personal journey as well as within the scope of broader universal situations that reverberate indeed backwards and forwards in time. These events are interconnected or in close proximity on the spiral of time, particularly within certain dimensions such as your own. This is a result of Soul Matrix involvement and the accompanying energetic balancing principles of karma and polarity, among other things, that continually pull upon them. Due to this, what befalls one event in time can actually alter and affect what is being played out at another point on the timeline and changes can therefore occur since these events are not static but dynamic in nature. Remembering that all time, or rather events in time, are happening essentially simultaneously at different coordinates on the timeline, one begins to understand that it is possible for an event at one point in time to be altered drastically based simply on what is happening at another seemingly disinterested but actually connected point on the timeline. Thus, though rare once a *probable* future thought form has generated sufficiently, it is possible for changes in terms of substance to occur. Although these will undoubtedly have a strong resemblance to the event originally foreseen, what is "predicted" or "prophesized" can have variations within it that sometimes render the actual event difficult to recognize based on the viewer's focus in the present moment.

We do not intend this as a disclaimer, but offer it only as an explanation as to why events can change both in terms of their time logistic and in terms of their makeup. While we will agree that there are many that would wish to mislead you, intentionally or not, or generate fear with their predictive offerings, it should be reiterated that those assisting you with legitimate intuitive abilities are often disbelieved for these very reasons. Be assured however, that there are many universal events based on the steady progress of past, present and future free will choices that have been made that in a sense are "destined" to occur. There are also ample current karmic and energetic factors that ensure, or predestine if you prefer, the materialization of certain future events at one point or another. We have attempted to focus on such timeline events.

Though we will try as best as possible to provide you with details and date approximations related to your current linear time measurements, please be aware that actual fluctuations are always present. Be aware therefore, that occurrences as well as specific date designations are subject to drift forward or backwards on the timeline depending upon the various alignments and combinations of free will, mass consciousness, natural energetics and actual time-space fluctuations.

While much is subject to change, what will not be altered are the basic principles of Ascension as an evolutionary process as we have detailed (see "The System Lords and the Twelve Dimensions"), or the fact that ultimately many of you will end your cycles of incarnation on Third Dimensional Earth as that lead timeline collapses and a new one forms. If you are "harvestable," in terms of your consciousness and vibrational quality, and willing, in terms of the choice of you and your Higher Self, very soon the majority of you will begin incarnations in a Fifth Dimensional reality on a Fifth Dimensional version of Earth known as Terra.

If we attempt the undertaking of a book such as this at all, it is to show you the multidimensional aspects of time, the purpose behind monumental events that affect you and your environment and the enormous potential inherent in your Soul's Ascension. Rest assured that we shall make every attempt to ground you in the higher purpose and universal reasons driving this great process rather than any way generating fear, especially as it regards the many possible challenges and changes faced on the continuing Third Dimensional Earth timeline.

Those of you already resonating at a higher vibrational frequency and achieving a more enlightened consciousness will naturally gravitate towards the information we provide in Part Two of this book related to the Golden Era of Human Angelics and life as it exists on Fifth Dimensional Terra. This is as it should be, for though continued incarnations within Third Dimensional reality might allow growth opportunities for those in need of lower vibrational and karmic lessons or skills, Ascension into a Fifth Dimensional reality on Terra should be considered the preferable and, certainly, the more joyous "future" to which you and your Soul wish to aspire. We wish you great joy and success in that undertaking.

PART ONE

THE PROBABLE FUTURE OF THE THIRD UNIVERSAL DIMENSION AND PLANET EARTH

 **CHAPTER 1**

ASCENSION AND THE COLLAPSE OF CURRENT THIRD DIMENSIONAL SPACE-TIME

As we have said in the past, Ascension is an evolutionary process, universal in nature and applicable (at one point or another) to each and every galaxy, solar system, Soul and Being within the known universal structure. It is in this way that the twelve universal dimensions we have described reach potential, expand and fold each into the other. In particular, Ascension is the process by which universal dimensions mature and evolve to greater dimensional frequencies in a never-ending return to Source, which resides at and even above the Twelfth Universal Dimension. When a universal dimension, which has the inherent properties of both lower and higher dimensional levels contained within it, evolves to the next highest level that its frequency and consciousness permits, it does so in a manner that in many respects remains one of the great mysteries of being for all those journeying through universal dimensional awareness.

While it is not necessary to understand details related to the mechanics that permit shifting and melding of the space-time waves that define dimensional boundaries, we do wish to emphasize that universal dimensions exist in harmony and unison with each other, and in many cases there is substantial overlap and even interaction. In basic terms, universal dimensions exist as divergent wave frequencies that emanate outwards from Source – All That Is, or God, if you prefer. Distinction and definition within these waves is defined by space-time mechanics, while much of the creative process within a particular dimension is derived from polarity, scalar momentum and motion, as we have formerly explained. For the most part, motion within the universal structure, the phenomenon of universal spin as we prefer to term it, regulates and is regulated by the principles and properties of matter and anti-matter, perhaps loosely recognizable to you in some of your basic concepts concerning gravity and anti gravity, which in large part remains an erroneous concept at best.

However, the concept of matter and anti-matter, which could be described as a kind of universal gravity and anti-gravity system of sorts, has a good deal to do with not only what is physically created in a universal dimension but also what is discharged through it as well. This includes the seeming passage of time and space that you experience. Let us explain. Polarities are formed and generated by "spin" that causes friction universally and energetically. This spin not only provides the basis for physical creation, it provides the on-going mass motion that you are aware of within your Solar System, your Galaxy and the Universe at large. When the resonant qualities, or "spin," of a particular dimension have reached a specific frequency and vibrational state, either through manipulation or natural universal energies, it begins the process of Ascension. Ultimately, this changes a dimension's vibrational signature, which further alters its physical make-up and especially its space-time wave and timeline coordinates. Once the spin has reached a certain point of oscillation, generally one that is concordant with the next dimensional vibration, the dimensional wave becomes synchronistic with the neighboring resonant energy (dimensional space-time wave) emanating from universal God Source. When this occurs, the energetic wave is transformed as it is merged and propelled into the next dimensional resonance, actually becoming *one* with its predecessor.

The photon energy that travels through a solar system is transferred into the system via its solar body. That energy's precursor originates from what we shall term "Hyper-Space," from outside of the particular dimension in which the Sun itself exists. This originating Source energy could be said to pass through a Sun's heart to become the core of creation, and the light generated becomes a vehicle for Source energy coming into the solar system that it is passing over and through. This energetic process, and more importantly these energy waves, scalar, electromagnetic and other, play a significant role in generating the space-time wave that ultimately defines the dimension that you know.

Now the energy responsible for spin propulsion, and therefore polarity, like the kind emanating from a solar body, is energy that can be said to be "matter-oriented." In other words, the solar body of a system, your Sun for example, can be said to emit "Source" energy (particles) that acts as the positive polar and creative Being, the "matter-engine" if you will within a system. Thus, there is a strong association with deity projected upon the Sun by so many ancient and modern cultures in your world.

But the energy a solar body, your Sun, emits also can be said to have a polar opposite that exists in direct opposition to it. That opposition could be called a solar system's "anti-matter engine." Simply put, you know these "anti-matter engines" as Black Holes. A solar body therefore, and in fact groups of solar bodies and stars within a specific space and time (although the number and influence vary greatly according to the galaxy, the time-space continuum and the dimension, among many other things), act as counter-point to the energy of the Black Holes within galaxies throughout the Universe, and the gravitational pull and polarity of the Black Holes are the antithesis of the Solar bodies.

Now visualize this using any basic polarity or duality model you choose. The Sun acts as the positive, Yang or male aspect of a particular system. It is balanced by that system's Black Hole, which represents the negative, Yin or female aspects of the model. Likewise, the Sun emits and propels energy coming from Hyper Space, or Source, into and through the system, whereas the Black Hole pulls the energy that has been emitted forth so that it washes through a dimension and is then returned out of the system back to Source. The Sun projects through the system the building blocks of space-time, which defines the dimension and its resonance, and the Black Hole, via its immense gravitational pull, absorbs the energy that reaches it after it has been used throughout the system for the purpose of creation. The energetic particles that constitute the dimension, as well as all matter created therein, is originally sent into the system via the Sun, and all energetic particles within the system are ultimately pulled through it and recycled back to Source by the Black Holes.

Although not technically identified by your science as such, or consistent with your current definitions of Black Holes (which you consider to be burnt out stars and, though they can sometimes be, are not limited to such), the "Black Hole" that can be said to predominate in your Milky Way Galaxy and which has the greatest influence in defining your Solar System's current dimension, is known as the Dark or Great Rift. Distant though it may seem, this rift acts as the balancing force, or the anti-gravity, anti-matter vehicle, that counter synchs with your Sun.

The Great Rift acts as such not only for your Sun but also for a vast number of other solar bodies within your Galaxy, all of which share the same dimensional reality. Your dimension is constantly acted upon by the gravitational pull of this particular Black Hole, and in a manner of speaking, energy constantly pouring into your system via your Sun -- energy that is utilized in the space-time creation process within your sphere -- is also being constantly pulled through it and discharged via the Great Rift. This is why many ancient mythologies identified this area of the Galaxy by various designations that referred back to their concept of "Source," including calling it the Gates of Heaven, the Eye of God, the Jaws of Hell and the Center of the Universe, to cite a few.

You are currently in the process of receiving new energetic impulses, and a higher level of photon energy is being emitted by your Sun and entering into your particular solar system. This has to do in part with the Earth's current positioning in the Galaxy, particularly as it regards its movement vis-a-vis the Great Rift. As specific alignments are made between the Galaxy solar bodies and the Galaxy's primordial Black Hole, the Great Rift in this case, higher energy levels can be said to pour directly from your Sun since they are being pulled forcefully by and into the Black Hole due to the solar system's new alignments. The energetic forces are being washed across you Solar System in a much more pervasive manner than is usual.

As this occurs, the space-time wave is, in a manner of speaking, being sucked directly into the Black Hole, and because of the nature of Universal propulsion and Ascension, a new space-time wave is being generated and created simultaneously with the collapse of the former space-time wave. The old wave -- time-wave, energy, time-space continuum or whatever you would like to term it – together with the old paradigms held within the quantum energy fields housed inside the dimension, are being expelled at an ever more rapid pace, just as a new space-time wave is being generated to replace it.

This is the technical reason that the measure of time appears to be speeding up for you, as the continuum you have known in the past collapses prior to the adherence of a new space-time (dimensional) coordinate that will replace it. There are other issues as well, some that have even been noted by your world. First of all, though global warming is a definite trend, you might consider that this is a phenomenon related to the natural heating up of your entire solar system as photon energy from your Sun increases during this process. This is not to excuse the fact that human culture does in fact contribute to environmental warming trends on Earth occurring because of a misuse of the planet and the environment's resources. Nor does it mean that this combination of factors is not consequential, and it should be remembered that anytime the planet entity upon which you reside is not respected and cared for, a dangerous potential for challenging karmic experiences exists. In truth however, the most significant current cause of your planet and solar system's warming directly correlates to the current positioning of your solar system within the Galaxy, its alignment with the Great Rift and the extensive new photon energies emanating from your Sun.

Moreover, generally when such a period occurs, there is the risk of substantial trauma within a particular planetary system based on the forceful photon and energetic pull being exerted upon and through it. This trauma is usually minimized by the fact that there is simultaneously an energetic elevation of all lives and Beings within the time wave in question, and each time wave carries with it new forming principles that raise the existing universal level to the next grade or energetic environment.

In such a case, Beings such as yourselves become "tuned-into" these phenomena and you are thus better prepared, wherever and whenever possible, to counter the physical devastation that is being created through higher awareness and the creation of your personal reality. In some instances, entire creature populations become extinct, sensing the changing reality and in many cases choosing to cycle off lifetimes on the planet awaiting the conclusion of these energetic transformations. Such is the case with the ever-increasing extinctions being experienced currently worldwide. At the least, generally all Beings incarnated within the system become better attuned to knowing where not to be and when not to be there within the context of ordinary daily existence. This is ultimately a life-preservation safeguard transmitted through the population's higher consciousness via their inner knowledge, genetic coding, thought-form catastrophobia and related energetic connections.

At a dimensional level, this same Ascension energy is exactly how what was previously second dimensional in nature is raised and evolves to become Third Dimensional, and how Third Dimensional reality is raised into Fourth Dimensional existence, and so on and so forth. To be clear, universal dimensions usually evolve into their predecessors and become unified with them while replacing them in an evolutionary manner, but linear advancement higher to higher is not always the case. That is particularly true as it regards a universal dimension that previously attained the attributes of the next highest dimensional level only to lose its vibrational quality and fall back to a lower dimensional resonance, which has occurred on rare occasions. Indeed, this was the case in the prior Ascension period leading to the current Earth period in which you find yourselves now.

As we described in our previous book, "The System Lords and The Twelve Dimensions," there was a time when the world you know as Earth, and the solar system of which you are part, was in fact dimensionally elevated and was Fourth Dimensional in nature. In fact, at the time of the last grand evolutionary Ascension period, there was a split that occurred in the time wave that pulled the dimension down from fourth to solid third density resonance.

This is commonly referred to within your religious and ancient mythologies as "The Fall." It was at this time that Human Angelics (interpreted as the "angels" of your religious myths) experienced a kind of de-evolution that resulted in literally a "Fall" from consciousness leading to a fall from Fourth to Third Dimensional resonance. It is within that denser Third Dimensional reality, the current one, that Human Angelics have incarnated ever since.

Thus, what you are currently experiencing is the reemergence of Earth's higher universal space-time wave and dimension. In truth, due to this many Fourth Dimensional characteristics are already being glimpsed within Earth's current Third Density reality, and we might add that it is for this reason that most Human Angelics incarnated in the Third Dimension currently will find their energy and consciousness raised to Fifth Dimensional resonance as the outcome of this current Ascension period. The extraordinary energies and alignments available during this Ascension period will transition the established space-time wave over the course of approximately the coming two hundred to three hundred years and merge it into what will become the continuation of a Fifth Dimensional timeline.

As we have said many times, Ascension is a matter of choice as well as a matter of consciousness. In this respect, there are some Human Angelic and other Soul matrices and entities currently incarnated in the collapsing current Third Universal Dimension reality that will continue on, out of need or desire, with incarnations in the emerging Third Dimensional space-time wave, which is being generated out of the evolution of the prior Second Universal Dimension. These entities will continue, if you will, to incarnate and exist within Third Dimensional consciousness, experiencing lifetimes and karma, sometime more intense than before, in ways similar to now. These entities, for reasons related to growth and known only to them, prefer not to Ascend during the current cycle.

Simultaneously, at this juncture the current Third Universal Dimension is destined to evolve and merge, becoming the Fourth and Fifth Universal Dimension. The creation of *that* new timeline will mean expanded experiences for incarnation by those Human Angelic Soul matrices wishing to Ascend, and many of these Souls have already begun incarnations on the higher frequency Fifth Dimensional Terra, despite the fact that Ascension shall take many more years to complete both with respect to life on Earth and life on Terra. This evolution will afford Human Angelic Souls vast new opportunities for growth and increases in consciousness. That new emerging and evolving time-space continuum is the world we shall explore in depth later in this book. Prior to those discussions however, we must explore the continuation of a Third Universal Dimensional timeline and world, even though in reality it also represents a new energetic space-time wave that continues on, one that is perhaps slightly different what you would choose to envision based on a lowered vibrational quality and direction.

A question that might be asked at this particular point is: "What happens to the current Earth, and the Souls incarnated there who have chosen to Ascend at the point when Ascension definitively occurs?" Our answer to this is that *the* Ascension process is not a momentary occurrence, and there is no grand "event" that can be identified as the Ascension. Thus, those waiting to be "beamed up" by alien ships or those expecting a rapture-like event may be sorely disappointed.

In fact, Ascension can be likened to the process of evolution known currently by your science that requires specific impetus, motion and space -- what you sense as the passage of time -- to occur. But rest assured that for most, the current or subsequent lifetime might be all that is required before personal Ascension is achieved. Thus our real answer to such a question is that for the most part Beings currently existing on a Third Dimensional Earth, even those wishing to Ascend, will continue to do so and complete the course of their prescribed lifetimes. Naturally however, they will do so in ways that are preparatory for them through the possibility of more enlightened realities (even in a Third Dimensional environment). The expanded energies coming from Source (the Sun) will allow these individuals, through their genetic coding and DNA awakening, greater alignment with higher consciousness, attunement to a higher spiritual reality and access to their own Truth.

Still, be aware that for now those entities destined by virtue of greater consciousness to Ascend to a higher dimensional realm shall exist side by side with the entities that *will* not necessarily Ascend. The latter will simply continue on in incarnations within some version of Third Universal Dimension reality they know now, while Ascending Souls shall not reincarnate within a physical Third Dimensional Earth vibration any longer. They will either await a time for Fifth Dimensional incarnation residing in the higher astral planes (sublevels) of the Universal Third Dimension, or they will proceed directly to Fifth Dimensional incarnations on Terra as soon as they are ready to do so.

Thus as this process continues, those entities being born into your world will at some point no longer be entities related to Souls that are destined, by choice and by consciousness, to emerge and incarnate into lifetimes within a new (to them) Fifth Dimensional reality. Instead, the entities that will be born within Third Universal Dimension reality in your linear future will exclusively be incarnations of Souls who wish to continue on, for whatever reasons, within Third Density. In this manner, over the course of approximately the coming one hundred to three hundred of your Earth years a practical and complete divergence and split will occur, with some remaining behind and continuing on within Third Dimensional reality and others, those Human Angelics ready for Ascension, evolving as the dimension merges with Fourth and Fifth Dimensional reality

Ultimately in the not too distant future, the emerging Third Universal Dimension, which remember at some point is actually the second dimensional reality elevated to a Third Universal Dimension vibration, will be exclusively inhabited by entities who retain and hold lower resonant frequencies. It will be populated by those entities, through choice or through need, that wish to continue to experience physical lifetimes in a lower dimensional realm where specific creative and karmic opportunities are available to them. Those entities that wish to be part of the current "schism," though they may continue for the present and though they will complete current lifetimes within Third Dimensional reality, will ultimately find themselves Ascended into new lifetimes that are based in Fifth Density. As this process of evolution progresses, what you know as the Third Universal Dimension will appear to continue on its current march unchanged, even though it will be altered imperceptibly to those still incarnating within it.

To explore this further, we must first look at current events being experienced in the Third Universal Dimension prior to Ascension and demonstrate for you the polarities and influences gaining access and strength in the collapsing space-time wave. We would like to look particularly at those influences coming from the life incarnations of the System Lords, those Ninth Dimensional Avatars and enlightened Beings that have chosen to return to Third Dimensional Earth incarnations in order to assist that dimension and its inhabitants in their growth. Such an analysis will assist you in understanding the most probable course in terms of events and world situations that the current timeline is following.

We begin that conversation as it relates to the symbolism of Christ and Anti-Christ consciousness, as well as the mythology of Armageddon, as it applies to the continuing Third Universal Dimensional time wave. But first let us quickly discuss the important concept of polarity again, which we have discussed at great length in our previous book. Polarity, as we demonstrated amply in our description of the polarity balances exemplified by a Galactic Solar System and a Black Hole, is a basic and fundamental construct of the Universe, one that is relevant, more or less, in almost every dimension. It is interesting to note that dual polarity (be aware that in many higher dimensions multi-polarity is more the norm), seen represented in the concepts of Yin and Yang, good and evil, north and south or positive and negative, also reveals itself as a principal precept of lower universal dimensions. This includes the Third Universal Dimension of which your current world and you are part.

In addition to this, the concept of polarity can also be seen embodied in the existence of incarnations of highly conscious universal entities, the two principal among these being those we termed that originate from the "Spiritual System Lord" and the "Physical System Lord." These enlightened Beings, and the many simultaneous physical persons and lifetimes that emanate from them, act as a fundamental counter point and balance each to the other. For the most part, the Spiritual System Lord incarnates in lifetimes to bring spiritual awakening and higher consciousness to the world, whereas the Physical System Lord's incarnations and personages are concerned with bringing about world geo-political and cultural growth, setting the stage for mass consciousness and a backdrop against which spiritual enlightenment and higher consciousness can evolve. Ideally, you see the symbolism of their efforts represented as the basis of your western Christ and Anti-Christ mythology, and we would even suggest that both Eastern and Western spiritual mythologies (Christ/Anti-Christ or Yin/Yang, as examples) are unconsciously derived from an inner knowing of the System Lord's relevance to most Human Angelic incarnates.

Naturally the concept and appellation we employ (System Lords) should not be understood as a description of actual "Time Lords," Overlords, Gods or rulers running any particular dimension. Instead, the System Lords should be experienced as a universal truth related to the concept of polarity, and these Higher Beings could in fact be considered the embodiment of that concept. They are Avatars of high universal consciousness expressing themselves through incarnations within lower dimensions for the purpose of shaping a dimensional realm in order to create parameters and opportunities for growth that all entities incarnated within that reality are able to experience. (We remind you that the actual physical incarnations of a System Lord are not necessarily conscious of their origins, and in many cases each incarnation lives lifetimes with goals, attributes and aspirations not unlike the vast majority of other Human Angelic Souls incarnated in a particular world or space-time).

It is through polarity, and more specifically the work of the System Lords in organizing the groundwork for mass conscious events that growth for incarnates of a lower dimensional reality is generally maximized and achieved. It is also in this manner that Soul matrices are able to choose specific positions in time and space within which they wish to incarnate. As an example, a Soul wishing to incarnate in a time and space on Third Dimensional Earth related to say the turmoil of war, for whatever reasons they may have to do so, would ideally be able to look through the space-time wave coordinates to find where the maximum synchronistic opportunities for growth may be present.

Following the general time coordinates of mass consciousness related to a Soul's desire for maximum growth, the Soul might then take a look at other opportunistic synchronicities. These could include the appropriate time periods when other entities from your own or a related Soul Matrices would be available to serve as parents, family or other procreative vehicles for the entity. In addition, the Soul might select time coordinates when Soul or Task Mates in the form of friends, associates and colleagues might be available to contribute to an entity's Soul purpose or mandate. All of this is considered in order to provide the incarnation with the most ideal situations to best explore and accomplish the life goals it has determined will be of value to its consciousness and growth.

As we have described, The System Lords are invaluable in shaping and reshaping recognizable space-time coordinates (backdrops) directing the mass conscious reality into positions that favor, or for that matter do not favor, particular themes, world events and situations presented to human kind, and all Souls incarnated within the dimension to provide potential for individual growth. If we discuss this at all, it is to demonstrate that in the coming time period, the linear time coordinate that lies just ahead of you in Third Dimensional reality on Earth, there is yet to become known in your world intense and important efforts being brought forth by the System Lords. These efforts, and the events and world direction they spawn, are required in order to bring a maximum amount of learning and progress to the Third Dimensional timeline, as well as all those who choose to remain in incarnations on a Third Dimensional Earth. It is no wonder then that speaking of these System Lords as polar counterparts working in unison with each other they will be closely associated on the coming timeline with some of the mythologies and revelations relative to both Christ and anti-Christ consciousness, nor is it inconsequential that their incarnations will act as progenitors in a period often prophesied as "End Times."

As we explained in the past, there is no specific deity or demon battling for control of the destiny of Earth. In the west, this is in fact a misunderstanding and even a misappropriation of any true understanding of the relevance of Christ and anti-Christ consciousness. More accurately stated, the idea of Armageddon is perhaps merely a way of referencing certain space-time coordinates, albeit in rather simplistic and naïve terms, and the coming period known as the 21st and 22nd century is indeed a time that has association with the great timeline schism that is occurring.

In that sense, it could be said that predictions concerning some sort of "tribulation" period are based on this happening. Moreover, it is the events that will be set up and placed in motion by incarnations of the System Lords during this period, operating under the guise of Christ and Anti-Christ symbolism, that will in fact provide some of the turmoil and depth of challenge known in those predictions as the timeline enters the not too distant chronological future, particularly as the Ascension process accelerates.

We will discuss some of that turmoil momentarily, but prior to discussing it we must begin by informing you, as we have already, that the current main Ascension period taking place between the years 1987 and 2250 is in fact a period where the proverbial fork in the road is met by all Beings in the dimension and even by Earth itself. Many who are currently passing through death of the physical body from your time and space are simply receding to higher Third Dimensional astral sub-dimensions, awaiting final transformation in order for them to continue to incarnations on Fifth Dimensional Terra. For some, this will occur at a time when the final transformation of the space-time wave is in place. Much of this is complicated to understand since you tend to be fixated on linear progression, but suffice to say there is a myriad of events that need to transpire, no matter when or what time period, in order for evolution and final Ascension to take place across the board.

Getting back to our story with regard to Third Dimensional Earth and the Third Dimensional timeline, as we stated earlier a limited number of Soul matrices that are incarnated in Third Dimensional Earth at the current time are not ready to Ascend or evolve to higher dimensional experiences. This is despite the fact that they may be Human Angelic Souls in origin. For the most part these are Souls that are young in nature and would prefer to continue with Third Dimensional karmic endeavors as the basis of their learning and growth. Due to this, these Souls continue to prefer a time gap between the time they think, feel and desire something and its actual creation or manifestation in physical reality.

This time or "learning" gap has long been a precept of Third Dimensional learning and actual physical creation in your world. It enables you to master control of your thoughts as creative forces, and prevents the random and haphazard manifestation of physical reality until such time as you are consciously aware of your co-creator abilities or ready for the experience. Souls still wrestling with this and preferring the comfort of the learning gap will continue to incarnate in Third Dimensional density, and once they pass from the current physical lifetimes they will reside within astral areas where it will be easy for them to reach and reconnect with the continuation of the Third Dimension, that is once the fermentation of Second dimensional life is complete and it is fused into and creates the new Third Dimensional space-time wave.

There are many humans on Earth presently. But, as we have mentioned before, though they are of the human family in shape, form and genetic make up, not all are derived from Soul matrices that are related to what we have termed the Human Angelic Soul species. Again, let us emphasize that we are not creating a special group here, and neither is there one particular human race, gender or creed that is the sole dominion of Human Angelic Souls. Human Angelic Souls are incarnated in every human form, gender, orientation, type and race existing on Earth at the current time. This is merely to point out to you that living along side you, and the multitude of Human Angelic Souls, who are considered the guardians of Earth and its dimensional portals, there are also alien Soul matrices incarnated in human form. This has been so since your beginnings but it is far more prevalent now and with far more impact on the current and coming time period than at any other point on the timeline, which you will begin to discover.

If we mention this at all, it is to inform you that because Human Angelic Souls are the guardians of the Earth realm in all dimensions where an Earth-based realm exists, **only** Human Angelic Souls together with the solar system and galaxy in which you reside are able to transcend and Ascend with your planet during the current Ascension period. In this way, when Second dimensional Earth ultimately merges with and becomes Third Dimensional Earth, and Third Dimensional Earth becomes Fourth and Fifth Dimensional Terra, it is the Human Angelic Soul matrices only that will begin incarnations in the higher dimensional vibration of this same region of space-time on Fifth Dimensional Terra.

All others, including all alien Soul matrices incarnated in human or genetic hybrid forms (yet to emerge) on Earth, will continue to incarnate within the emerging lower vibrational Third Dimensional Earth realm. This is particularly true in what you term the "Third World" where populations, led by economics and improvements in health and longevity, are exploding. We suggest that prior dramatic increases in Asian populations and especially increases in populations on continental Africa that will take place over the course of the 21st and 22nd Century are directly related to the phenomenon of an influx of physical human incarnations by non Human Angelic Souls.

Understand as well that these coming Fifth Dimensional incarnations are not found "elsewhere" or in some foreign place removed from the current positioning of Earth, speaking in terms of universal time and space. For the most part, these incarnations continue on within the region and realm designated for Human Angelic guardianship, which in the Third Dimension you know as Earth, but in the Fifth Dimension is known as Terra. Terra is not some foreign, relocated planet (to you), but is Earth at a Fifth Dimensional vibration or oscillation, just as Earth, or more accurately, Terra, at a seventh dimensional vibration is known as Gaia. If you were to look at it from a much higher perspective however, you would see that all these names are synonymous with the planetary being known to you as Earth, existing as all of you do at multi-dimensional and vibrational levels, all related to you and in many cases overlapping each other.

Those with a penchant for ancient myth will note that these names for Earth are represented in Greek and Roman mythology to designate varying levels of consciousness of the primordial mother, and it is further interesting to note that for the Greeks, Gaia is the name used for the mother of the world whereas for the Romans, Terra is the designation used. This is interesting in that it represents a vibrational symbolism of sorts, with the Greek myths being more closely associated with more ancient world mythology that reflected the higher seventh dimensional aspirations and focus. The Romans on the other hand who were more worldly oriented and less spiritual in nature were a younger Soul group attuned to more physical Third Dimensional views of the "mother," Earth. Not only does this represent the spiritual and vibrational make-up of these cultures, in a way it could be said to indicate an unconscious alignment with the vibrational signature and symbolism that is found in the sound signature of every name – person, place or thing. For our purposes, and name designations for Earth aside, all of these names represent the overlapping facets and vibrational aspects of the same world at different dimensional resonance.

The idea of different names given for different vibrational aspects of the same thing also provides a clear picture of how universal dimensions overlap and co-exist. For in truth, the Fourth and Fifth Dimensional versions of Earth, in those respective dimensions, exist as an overlay to Second and Third Dimensional Earth, just as seventh dimensional Earth, known as Gaia, is an overlap to fourth, fifth and sixth dimensional Earth within the same time and space.

What makes the difference is the vibrational quality of the overlap. While these dimensions are much closer than you would ever anticipate, for all intent and purpose they are invisible to you. However, as we have explained before it is indeed possible for a being existing on seventh dimensional Gaia to be aware of and in many cases, if desired and tuned-in energetically, to peer-in on Beings in the sixth, fifth, fourth or even Third Dimensional versions of Earth. While those Beings existing in lower dimensional existences have no specific relevance to them, in much the same way a stone existing on the other side of the planet has no immediate relevance to you currently, the dimensional overlaps are in fact unified structures distinguishable only by the parameters of the dimension. This includes oscillation, vibrational frequency and what you know as time and space, which is a construct derived from dimensional oscillation and spin.

To continue our story, over the course of eons Human Angelics have been going through the process of growth and consciousness expansion. They have been housed within the spheres of the many Ascended and evolved versions of Earth, each at a different oscillation and vibrational quality rising up to Source via the different dimensional levels. While these dimensional levels exist simultaneously and coincide with each other, just as there is programming from various networks residing within your cable box simultaneously, you are only witness to the one that you have signed up for and then tuned in to watch. However, as a Human Angelic entity, you could be said to have the ability at some point to tune into any of the channels available and you are destined to continue your evolution as a guardian of the Earth realm regardless of which dimension you happen to be tuned into at any given point in your Soul's journey.

While we do not wish to imply this as a blanket assertion concerning all Souls, for the most part over the coming two hundred to three hundred years this Ascension period will see most Human Angelic Souls leave incarnations in the Third Universal Dimension behind and rise to incarnations in higher dimensional levels and realms. In contrast, those alien Soul matrices that are either peeking in on your world or that are coming into physical incarnations on Third Dimensional Earth for their own purposes of growth are not generally destined to Ascend at this time, nor do they particularly wish to Ascend together with Earth and its Human Angelic Soul population.

As a result, these entities have the option of continuing incarnations within a lower Third Dimensional level on Earth, or completely cycling off incarnations within the proximity and sector of the Universe. Most of these Soul matrices will opt to return to the solar system or galaxy of their preference or Soul origination. In general, a great many of the entities incarnated in human physical form on Earth that are of "alien" (to you) extraction are in fact Third Dimensional Beings from distant areas of the Universe that are not related to the Ascended growth of your particular realm or planet. They wish therefore to remain within Third Dimensional incarnations, whether that is experienced in the space-time wave that will be the same as continuing Third Dimensional Earth or in some other sector of the Universe more closely associated with their Soul origin.

If we explain this at all, it is an attempt to help you understand that these Beings, together with the Human Angelics and guardians that choose to remain in Third Dimensional density, will continue on with incarnations for as long as possible on an emerging Third Dimensional Earth. That is to say, they will continue having incarnations on a Third Dimensional Earth that evolves over time and is comprised from the Ascension of Second dimensional Earth. It is the pending story of these Beings and their probable future that we will discuss with you shortly as we delve into what will happen to the current and emerging time-space line as it continues within a third dimensional density vibration and consciousness.

It is for this reason that we discussed the concept of Christ and anti-Christ consciousness, since it has powerful relevance in the coming Third Dimensional timeline. It is also why we have informed you about the pending important aspects of Soul incarnations related to those energies, which, frankly, will set the stage for what has become widely popularized for generations as Earth's Armageddon.

Now Armageddon, as we have said often, is greatly misunderstood. Most assume it to be a great struggle between good and evil for control of you that ultimately destroys your world and leads you to a Golden Age, one that emerges after a period of great tribulation when a Christ figure, or Christ consciousness, rides onto the scene and saves followers leading them to glorious realms. Though the metaphor of death, Ascension and rebirth into a higher realm of consciousness is perhaps appropriate, unfortunately most accepted interpretations of such a concept are woefully lacking, if not a childish way of understanding events to come. We do not wish to disappoint anyone, but first of all let us set the record straight by informing you that the historical figure known as Jesus will not be appearing any time soon to rescue or "resurrect" followers. Nor for that matter will any religious or spiritual figure ride into your town on a golden steed, carry you to more charming destinies or provide you with palaces and veiled virgins somewhere beyond the clouds. Should one seem to appear, we suggest you be highly suspicious of such activity.

What will happen instead within Third Dimensional reality is that Christ and anti-Christ consciousness, the Spiritual and Physical System Lords if you please, will, through various incarnations already present and polar in nature, create the events that will become the basis for the emerging new Third Dimensional timeline and reality. This will seem to all living through it as if it is merely the continuation of the same space-time wave and timeline, albeit a somewhat sped up reality. In fact however, this is already beginning to emerge around you as the current timeline collapses and is imperceptively replaced. We assure you that over time you will come to know that what is occurring serves as the basis of a renewed and quite different Third Dimensional reality.

In this way various incarnations of the Physical System Lord, some of whom are already incarnated on Earth as of this writing, will begin to appear in world events. While not necessarily negative and certainly not "evil" in a real sense, the Physical System Lord is nevertheless the energy you most readily identify with "anti-Christ" behavior and anti-Christ consciousness generally. This entity, along with other entities that are incarnates of the Physical System Lord, each of whom are also adjuncts to each other, will set the stage for a massive reversal and re-orientation of current human consciousness and culture. Following the collapse of the current mindset and paradigm, a resurrection of consciousness is then possible and such a change will be initiated globally via the appearance of a new future incarnation of the Spiritual System

Lord.

The incarnation of that entity will represent the embodiment of "Christ-like" consciousness even though the Being itself will have little to no outward association with either the religious or historical figure of Jesus or the resulting churches upon which those philosophies are based. What is of importance however is the fact that this figure's emergence will ultimately pave the way for a new Third Dimensional thought form and reality. Religious mythology describes this as the "Second Coming" despite the fact that, as we have attempted to explain, it will not be experienced in the manner many think with respect to a returning religious personality (even if these entities are in truth related since they are truly different incarnations of the same Spiritual System Lord Oversoul). This recalibrating of consciousness will enable continued spiritual growth of the Third Dimension through the fundamental balancing principles known to you as karma, as this remains the learning method of choice for Souls experiencing lifetimes in lower dimensions and denser realities.

In a manner of speaking, the idea that certain groups, religious or otherwise, will be "saved" by their leaders stems from an inner knowing, albeit misunderstood, of Ascension. It is a merging of timeline consciousness, a bleed-through if you will, that leads one to feel that the struggle of a Christ and anti-Christ personality, a cosmic force of good and one of evil, Christ and anti Christ mass consciousness (which is the most relevant), will bring deliverance into higher dimensional realms.

In reality, those who are destined to incarnate into higher dimensional realities will do so regardless of what is going to occur in the timeline we are describing and certainly these entities will have no need to believe in or wait for any figure, on a white horse or otherwise, however majestic that symbol might be. What is clear is that when these concepts are examined they become an important and valuable informational (if not inspirational) message. The message behind these biblical and other symbols is quite naturally related to Ascension and what will happen to those entities who through higher consciousness and adherence to spiritual growth, Ascend into higher dimensional realms. In this case however, we are speaking of an Ascended Being's incarnation on the timeline of Fifth Dimensional Terra rather than a mysterious evacuation to "heaven" as biblically detailed. To be sure, as you will see in Part Two of this book, certain aspects of Terra could certainly be said to be heavenly, especially from your current vantage point.

Our first goal will be to describe for you some of the events currently projected forward in terms of the most probable timeline based on the trajectory of energies now found and newly emerging in the Third Dimensional world. It is our objective to discuss with you details of symbolism around the arrival of both a "Christ-like" and "anti-Christ-like" figure applicable to your world mythologies, the great global cataclysm that shall ensue and the potential for misguided world unification leading to worldwide political disintegration and destruction of the current geopolitical map.

We shall include discussions around the coming great and violent Earth changes that will ultimately result in the demise, over time, of your current epoch civilizations and cultures. Later, for those Human Angelics that are in the process of Ascending to higher vibrational incarnations on Fifth Dimensional Terra, we will provide you with a glimpse of how life on Terra appears based on the most probable current energetic trajectory of the Fifth Dimensional timeline. Intriguing though the destiny of Third Dimensional Earth might seem, we would be surprised if most of you are not more enamored with and find preferential the life of Ascension that awaits you on Fifth Dimensional Terra. This is particularly true when seen in contrast to the physical lifetimes that many alien and other Souls will experience while moving forward on the new and emerging timeline of Third Dimensional Earth.

Chapter 2
A Third Universal Dimension Future

There are two important things to understand with regard to the future of the Third Universal Dimension. First of all, it is important to know that as we have explained already, universal dimensions overlap and are contained one within the other in an expansive model that is best visualized in the proverbial Russian "doll within a doll" nesting (Matryoshka) sculptures that you have seen many times. In this respect, First dimension resides within the Second, Second resides within the third, the third resides within the fourth, fourth in the fifth, fifth in the sixth, sixth in the seventh and upwards until the ninth at which point there is modification of our model, although for our purposes, and to avoid confusion, let us assume that this continues up to and including the twelve known universal dimensions. You experience a universal dimension from within and therefore seeing life in the fourth or Fifth Dimension is not possible to do from the Second or Third Dimension, since the Third Dimension is actually contained within the fourth and Fifth Dimensional fields, as per our model. Also, as we have said and just as our model indicates, the Fourth Universal Dimension knows that it contains the Third Universal Dimension but the Third Universal Dimension may not be aware of this, knowing only that it houses the Second and First. In this respect, universal dimension and dimensional awareness becomes a matter of perspective and witnessed reality.

Usually, the universal dimension in which you find yourself becomes your chief focus, and from your perspective what happens within the dimension that encompasses you is truly what drives you. On rare occasions, you look either up or down outside of your own time-space (doll positioning) but for the most part these are abstracts and your world revolves around your linear dimensional awareness, particularly the dimensions that are understandable and witnessed by you, which tend to be lower frequency dimensions. But the focus you enjoy does not mean that time and space does not unfold equally in every other dimension, it only means that the time and space of other dimensions is not concurrent or similar to the time and space you know as your own.

Secondarily, as we have discussed in our prior book, all universal dimensions are subject to polarity in some respect. Polarity, which is a dynamic that causes the spin that creates the mechanism for attracting reality to you, is in fact one of the principal reasons a universal dimension seems as though it moves forward within a linear time measurement. More importantly is the fact that polarity implies the existence of distinct and different balancing energies, which we have metamorphosed for you as the System Lords. These energies act in concert, or spin, with each other and create the basis for momentum. This momentum is not only relevant to creation of the movement of time space, but also has impact on helping to materialize the choices and events that occur within reality. In this way, incarnations of the Physical System Lord bring opportunities for growth by inspiring momentous and divergent changes to the political and cultural make-up of your world, whereas the Spiritual System Lord's incarnations bring opportunities for spiritual and emotional awakening by renewing a commitment to higher consciousness and growth in your world. These fundamental "polar" energies work together in great harmony with each other.

Getting back to our original discussion with respect to universal dimensional structure being symbolically linked to the form of a doll within a doll, it becomes clear that Third Dimensional existence is contained within fourth, fifth, sixth and higher dimensional existence, and this is a matter of perspective; that is to say, it is a matter of focus and the ability to observe a particular dimension is based on your perceptive abilities and positioning, which is also related to your ability to resonate (oscillate) at similar frequencies. The close overlap dimensions have, and the fact that witnessing a dimension is related to your own frequency or consciousness, means that evolution is possible. Thus, Ascension could be seen as the ability to raise your perspective to the point where you are able to witness Fourth and Fifth Dimensional realities.

When this occurs, you become privy to higher dimensional awareness much the same as when you remove yourself from the model of a doll within a doll, where you are able to see the resonance that contains you as well as the resonances that oscillate beneath you. Thus, Fifth Dimensional existence has its own perspective, as well as a very close association with Fourth Dimensional perspective, and in the same manner Third Dimensional perspective (the perspective you currently enjoy) is privy to and has strong links to Second dimensionality. Through the process of Ascension, each dimension already existing within our model becomes accessible to those Beings incarnating within it based on their ability to raise consciousness and frequency, which provides the higher dimensional perspective that allows them to incarnate in the dimension in the first place.

Our point in describing this is to answer the question of what happens to Third Dimensional reality. Third Dimensional reality continues on and those within Third Dimensional reality who have raised their resonance enough to evolve their DNA, a prerequisite for raising perceptive abilities and consequently perspective, will then resonate at higher levels of perception. It becomes easy to see that those who do not evolve their resonance, and thus do not evolve their genetic structure and DNA, cannot expand their potential perspective, and thus they will retain a Third Dimensional focus that continues to be based on their perspective (consciousness) abilities.

Of course, as we stated, the Third Dimensional reality in which they remain is now added to and expanded by Second dimensional entities and Beings that have raised their level of resonance (perspective) and are then able to proceed with new incarnations and awareness that are focused within Third Dimensional perspective. In this manner, Ascension continues to be possible within the dimension as a whole, as well as throughout the Universe. Suffice to say however, that those who do not leave incarnations in one dimension and rise to higher dimensional awareness through the enlightening of their perspective will remain at the same dimensional level. This will be so whether or not they realize that it is a newly formed edition of their preferred dimension, or they believe it to be the same time and place since it displays all the same characteristics as the one currently known so well.

These entities, more specifically their Soul matrices, continue to incarnate and exist within a Third Dimensional reality. In this way, those who are not prepared to evolve at the current time are destined, through free will or otherwise, to continue on within a time-space continuum that is Third Dimensional in density. It is also appropriate that the System Lords we have discussed continue to be present within a newly emerging yet continuous Third Dimensional reality. These System Lord incarnations will work to provide opportunities for growth for all Soul's seeking to proceed through experiences in a Third Dimensional physical reality, assisting them to generate the necessary opportunities and avenues needed for maximum growth (enlightenment) by helping to create world political, cultural, emotional and spiritual energetic structures used as a backdrop and impetus for a Soul's physical life mission. Naturally, such work and guidance is always intended to continually move Beings incarnating within the dimension towards an elevation in creative consciousness. That elevation will ultimately lead them to their own dimensional Ascension, perhaps at the juncture of a future Ascension period if that Soul matrix and the entity is so inclined.

Those who continue on in Third Universal Dimension reality, even though it will be intrinsically birthed from the elevation of Second Universal Dimension consciousness, will continue on within a physical reality that is similar to the physical reality you and they currently know. What is different however, and will become clear as the timeline progresses, is that the reality, as a new Being itself, will have some distinct variations and new properties that are noticeably altered from the current Third Dimensional properties you now know. Since this is not an overnight occurrence as perceived by you, few will realize that essentially there is a collapse occurring of the time and space reality that is known.

Most will see this collapse as history unfolding. Indeed, it will be commonly viewed as the end of one era and the beginning of another. This is not to be confused with one culture raising its consciousness and rising to fourth and Fifth Dimensional value, but we are speaking in terms of a Third Dimensional Earth culture coming to an end and a new Third Dimensional world culture emerging out of its ashes. The symbolism of the Phoenix is well taken for it is from the ashes of the prior Third Dimensional culture that the new Third Dimensional culture will be established.

In this respect, many of the things you see happening around you currently are related to that collapse, which also coincides with a collapse of time and space, paving the way for the emergence of a new Third Dimensional reality. It should be understood that entities will continue to exist in Third Universal Dimensional incarnations and it is these entities that we shall discuss next with respect to the collapse of your current world civilizations and the emergence of a new Third Dimensional civilization, as the collapse takes place over the course of the coming several hundred years on the Third Dimensional timeline.

The history of your world is one of civilizations rising and falling. Unfortunately, from your current perspective it is difficult for you to see the inter connectedness of history and time, which would appear to you as almost a dimensional looping spiral cornucopia if you were able to see it from outside the timeline. This means there are historic periods that coincide and correlate, or at least have close proximity to each other, regardless of the distance measured in your time on a linear scale. In addition, it is difficult for you to see the System Lords cooperate through the timeline in the rise and fall of cultures, mass consciousness and civilizations. Endless speculation occurs around why cultures and civilizations disappear or parallel each other so closely despite large separations in time. This is because you are not privy to an outside perspective and therefore cannot fully comprehend how one civilization relates to another, distant though it may seem, or how a civilization collapses and a new one supersedes it.

For the most part, these rises and falls are cyclical in nature and in some instances they coincide with the approximately 26,000 year solar cycle, the approximately 260,000 year galactic cycle or even the 2.5 Million year universal cycles that we've discussed in the past. Of course, others may not coincide with these periods and instead are merely orchestrated by the System Lords to provide new opportunities and new situations for growth in the world where the prevailing

Soul matrices incarnate.

Case in point is the world civilization we discussed in "The System Lords and the Twelve Dimensions" known as the empire of Atlantis. The demise of the Atlantean civilization occurred gradually over many millennia but took place primarily after a grand Ascension galactic cycle of approximately 260,000 years. However, its fall also took place at various other intervals after the galactic Ascension cycle, including over several 26,000 year solar cycles.

You will recall that the 26,000 year solar cycle is one that enables Ascension and evolution within the sublevels of the dimension itself, whereas the galactic 260,000 year cycle permits Ascension on a broader plane where universal dimensions themselves are able to Ascend. You are currently not only living at the junction of a 26,000 year cycle permitting Ascension within sublevels of the Earth sphere (know to you as the Astral planes), but also at the junction of a grand 260,000 year galactic cycle, which permits Ascension to occur universally from one dimension to the next. It is for this reason that Ascension and evolution can occur within the Third Dimension, thus allowing Souls to continue on with incarnations on a renewed Third Dimensional Earth. This is also the reason Souls previously incarnating in the Third Dimension now have the potential to incarnate at a higher, Fifth Dimensional vibration on Fifth Dimension Terra.

The reason we are discussing this is not only to give you some insight into the interconnectedness of cycles and the reasons civilizations rise and fall within your world, it is to further set the stage for describing what is about to transpire on the Third Universal Dimension timeline, in other words the coming history of your world. As we have said in the past, System Lords incarnate in cooperation and unison with each other. You know by now that the Physical System Lord incarnates for the purpose of providing changes to the geopolitical structure of your world. The Spiritual System Lord generally arrives as a follow up to these geopolitical changes in order to bring about a reboot of the social and spiritual consciousness of your world. Generally, although this is not always the case, in this way the Physical System Lord usually paves a way for the Spiritual System Lord's appearance.

Your epics regarding Armageddon or concerning what you term the "End of the World" are a compilation of misunderstood information. These epics are related first to the fact that cyclically the Physical and Spiritual System Lords arrive in your plane of reality to create a backdrop against which Souls can incarnate and, Second, the fact that the current Third Dimension is collapsing and will soon be replaced with a new version of itself. It is also a vague if not ill understood composite of information related to the end of Third Dimensional incarnation for most Human Angelic Souls, and their Ascension into Fifth Dimensional incarnations. How this information is being disseminated however, through the lens of current religious or other superstitious belief is erroneous at best, particularly the many "New Age" tales describing how the current Third Dimension's Ascension will be an event that physically propels everyone and everything into a fourth or Fifth Dimensional existence at the blink of an eye.

If you are to understand the process further, it is important to separate out that which is true and that which is not true with regard to continuation of the Third Universal Dimension's timeline. In order to do so, it must be understood that mythologies related to the End Times, or what you call the end of the world, are unfounded and generally untrue. For the most part these will not come to pass in the manner in which they have been described. Therefore the conflict you have been told that exist between the forces of good and evil is actually a misinterpreted description of the polarity relationship between the

Physical System Lord and the Spiritual System Lord, Yin and Yang if you will. It is also representative of the Phoenix mythology, since as we have previously described the Physical System Lord does sometimes pave the way for the Spiritual System Lord by annihilating and destroying the existing geopolitical structures, social orders and related cultural paradigms in order to create an opening for new spiritual and emotional consciousness. This allows the ashes of the previous world to spawn a rebirth of civilization and its structures.

Make no mistake however, this is within the context of a continuation of the existing dimensional parameters and is not a description of transcendence, where annihilation of the Third Universal Dimension leads miraculously to life in the Fourth or Fifth Universal Dimension. With that in mind, it is important to understand that the Third Universal Dimension is not scheduled to expire in the Twenty First Century, or for some time thereafter. To be precise, there is indication of a timeline anomaly in the continuing Third Dimension that leads to the partial destruction and rebirth of your entire planet in approximately the Twenty-sixth Century, but that event is not necessarily related to current and coming changes that will be occurring in your world over the next several hundred years.

As we have said in the past, understanding that we are strictly discussing the Third Universal Dimension and its continuation, the Physical System Lord has incarnated in several locations and is emerging with respect to a plan that was put into motion millennia ago to coincide with this particular period. These incarnations also coincide with the mass Ascension that is about to occur and is related to what could be referred to as the demise of the current civilization, a necessary component of the transformation that will ultimately be the future timeline of the continuing Third Universal Dimension. That future timeline could be said to be imminent, and you are already experiencing many factors related to this.

In fact, although many of the natural disasters that are occurring are either caused by the transcendent energies meant to propel the current Third Dimension into fourth and Fifth Dimensional density or they are unnatural occurrences related to the manipulation of natural energies by those that have access to technology that can manipulate these planetary factors. Even so, it is important to understand that what you are experiencing is part of a greater purpose. That greater purpose is behind creating a new and emerging reality that will soon become the norm for those Soul matrices that wish to remain in Third Density and continue to incarnate in that reality.

Again, let us reiterate our caution against believing that one universal dimension is better, more perfect or has greater good than any other (lower) dimensional level for this is not the case. Each dimensional level, and each dimensional sublevel for that matter, serves its purpose for the greater good, and each has merit and value. Those Soul matrices of Human Angelic origin or otherwise incarnating in the Third Dimensional Earth realm today are not necessarily of lower importance than any Soul matrix that will Ascend to fourth and Fifth Dimensional reality, such as the one we will describe shortly known as Terra. All existence is achieved for purposes related to Soul growth, and those purposes are completely individual and unique to each entity and each Soul. Therefore, should you harbor any attachment to hierarchies with respect to those who remain in Third Dimensional density and those that move onto Fifth Dimensional incarnations, or the dimensional realms itself, let us dismiss such notions before we continue our conversation. Similarly, be advised that the emerging Third Dimensional timeline's events are not to be considered faulty, bad or less desirable despite the coming challenges they seem to present to those incarnates still focused within it.

Having said that however, as is the case when considering the nature of vibrational frequency, because Third Dimensional reality is denser and oscillates at a rate that is lower in nature than higher dimensions, the events and situations that transpire there are much more impactful with respect to physical bodies. Because of this they are much more difficult in terms of the challenges presented. Suffice to say that in higher dimensional levels particularly above the fifth and especially beginning at the Seventh Universal Dimension, physical challenges are not experienced in the manner they are in lower density due to the fact that entities in those realms are more spiritual in nature. In fact, beginning in the Fifth Dimension an entity's awareness could be considered telepathic and in such an environment it becomes difficult to "pull-the-wool" over a higher dimensional Being's eyes. In a realm where each entity knows what the other entity is all about and feeling, experiencing or wanting out of the incarnation, it is easy to step aside and not incorporate that entity's reality into your own. Higher dimensions make the creation of reality far more personal and in many ways private, or at the very least they are less subject to mass involvement the way incarnates in the Third Dimension are.

While experiencing life in Third Universal Dimension reality, it is very difficult for you to actually remove yourself from the events that transpire around you. This is whether the events are occurring in the world at large, occurring within your own neighborhood or occurring in the lives of family, friends and associates. It is even more difficult in Third Density to remove yourself from the planetary and geopolitical challenges that may occur. That is to say it is more difficult for you to know the inner truth and real reason behind what is happening in your world, and thus it is more difficult if not impossible for you to remove yourself from the proximity of the challenge. Moreover, the physical structure of things and the nature of physics involved in your world make this problematic as well. In the seventh dimension for example, as the antithesis of this, entities are able to literally transport themselves, telepathically and otherwise, even in a physical manner, out of the line of fire of anything they do not wish to participate in.

You do not have such a luxury in the Third Universal Dimension. In your dimension, due to the dense nature of matter and the actual dimensional physics involved, the inability to be able to transport or telepathically remove yourself means that in the absence of a car, a bus, a plane or a helicopter, you are destined to be part of and in many cases play a role in the mass conscious environment being created around you. In this respect, the Physical System Lord is an important component of your reality because in a certain sense, this is the means by which focused energy is able to bring structure out of chaos. These sons of Gods, if you will permit this appellation, in fact assist with creation in the realm in order to permit those entities incarnated within the reality to enjoy their own existences and learning experiences. This is true even in the event that the work being accomplished by the Physical System Lord appears on the surface to originally bring destruction and chaos.

It should be remembered that the Avatars known as the Physical System Lord act only in unison with the Spiritual System Lord, whose incarnations act as protector and guide in order to bring the world to new levels of awareness and consciousness that rises out of the ashes and chaos most often orchestrated by incarnations of the Physical System Lord. It is for this reason that, as we said in identifying them with mythology related to the sons of God, the System Lords can be seen in western thought as the energies most akin to Christ and Anti-Christ consciousness, with the Physical System Lord closely aligned with anti-Christ consciousness and the Spiritual System Lord most closely aligned with the energy of Christ consciousness.

We would ask for a moment that you suspend the connection, obvious or not, that these energies and the denomination we give them might have with certain Christian sects or the Catholic Church. In reality, though Christ energy is most commonly identified as being representative of the Master known as Jesus whom we described in our book "The System Lords and the Twelve Dimensions" and who was an incarnate of the Spiritual System Lord, we use Christ consciousness to describe an energetic consciousness of Truth. This energy could just as easily be identified as Yin consciousness, and in that respect anti-Christ consciousness could be said to be identifiable with Yang consciousness. Yang and Yin consciousness then, with Yang energy being the more physical side of nature (male) and Yin consciousness being the more receptive, spiritual and esoteric side of nature (female), are again appellations for the same universal energies, energies that exist in polarity with each other and are universal in form and structure.

If we make this distinction it is because your world, particularly in the West, is so seeped in the notion of a Christ and Anti-Christ conflict that will bring an end to the world that we wish to dispel the idea that some kind of battle is forming that will soon be played out between a Christ-like physical Being and an Anti-Christ-like Being. To be sure, incarnations of the Physical System Lord will certainly be paving a path that will interact and may even conflict with lifetimes created by the Spiritual System Lord. But though you might wish to see this as a kind of cosmic battle, it is not truly a war in the manner that you think.

However, in discussing this it should be known that situations related to the emergence of Anti-Christ consciousness, or what we term Anti-Christ consciousness, will in fact lead to what can only be described as the demise of your current civilization. This will pave the way for Christ consciousness to reappear through incarnations of the Spiritual System Lord to rekindle true spiritual and higher awareness. It is this new and different sense of reality that emerges as a result of the turmoil experienced on the future Third Dimensional timeline that serves as the backdrop against which our story concerning the future of Third Dimensional reality is told.

This is, of course, easy to tell here but actually is much more complex in terms of how the events we will describe actually will affect the future Third Dimensional timeline. This complexity is increased by the fact that you currently have those incarnates that will be continuing on in Third Dimensional reality after the current lifetime living alongside those incarnates that will Ascend to higher dimensional incarnations. The emerging differences between those entities is also the reason there is such obvious conflict and philosophical difference stirring between those entities remaining in Third Dimensional reality and those poised to move on to higher dimensions. If has no doubt been noticed that over the past several decades there is a growing distinction between those entities that wish to adhere to what can be termed traditional or fundamentalist views with outmoded cultural models and those who want nothing at all to do with fundamentalist restrictions, conflicts and rules based on childish stereotypes and the writings of long-dead historic personalities.

It becomes evident today that there are a growing number of individuals and societies that, armed with Hebrew Bible, Christian New Testament or Islamic Koran in hand, for example, wish to oblige everyone to think in the same manner as they do. For the most part it becomes clear that those individuals and societies becoming more entrenched than ever before in naïve positions regarding belief and adherence to archaic laws and social structures are in fact entities intending to remain within incarnations in the new emerging Third Dimensional reality, a reality where karmic principles of balance are the basis for growth. On the flip side of this, those who cannot tolerate judgment, be bothered with sticking to someone else's master plan and have grown beyond such limited thinking, wishing only to live life in peaceful harmony and freedom that allows each to grow at their own pace. These individuals represent those who undoubtedly will be transferring their Soul energy to higher dimensional realities when they incarnate in coming lifetimes.

This disparity between essentially Third Dimensional-based entities and entities ready to Ascend to higher dimensional densities is perhaps the single greatest unseen force behind the conflicts, locally and internationally, that are now appearing in your world. It is also for this reason that some groups and societies seem to be entrenched in thought patterns that are so disparate, appearing even nonsensical to some but not others, depending upon your position and the nature of your Soul's consciousness.

You will find that this gap continues to broaden in your future. If you understand the relevance of it, you have the option and the probability not to take part. Yet it is important to know that these struggles, polar in nature once again, represent that the timeline is changing and continuation of the current Third Dimensional timeline will become nearly unsupportable very soon. If you wish to see this as the end of the world, the collapse of civilization and a restart or a new beginning, then certainly this is what is occurring.

As you would say however, life goes on in the Third Universal Dimension. Whether you are speaking of the trajectory of Western or Eastern culture, the shift in power and energy in your world to new regions and cultures or the collapse of energetic systems and power structures -- political, monetary or otherwise -- you are in fact witnessing the transition of the old Third Dimensional world and the emergence of a new Third Dimensional timeline. That world will be far different from the world you currently know. In order to best describe coming events projected on the emerging timeline, let us begin by segmenting the world into different regions in order to describe specific changes in those areas of the world that will be taking effect beginning now and through the coming decades and centuries. We will begin our journey by discussing the future of the North American continent, home of the society and culture known as America. But before we do so, let us take a moment to discuss the energetic forces and influences that prevail in your world that have been at work since the beginning of the current timeline and even before that.

 ## Chapter 3
The East to West Passage of Energetic Flow and the Beginning of Our Narrative on the Future of the Third Dimensional Timeline

Most of you who have incarnated in the western hemisphere over the course of the past century, and particularly those of you who have incarnated in North America, view the world from your central point of positioning. It is from this vantage, with the occasionally ethnocentric and nationalistic perspective it has commanded, that you see and analyze almost the entirety of global affairs. Unfortunately, this positioning does not take into full account those elusive and shifting universal energies that are ever present in your world. These influencing energies make their way from East to West naturally augmenting and altering the circumstances of mass consciousness, populations, cultures and continents as they flow.

Normally, these energetic waves (influences that might partially be likened to the forces described by astrological movements, although the waves we are discussing are more electromagnetic in nature) move across your planet at an imperceptible, crawling pace. It is because of this that they are only noticed when one looks back over long periods of linear time or when one estimates the consequences of events (history) after the fact. It is for this reason that when you contemplate the totality of what your historian usually call the modern period (from about 5000BCE to now), you tend to study history as it migrates from East to West, from the Pacific (early China), Indus and Mesopotamian cultures and regions, to ancient Egypt, to ancient Eurasia, to ancient

Greece, Rome, European empires and, ultimately, to the current North American region. A progression that appears to find cultural and historic dominance migrating from East to West, ending where you find yourselves today in the current moment.

Recently though, due to the extraneous and increased photon energies coming from the Galactic center through your Sun and resulting forces, these energetic influences that seem to favor aspects of culture and history are sped up enormously. Thus the passage of importance and influence, as well as the seemingly concurrent shifting of focus from one continent or civilization to the next as the case may be, is becoming confused if not commonplace. In fact, this shifting from one sphere of influence to the next (following our east to west pattern of flow) is now becoming noticeable within the span of a single lifetime. It is no accident therefore that although the energetic forces we are describing took centuries or even millennia to pass from say Egypt to Rome, or from Europe to the Americas, as an example, the passage of such energetic influences from the American continent to Asia, now in full swing, is being made visible and relevant to you in only a few short decades.

You have been led to believe that for the most part today's historic origins begin in what is called the cradle of civilization, an area from Babylon, in modern day Iraq, and south. There is a good deal of enthusiasts of the Babylonian-Sumerian culture that think of this as a precursor to recognizable culture and civilization, and thus they think of this as the birthplace of your current age. However, this is not actually correct. The Sumerian civilization was a noted one, as has been reported by some, and it was indeed an ancient culture that had originally been founded in cooperation with an off-planet race that temporarily invaded your world for their own interests. They would ultimately abandon it by the end of the great Atlantean turmoil sometime before

12,000 BCE. Thus, the ancient artifacts you know as remnants of early Babylon and Sumer come from a much later time period and are essentially only the faded remnants of that civilization, which ceased to exist except in primitive form by the end of the final worldwide Atlantean tribulations.

Our point here is that while the Sumerians of 5,000 BCE may be of interest to you, they are not the originating point of your history or the cradle of today's known world civilizations, most of which emerged long after the final fall of Atlantis and even after the period of the great global floods in approximately 12,000 and again in about 10,000 BCE. On the contrary, your current world history and its origins could be said to be more closely related to those civilizations that emerged millennia before the fall of the Atlantean civilization and traced to the Pacific regions of your world.

Most notably, these origins began in territories that many tens of thousands and even hundreds of thousands of years earlier were known as the Lumerian civilization, existing in the lands of MU, a true precursor civilization, even, in some respects, to the Atlanteans. Now if we are detailing this it is not only to make reference to the fact that the planetary "energy" waves we are describing did not originate in the lands of the Sumerians but also to highlight the movement of said energies, from East to West on a cyclical basis.

In fact, the movement of these energies could be said to coincide somewhat with the 26,000-year solar cycle that we have discussed in the past. Thus, you have an energetic wave that began in the Pacific approximately 26,000 years ago at the beginning of the last cycle, has toured the world over the past 26,000 year period, and is now set to return to its place of origin – the Pacific regions. If one were to look deeper, it is also possible to see that these periods of energetic waves, passing from East to West, demonstrate an even greater energy wave that also coincide with the 260,000 year Galactic turning of which we have spoken. That said it is interesting to note that both the approximate 26,000-year solar cycle as well as the approximate 260,000 grand cycle are currently coming to completion in your galactic sector simultaneously in the current era.

This is meant to demonstrate that although there is little ability to correlate these waves to historical time periods you would easily recognize, the cycles that previously took tens of thousands of years to complete are now, in their final phases, taking only hundreds of years or even a few decades to accomplish the same passage. Those who understand the work of the time keepers, the Maya, distant inheritors of Atlantean time keeping wisdom handed down from generation to generation, will understand this concept in that the time cycles detailed by the Mayans actually become shorter and shorter as they near completion. This in turn follows closely the elliptical nature of your Solar System and your Galaxy's progression through the cosmos. For those familiar with current day celestial turnings and the journey your system makes through the astrological signs, as Earth and your Solar System's planetary journey shortens, approaching completion of its long cylindrical trek, the energetic waves effecting them become more augmented and this has a more intense influence upon the planets in your system as well.

Staying confined to our discussion, this translates into a speeding up of all influences, gravitational, electromagnetic and otherwise, throughout the Solar System, and on Earth in particular. Thus, whereas an "ancient" Earth world civilization such as Atlantis might have held dominance in your world for many tens and even hundred of years, more recent world civilizations, such as the Hindu, Egyptian, Mesopotamian or Persian civilizations, may have lasted only three to five thousand years.

Continuing to follow this line of thought, an even more recent civilization chronologically speaking, such as the Greco-Roman one, might have only predominated and held influence for a few thousand years. And following this further, a major civilization of today, for convenience sake let us identify the American civilization, may only enjoy a hundred year lifespan or, currently, only be present within the energetic sphere of influence for a decade or less, until such time as the energetic wave-influences under discussion have moved past them.

This is precisely what you are witnessing today moment by moment as these energetic waves of world focus pass from the United States and North America, where it has resided since only the early to mid 20th Century, and begin influencing the Asian Pacific regions once again, ending where it began and readying itself to begin anew. This signals the 26,000-year wave cycle world-passage completion, and, in the current period, also the approximately 260,000 year grand cycle completion. In addition to the energetic waves we are discussing (and though some might argue the point and dislike the analogy), another way of looking at the devastation of Europe and parts of Asia during what is known to you as the two World Wars of the 20th Century would be as a way for influences we have discussed as the "System Lords" to clear the decks, so to speak, in order that North American culture emerge, flourish and predominate during a large part of the past century.

This is especially true as evidenced over the course of the latter part of the 20th Century, when one considers all energetic influences in play, where the American civilization emerged into full world prominence. In that respect, although the European continent and much of the rest of the world was by no means disintegrated or disengaged, it is clear that shifts in the balance of power were the result of dramas that occurred just prior to that time during both the first and second World Wars. We would suggest that these dramas and the aftermath period were in large part a result of the passage of electromagnetic universal energies as well as the planned necessities and influences of the System Lords. Of course, if you prefer to maintain a limited worldview point, then by all means attribute history and the flow of spheres of influence to the vial actions of this or that dictator, army or culture.

We prefer however, the broader view that energetic influences acting upon your galaxy, your solar system and your planet are in large part at the root of events and circumstances, if not specific occurrences, certainly the general direction and emerging spheres of dominance. When these influences are orchestrated in conjunction with the many incarnations of the Physical or Spiritual System Lords, who are acting in harmony with the universal energies prevalent at the time, physical reality-potential is maximized (those that practice astrology might understand this as events happening as part of the working of "astrological" preponderances). In the case of 20th Century events, all of these equated to the enhancing and emergence of North American world power, and this economic, political and military shift to the Americas has served as a backdrop for Soul incarnations, growth and development from approximately the late 19th Century to the present day.

With the current increase in Galactic photon energies, which could be said to prevail even over the cyclical energetic winds and influences we are discussing, you are witnessing today a sped up version of what essentially transpired in the not too distant past as power shifted from Europe to North America. This time however, remembering our East to West energetic wave motion, the shift happening is one that will ultimately diminish the American civilization's influence in the world. In

Timeline Collapse & Universal Ascension

direct opposition, it will augment an Asian Pacific influence on the world throughout a large part of the 21st Century. This shift will continue to take place both on the present (collapsing) and emerging (coming) Third Dimensional timeline, and much of the karmic energetic balancing (on both sides of the influences) that accompanies it is already well underway. That karmic balancing will also result in the final deterioration of a world culture and civilization that has predominated on Earth since the late early to late 20th Century, and held sway over your world for most of the past seventy-five to one hundred years.

If we mention this at all, it is because this is a starting point for our discussion of the future of the Third Dimensional timeline, beginning with information pertaining to the United States, North America and the North American continent. Naturally, this story also includes those who are incarnated in the North American arena or who find themselves present there during the coming period. Remember that these individuals have come to this specific time and place first and foremost for their own personal reasons related to Soul growth, interest and commitment. Secondarily, they are there in order to participate and contribute in what we shall call the cascade and final disintegration of a predominant society that acts as a catalyst for the continued evolution of mankind on Earth, highlighted by the potential Ascension of most Human Angelic Souls during the coming one hundred fifty to two hundred years.

Unfortunately, it must be clear by now that on the emerging Third Dimensional timeline, as you will see shortly, North America is no longer the world center of economic, political or military might. A shift from North America towards the West is certainly evident even from any layman's perspective today, with that front being focused on the Pacific Rim and Eastern regions of your globe. This transition, quick though it may be, will continue and the potential global conflict that is coming will ultimately seal the fate of the United States and herald the emergence of what we shall call the North American League in the face of its centralized collapse.

Eastern and Asian cultures and civilization will, once again, predominate on the evolving Third Dimensional timeline. This is not, however, so easily recognized from a static point of vision, though in fact the shift of power has long begun. This shift will continue to cement itself within the world psyche over the course of the coming few decades, until such time as its relevance can no longer be denied primarily under the weight of political and economic disintegration and the shrinking influence of North American civilization that results.

We begin by stating that as is so often the case, one need only provide enough rope to one's adversary and await entanglement in order to succeed. This is in fact a culturally based strategy of Asian civilizations, one particularly revered and exploited by the powerhouse nation of China. For some time, Asia has adopted a deliberate strategy towards the West that prefers providing its nemesis with enough rope to hang itself, awaiting the outcome, rather than establishing its dominance through a frontal, blatant attack so often the method of choice and, moreover, the customary expectation of North America and its highly influenced Western European partners. That said it becomes fairly clear in your world that those who intend to master tomorrow need only remain in the wings long enough for the inevitable collapse of an advisory under the weight of extraordinary hubris and a general disregard of the truth. Of course, it is important as well to be prepared and able to pick up the pieces at the appropriate time. It is not coincidental that this might also be found to be the favorite strategy of modern western-style investment tactics, and perhaps those with a degree of objectivity will see the potential karmic effects inherent in such behavior.

While this is symptomatic of and a clear outcome of the coming world situations that will be orchestrated into existence with the assistance of the System Lords, it must be understood as well that this is not in fact a *strategy* of the System Lords. There are certain parameters within which all exists and the continual evolution and transformation of energy, as well as the shift of power westward, remains a prerequisite for happenings within the dimension. However, as we have said it is primarily the role of the System Lords to incarnate in positions where they can facilitate and influence the learning experiences of those Souls incarnated within a specific timeline. As we have also said many times, the Physical System Lords do so through incarnations that change the political and economical structure and culture of the world, while the Spiritual System Lords do so in order to evolve the consciousness and spiritual understanding of the realm as a whole. Again, these events and their estimation should not be rendered subjectively or reduced to simplistic notions of good, bad, right or wrong. Each has its purpose, and, as we have said, in most cases these things are made manifest in your world for reasons that, often, rationality cannot discern.

What you see happening in your world is a continuation of this pattern of the Physical System Lords changing the geo-political and economic makeup of the world in order to pave the way for the Spiritual System Lords to open up new consciousness and spirituality for all Souls. In doing so, not only do they work in unison, they are, in a sense, purveyors of specific karma (energetic balancing) that may be relevant to occurrences across the millennia.

It is difficult for us to tie together the elaborate existing threads of group, cultural and community karma here, but we will endeavor to at least demonstrate how connections are made. In the West today, you live in a world that has become polarized and seemingly motionless.

This, however, is not necessarily the case in the East, and were you to explore the Asian continent presently, extreme viewpoints that may exist in pockets taken aside, you would find a thought-process that is fairly similar and essentially non-paralyzed. Now the paralyzation and polarization of much of the western world is based primarily on the emergence of fundamentalist viewpoints on both sides of the equation.

Fundamentalist myopic (fiercely unilateral) viewpoints are, as we have said, most often found in Souls that have chosen not to Ascend during the current cycle, and instead their intention is to continue on with their physical incarnations within Third Dimensional reality. In order for them to do so, there must first be a clearing-out of those Souls that will "Ascend" during the coming time period. This culling is achieved through a fundamental balancing of group karma, which in this respect can be seen as a struggle between two opposing sides and viewpoints. However, it must be clear by now that there is little difference between those who exhibit fundamentalist thinking in one part of the world with those maintaining fundamentalist viewpoints in another (expanding our perspective from those in the same neighborhood or country to a larger world view for a moment). Though their languages or cultures are different, some seeming primitive and some seeming not so primitive, if you were to look beyond the current physical limitations and logistics, you would see that in fact these Souls are not so very different – particularly in terms of Soul age and therefore, outlook. One might even conclude that they are distantly related, the way opposite sides of a coin are related, and despite their expressed outward hatred of each other, those animosities in fact lead each group to the same conclusions, filtered through their own lenses and in keeping with their own tribal or local belief structures.

In such a scenario, an Islamic fundamentalist might have an extreme hatred of, as an example, a Christian. Similarly, a fundamentalist Christian might demonstrate extreme fear and loathing of an Islamist group, the religion as a whole or perhaps even the region of the world (the Middle East) most closely associated with the group. Though these two groups might oppose each other vehemently, is there really such a large difference in their thought process or way of dealing with the reality around them? Does one not want the other to be or act just like them – by force if necessary?

In fact, these two opposing groups could be said to both be cut from the same cloth, and they could also be likened to Souls that generally gain maximum spiritual and consciousness growth almost exclusively through Third Dimensional opportunities (usually eye-for-an-eye type energy balancing events). Remembering that there is no good or bad in this, and we do not wish to place these Souls in a "lesser" light, these Souls may simply wish to continue on in Third Dimensional lifetimes because that is the dimension that offers the kind of necessary growth opportunities that best meet their needs. It is clear therefore, that these Souls would prefer *not* to move on to higher levels of consciousness just yet through the process of Ascension (the means of evolution by which Souls and whole universal dimensions "Ascend" to higher levels of oscillation, consciousness and growth). Looked at further, one could attribute such a choice primarily to Soul age, with younger Souls wishing to retain access to a Third Dimensional timeline in order to achieve karma-based lessons on an Earth similar to the one you currently know. Naturally, this is in contrast to the many older Souls that have wearied of Third Dimensional karmic-style Earth lessons and wish to Ascend to higher levels of learning on a higher-dimensional form of Earth.

While the dichotomy of younger and older Souls is present worldwide, and can be seen in countries or even neighborhoods with Souls of every type and purpose present therein, the broader push and pull of younger Souls wishing to remain in Third Dimensional struggles and older Souls wishing to Ascend to higher dimensional lessons in augmented oscillations becomes a central theme for any discussion of the current timeline. It also becomes the starting point for many of the challenges projected to emerge on the Third Dimensional timeline in your near future. Moreover, this sets the stage for struggles that are especially orchestrated to benefit the younger Souls from all sides, and these struggles can be specifically identified in real terms as the emerging great conflict that will arise between the Western and the Middle Eastern worlds. Such conflict, the primary precursor to creating a world dominated by basic karma and destined to be the staple of a coming Third Dimensional timeline, will lead to the diminishing and, ultimately, the demise of Western (North American) influence and power in the world as you know it, on that timeline and in that dimension.

Ironically, this struggle will be orchestrated by like-minded Souls on every side of the conflict, brandishing unswerving fundamentalist viewpoints, albeit perspectives that may appear outwardly to be diametrically opposed to their "Soul" brethren on the other side. Also ironically, the conflicts will be shaped by incarnations of the System Lords in order to pave the way for new influences in a continuing Third Dimensional world, as well as inspire those older Souls that are ready to Ascend assisting them to achieve that choice at this current junction.

It is the demise of the West and particularly North America that allows a complete and final shift of energetic power from the West to Asian and Eurasian centers of your Earth. It is this same collapse that heralds a more challenging Earth situation as it proceeds on a continuing Third Dimensional timeline, and signals to older Souls that for them the moment of Ascension has arrived. Older, Ascending Souls will be, in a sense, forced into transcendence, greater consciousness and growth and they will find themselves drawn (or harvested, a term that is preferable) into a higher dimensional existence, which they will experience through new incarnations that have already begun on a Fifth Dimensional Earth called Terra. We will discuss Fifth Dimensional Terra in the second half of this book, but first let us begin by detailing the future life of the continuing Third Dimension and its timeline – the one being created by and for those younger Souls wishing to remain for the coming age through incarnations on some form of the current Earth. Here we start our narrative, told to you from a position in the future, concerning the decline and fall of North America and the impact this will have on the future of the world you know now.

 ## Chapter 4
The Unraveling of North America and Failure of the United States on the Continuing Third Dimensional Timeline

Few realized in the early years following the turn of the 21st century that by the early to mid 2010's the polarization evident in American politics paralleled closely the polarization that had developed between the United State of America, its allies and countries in the Middle East or elsewhere gathered loosely under the banner of the Islamic Faith. Nor did anyone notice that the continuous internal conflicts being fought between political parties, fundamentalist national factions (either conservative or liberal) and specific races and ethnicities would have as much impact on the demise of US world prominence as the great external conflict orchestrated internationally and waiting in the wings.

Polarization on the home front increased through the late 2010's, as American resolve became thwarted by a lack of direction and an inability to act swiftly, or sometimes to take action in its best interest at all. Similarly, as pressures mounted on the world front and ideologies became even more entrenched and heated, particularly with regard to western efforts towards a new Islamic Crusade to stem the Islamic Fundamentalist problem, it soon became clear to the world that America could no longer be counted on to sustain its footing as *the* unilateral powerhouse. Numbed by its own inner struggles, devastated by continuous Earth Changes that reaped havoc throughout North America (natural and un-natural changes we will discuss fully in a later chapter) and plagued karmically by its many past intrigues, most of which were based primarily on the country's efforts to retain a faltering power structure and disintegrating world position, a once proud nation quickly turned apathetic, disoriented, vulnerable and disconnected from the goals of the rest of the world. In that state it was easily baited into all manner of misadventure and turmoil both internally and internationally – adventures it would discover by the mid 2020's that it could not emerge from intact.

If the definition of World War is the massive upheaval of order and a realignment of world geopolitics and events, then certainly it was the great world conflict that arose in this period, in essence the third continuation of the two previous World Wars that ultimately threw the world into the greatest turmoil it had ever seen. This conflict would not only cause the realignment of the world's national, regional and geopolitical orders, in time it would also prove to be the keys to the fall of North American culture. In particular, the United States of America would experience a calamitous chain of events from the early to mid 21st Century that would, for all intent and purpose, lead to final disintegration of that great union before it had reached the 300th anniversary of its establishment.

In a broader context, particularly for the West, that great World War, which was the third of its kind on such a scale, represented a continuation and ongoing karmic balancing of many conflicts, including the second World War, the first World War, the Crimean War, the US Civil War, the Napoleonic Wars, the Wars of Religious Reformation, the Ottoman Wars and the Christian Crusades, among others. In addition to this it could be directly linked in terms of Soul group participants (in various incarnations throughout the world and through time) to many prior struggles of ideology, particularly and probably most ironically, the invasions that overran and brought about the final unraveling of the Imperial and Byzantine Roman worlds at the hands of so-called "barbarians" of that time.

As we have said before, it is the role of the Physical System Lord's incarnations to alter the geopolitical structures of the time in order to pave the way for a spiritual and consciousness rebirth brought about by an incarnation of the Spiritual System Lord. Surely it is clear that however devastating and ruthless at the time, the dismantling of Roman world culture by so called "barbarian" invasions helped paved the way for the rise of a geopolitical structure in Europe based on the spiritual principles and practices of Christendom. Similarly, throughout Eurasia and the Middle East, Islamic principles and practices emerged in the distant wake of the "barbarian" vacuum creating the foundation of geopolitical structures in that part of the world. Generally, this remains the basic geopolitical and spiritual dualities upon which the Western and a large portion of the Eastern world are based today.

Removing for a moment any discussion as to whether or not the results of either the increased consciousness or renewed geopolitical structures created were truly what was intended by the various incarnations of the Physical and Spiritual System, a discussion hampered by the natural tendency to see right and wrong, good and bad in what befalls mankind based on your perspective, suffice to say that the impact through time is becoming clear. Taking this idea further, were you to substitute the colloquial term used in the "civilized" world in the 1st Century -- "barbarian" -- for the colloquial term used in the civilized world in the 21st Century, -- "terrorist" -- to describe a violent group appearing highly backwards and slightly stunted in consciousness, you would find you were describing very similar groups and situations. In fact, from the Soul's perspective, taking into consideration once again our discussion concerning those Souls of lower consciousness wishing to remain in a Third Dimensional incarnation process, this may in fact have more validity than you may realize.

The continuing struggle after the fall of Rome at the hands of "barbarians" was resurrected soon after during the apex of the Middle (Dark) Ages under a different guise that was to become known as the great turmoil of the Religious Crusades. It was perhaps the karma generated in the Crusades to liberate Jerusalem from the "barbaric" Muslims and the equal push by Islam to eradicate the Christian "infidels" that created such enormous strife. In fact, the many centuries of conflict between the West and East, civilized and barbarian, established and emerging, have's and have not's, Christendom and Islam -- in short, the Crusades – might well be identified as the greatest spark and karmic generator existing in the modern era as a basis for the conflagration to be known as Earth's Third World War.

What we have attempted to explain here is that although your history carefully constructs historic conflicts so they can be placed within specific regions and time periods, seemingly without connection, the truth is that from a Soul and karmic perspective these things are far more universal, ongoing, interconnected, unending, ebbing and flowing than they may appear. In fact, they transpire over many hundred and even thousand-year intervals with the participation of Souls who keep coming, going and returning, again and again, for their own purposes related to continuing their own Soul growth and karmic balancing.

In this context it's easy to see that the great Third World War not only had origins much further back on the timeline, it could even be said that it represented a continuation of struggles that originated and occurred throughout modern history, which began at the end of what we have called the final Atlantean period. In general, one could also say that the *real* struggle underneath this conflict, which is seemingly endless and eternal in nature, was and is the duality resulting from ideological conflicts between two groups of Third Dimensionally-based incarnated Souls.

Specifically, as we have discussed in the past, this also represents the duality struggle found to be inherent and existing between Soul groups originating from matrices oriented towards "Service-to-Self" and Soul groups whose incarnations are rooted in diametrically opposed matrices that are oriented towards "Service-to-Others." It is important to understand that in one form or another this polar clash (not really a clash in the true sense, but rather a gravitational polarity around which opportunities and events for growth are built in your world) has been in play since not only the beginning of your modern era, which we identify as the end of Atlantean civilization following its third and final collapse in approximately 13,000 BCE, but since the dawn of perfected human physical incarnations in the current and, in many ways, previous 260,000 year galactic cycle periods.

This duality, and the conflict that represents it, demonstrates clearly the karmic polarity and duality that arises naturally between Soul groups (expressed physically through a wide range of political, social, cultural, religious, economic, ethnic and even racial differences) looking for opportunities of consciousness growth within the context of Third Dimensional incarnation. The ongoing nature of such polarity ensures ample opportunity for Soul growth and leads one to the vibrational consciousness necessary to prepare for Ascension periods such as the one you are currently facing. Symbolically, much of this could be said to be highly representative of the age-old struggle known to your world mythologies as the struggle between light and darkness, good and evil, the Titans versus the Olympians; remembering of course to dismiss any subjective connotations (good, bad, right, wrong) you may naturally assign to the side of your preference in such representations and symbolism.

In effect, the third great world conflict of the modern era, which began subtly in the Middle East around the mid 2010's and continued through the 2020's, was a turning point acting as a seemingly endless vortex that once initiated was not extinguished until it had pulled the entire Middle East, Europe, the United States, England, Australia, Russia, China, large parts of Asia and parts of Africa into the conflict. Ultimately it would alter the state of the known world structure at the time. In many ways, and certainly in retrospect, it should have been easy to see this conflict, with its first rumbles occurring through the most ancient areas of Syria, Iraq and Lebanon, as the precursor to the symbolic Biblical conflict known as Armageddon, colloquially known as the massive battle that would bring "the end of the world" and herald the return of a spiritual Master.

While many reading this are no doubt expecting us to tell them that the historic Jesus was the Master who returned at that time, and though there may be spiritual connections of a sort, those of you with a broader understanding will recognize that true spiritual "Masters" do not have religious affiliation or dogma associated with them and, rather, are the derivative physical incarnations of a group of Ninth Dimensional Beings we have called, for convenience sake, the Spiritual System Lords. Symbolically identified universally as the "Sons of God" due to their high consciousness and dimensional resonance, these enlightened spiritual Beings (Avatars) unselfishly incarnate in physical form within lower dimensions in order to provide conscious awakening while influencing the spiritual course of a dimension such as your own as it expands and moves forward (see the System Lords and the Twelve Dimensions for more information) on the timeline.

Returning to our story however, to be sure there were many events up to and directly resulting from the beginning of the great world conflict of the early 21st Century that in fact bankrupted the American system and led to the early and, in many respects, lightening-quick disintegration of the United States. This was due in large part to its Federal government's global overextension that had been ongoing since the later part of the 20th Century.

Unbeknownst to most at the time when the military crisis began and quickly enveloped the world, the US and its economy had been teetering on and off the brink of bankruptcy since approximately the turn of the century in 2000. The overwhelming events of the great war of the 21st Century, combined with the simultaneous chain of shattering natural and un-natural Earth events in the Americas and elsewhere, acted as the straw that broke the proverbial camel's back hastening the country's ultimate decline. Moreover, widespread economic disillusionment readily combined with mounting regional and State efforts to obtain autonomy and independence from a faltering and dysfunctional Federal overseer. This, together with the population's extreme political, regional, racial, economic and cultural polarization, quickly brought the country to a place where an impotent Federal entity was no longer able to extrude itself from a worsening, if not wholly intolerable, local, regional, national and international position.

With the emergence of several incarnations of the Physical System Lord at the time in several Middle Eastern countries, particularly those associated with the regions of Iraq, Syria, Lebanon, Afghanistan, Pakistan, Turkey, Iran, Egypt, Israel and various North African and Arabian states, events quickly accelerated and became insurmountable by the mid to late 2010's leading to declarations of war all around. While this period was not to be called "World War III" at the time it emerged, and, in fact, this heading was kept from popular awareness by the political and media structure for many years and perhaps a decade or more after it began, make no mistake that *this* was the true appellation for the global conflicts that began unfolding in the mid to late 2010's.

This was particularly true following fresh terror-style attacks that took place on European and American soil beginning in that same period. Orchestrated on a calculated scale with alliances made between crime cartels and Islamists, once these targeted attacks began occurring within the boundaries of the US and European homelands, conservative national factions looking to ensure the population's fear and fury, as well as gain deeper US involvement in the global conflicts, demanded action to stem the increasing terrorist and Fundamentalist threat now emerging within their own borders. Ironically, these same factions not only had a covert internal hand in many of the domestic attacks that began to occur in the mid to late 2010's, they were also the group that had originally manipulated and facilitated various Islamic Fundamentalist's rise to power in the Middle East and elsewhere. As fear mongering increased worldwide, conflict expanded at an accelerated rate, incited by different Physical System Lord incarnations on both sides of the fighting.

Hardly anyone living in the West realized at the time that much of what was occurring had been unleashed originally behind-the-scenes as a covert plot by their governments and western agencies to distract the world from the West's worsening financial state and faltering economies. In addition the plan was to use ancient Middle Eastern national, cultural and religious differences and prejudices to disrupt, defuse and disintegrate the entire region pitting sect against sect and factions of Islam against each other in order to keep the area mired in its own localized survival conflicts to control and minimize expansion and further export of violent fundamentalist perspectives. Few anticipated that public calls in the West to eradicate the rising terrorist and military threats in the Middle East would not only prove impossible to achieve but ultimately would lead to the long term unraveling of Western civilization from the inside out in its wake. For many it would prove a valuable lesson as fear begat ever increasing levels of fear, distrust and loathing worldwide.

Once out of the control of its original handlers and instigators, the Middle Eastern conflicts quickly degenerated and spread resulting finally in one of the most devastating nuclear events ever unleashed on your world. Those first exchanges confined themselves for a time to the contested Muslim centers of conflict within regions of Syria, Iran, Iraq, Turkey and Lebanon, but the destruction they evoked marked a dramatic and immediate shift in world political power, structure and organization. As western involvement in the conflict increased in pitch and actuality, it soon turned moderate Islamic nations as a whole and Muslims living worldwide. Before long even those less ideologically focused than the hardcore Islamic Fundamentalists, who were known for their ruthlessness, irrevocably turned against the West and western governments, especially in the United States and Europe.

The devastation this caused did bring silence to the world for a short time thereafter. However, few living realized that the fairly limited regional nuclear exchanges in the Middle East and their silent aftermath would not only set the stage for national, international, cultural and religious finger-pointing but would also act as a precursor to the free-fall of world political structures. This was destined to deliver global disintegration on the grandest scale ever envisioned by modern humans.

The silence stifled, initial exchanges and subsequent augmentation of nuclear use by Islamic state sponsored terrorist groups would bring the conflict to Europe's doorstep in the form of limited nuclear occurrences in parts of Europe. These events would be responsible for widespread western disarray and, in their wake, the return of large swaths of European culture and society to the Dark Ages. On the heels of this world outrage, new destruction and devastation that occurred in some of the major centers of the North American continent, particularly the West and Southwestern US, would not only bring the conflict squarely to American soil, it ensured once safe havens would now hold a focus for the conflict's continuation. By the early to mid 2020's, it was clear that the dismantling of everyday life as previously known in North America was fully underway, as American Federals implemented police-state measures and out of fear disbanded individual constitutional protections, effectively making the country a nation under siege from the inside out.

These factors, combined with the existing economic malaise, ongoing dualities and increasing polarization caused tremendous shift worldwide in terms of political and economic structures, and nowhere was this felt more intensely than within North America and the former United States. Despite some half hearted and brief attempts to stem national disintegration through efforts to unify the North American continent into one mega union, it was mainly at this time, from the late 2010's through the 2020's, that North America and particularly the United States fell into generalized chaos.

The deepening global war, internal political authoritarianism and national economic crisis quickly made America, and in some respects North America, a place where for all intent and purpose it was every man for themselves. Though not an overnight occurrence, the natural separation and division of the United States into specific regions, only loosely identified with or associated with Federal authority initially, was the first real sign that historic change was occurring and a shift in power from a Federal to a regional and State basis was happening. As the Federal government lost its ability to regulate all but a meager national defense effort, bankrupt under the weight of its enormous debt and unable to raise or oblige federal tax compliance, it became clear that its end was only a matter of time and world power had relocated focus to the relatively war-untouched Asia Pacific.

Disarray worsened late in the 2020's, and States began to turn to new loosely formed American regional alliances to promote their own interests and rights, aligning themselves with other States or areas within specific regions for economic and political strength. Though the first introduction of various State currencies backed by independent State and Regional Central Banks emerged as early as the mid 2020s following the value collapse of the America dollar, which was preceded by the recession of the late 2010's and the great US economic collapse that followed, by the 2030's only state or regional currencies backed by real assets were being recognized nationally or internationally. Although many regions and States in this emerging American Union continued to elect Federal "representatives" and discuss national defense, they had little real focus or authority, and by the end of the 2020's references to a central Federal government were perfunctory, even nostalgic.

True power was now firmly seated within a handful of powerful economic and political regions that formally had been collectively known as the United States of America. Where one resided within this collective by the early to mid 2020's was to become very significant, and for the most part this is where one would most likely reside not only through the remainder of the third great world conflict but through the invasion and occupation of central North America still to come.

This factor had far reaching consequences and was the cause of much hardship for friends and families separated by the newly emerged boundaries. Indeed, it would be an understatement to say that life was growing more and more of a challenge for those people still residing in States and regions where natural disasters and lawlessness increased seasonally or where unified economies, assistance, subsidies and legal protections were no longer to be found. It quickly became evident that many former US States would be hit hard by the federal unraveling. This was particularly true in areas dominated by individuals still fighting to preserve their fundamentalist perspective and Service-to-Self orientation, most likely places populated by those very Souls that would choose further future incarnations in a Third Dimensional-based reality.

As some former American States, now fractured and disorganized, bonded together into stronger regional powers, the success of certain regions, such as the region that constituted the New England States or the region of the Pacific Coast, predominated and became the economic winners in the fall out that ensued. By the dawn of the 2030's, most of these regions had militarized and established regional armies for their own protection primarily to protect them from newly formed and ungoverned militias acting almost as outlaw "raiders" emanating from poverty-stricken North American territories. The poverty, disillusion and lawlessness rampant in these depressed regions, former States now non-aligned, was made more poignant by the prosperous regions' refusal to allow immigration or organize disaster aid of any kind. Naturally, this caused mounting resentment that would serve as the seeds for the coming second North American Civil War, not to mention the foreign invasions that civil disturbance would ultimately trigger. These so-called peace keeping invasions would serve once and for all to end the American culture that existed prior to that time.

The second American civil war served as the final coup de grâce for cohesion and unity on the North American continent, and its impact was second only to the devastating natural disasters taking place and the final fall of the US Federal government. As the first Civil War had done previously, the new civil war pitted brother against brother and family against family. In doing so it brought about the destruction and elimination en masse of certain ethnicities, races and other populations living in certain regions on the North American continent.

Although the nations of Canada and Mexico, still relatively intact as nation states, attempted to refrain from any connection or involvement, it was incursions by the outlaw, poverty stricken independent former-US States at this time that would ultimately engulf the entire North American continent in conflict. While Europe and the Middle East were still recovering from the nuclear holocaust and devastations they had experienced, mostly with the aid of Russia and China, much of the world was at this point disinterested in the former United States, leaving it to respond to its own devices and karma. However, the incursions into Mexico and Canada by rogue former US state militias changed attitudes and caused both Asian and Russian populations to demand assistance for the people of Canada, Mexico and Latin America. Russian and Chinese interests in Latin and South America had augmented continually since the beginning of the 2020's, and thus political forces in these nations saw the incursions by former American citizens in those regions as terroristic attacks on their own interests.

Ironically, the offending former US citizens and regions that banded together into militias and were now raiding Canadian and Mexican territories out of economic necessity, the very same groups that not long before had been quick to label any group fighting a cause alien to its own interests as "terrorists," were now labeled as international terrorist organizations themselves. In addition, both the Chinese and Russians, who only reluctantly aligned to come to the world's aid during the great conflict, were still dealing with the sting of that conflict and many held the former US populace and government representatives responsible for originally instigating the world war via secret and clandestine government actions in the first place. Now, China and Russia assumed the role of world police focused on policing rogue regions of the former US, a position once stubbornly adhered to by the United States worldwide. The balancing of this particular energetic karmic debt was obvious to most, and the irony of that situation was not lost on historians of the time.

It was not until the second Civil War in America was underway however, that Asian and Russian political structures, through incarnations of the System Lords, began to consider and finally act upon a goal to successfully colonize parts of former America. Russia had already been provided with virtual free access to large parts of the devastated European continent, as well as large areas of Turkey, the Middle East and North Africa. For its part, particularly in light of the disastrous Earth changes that had occurred in Japan, Taiwan, Korea and the Philippines, which diminished their regional and world influence almost completely, China had freely capitalized and economically benefited from its dominance in Pacific Asia, as well as South East Asia, Australia, Africa, Mexico and, particularly, Latin and South America.

In terms of functioning regions in the former US, for the most part the country mainland had spilt into the New England regional states, the Western Coastal region, the Texas union, and the Chicago-led upper mid-western territories. States or areas found outside of these newly formed regional territories were considered lost (due to the overwhelming natural or manmade disasters that had befallen them, particularly in the western, mid-western and southern portions of the country) or ungovernable. For the most part it was these areas that were mainly responsible for the activity called the second American Civil War and they would also be the areas where the conflict and challenges raged most intensely. While the New England and West Coast regions were economically, politically and militarily savvy enough via foreign alliances and associations to fend off regional or foreign invasion and remain independent, it soon became clear by the mid 2030's into the 2040's that other areas would not be as lucky. Indeed, many US territories were ripe for the taking, as both the Chicago and Texas unions would soon discover.

By the year 2075 any resemblance that may have existed up until then to the United States of the late 20th Century was virtually non-existent. However, before we continue our discussion of the fate of former US regions, let us first take a look at the emergence of the Eurasian Enlightenment, a time of historical importance that emerged on the Third Dimensional timeline in the mid to late 21st Century.

Chapter 5
The Emergence of the Eurasian Enlightenment

The Third Great War as it became known, was relatively short lived in terms of its duration but was of a destructive nature that had never been seen on the face of planet Earth prior. Its impact was felt worldwide for nearly a century and a half thereafter. The destruction it caused was most intense in those specific global regions where religious, political, philosophical and other cultural influences had created a metaphysical impasse of sorts. For many it was the inevitable course necessary to shake up the entrenched duality that had been created, where modernity, advancement and change were not only difficult to achieve but, if obtainable at all, were impossible to ground.

That shake up however, was vital if the philosophical and spiritual inroads necessary for growth in the newly emerging Third Dimensional timeline, with the assistance of incarnations from the Spiritual System Lord, were to be possible. It would be up to incarnations of the Physical System Lord (incarnations motivating mass consciousness towards geopolitical and rational-brain evolution) to break the blockage via the great world conflict that ensued, and thus a majority of physical incarnations were undertaken by that entity beginning in the late 20th Century and well into the third quarter of the 21st Century. Many of these could be said to be at the heart of the motivating factors surrounding the great World War of the 21st Century.

Despite this however, the Spiritual System Lord (physical incarnations directing mass consciousness towards social and spiritual, or right-brain evolution) also materialized within the realm in numerous forms during the period, although the bulk of these incarnations were post World War III and after the decade of the 2020's. These incarnations would have a direct impact on elevating technical achievement, creative output, cultural renaissance and artistic sensitivity worldwide bringing new forms of wisdom and higher consciousness following the great world conflict.

The philosophical and spiritual rebirth that took place post World War III would lead to a convergence of humanitarian thought and talent centered in areas of Euro-Asia, in particular regions of southern and western Russia including the Ukraine, areas of Eastern Europe, the Balkans and the Baltics. Surprisingly, western Russia and most of its historic Eurasian and Eastern European satellites became the central region to emerge from the Third Great War with economies and infrastructure relatively intact. This was mostly because Russia had previously been forced to develop its own independent economic and political unions after political and economic isolation was imposed by British, West European and American concerns as a punishment for hardline Russian political strategies that began to take hold in the mid to late 2010's. At the same time, the Russian league's isolation made it less reliant on global interface. Thus, ostracizing from the West together with a leadership that pushed for ultra autonomy in world affairs helped it to narrowly overcome the overwhelming economic losses imposed on it and, because of it's isolation, escape the even heavier war devastations that would be felt throughout Western Europe, the Middle East, Eastern Africa and, later on, North America.

Protected by a newly fortified and emboldened Russia, together with allies, the federation was able to remain relatively quiet and on the sidelines for the beginning of the Third Great War, rushing in to save the day only after seeing other players had all but exhausted and bankrupted themselves. It was a conscious tactic historians and strategists made note of remembering how America came late to the European front and was then able to entrench its influence in Europe and to an extent Asia throughout the post World War II era.

Seeing itself as a world cultural "savior" of sorts, beginning in the late 2020's and through the 2030's Russia capitalized on what it saw as its ability to bring order to a crumbling and demoralized world, particularly in areas to its west, southwest and south, turning situations to its advantage through cunning, influence, leadership, philosophy and artistic endeavors. Ongoing relaxation of its primal, conservative and seemingly fundamentalist values throughout the period, which was aided by an influx of incarnations of highly enlightened Souls and at least two incarnations of the Physical System Lord in the region beginning in the late 2000's, helped push the federation populace to slightly augmented consciousness. As a result, following a short period of internal social and political strife during the mid to late 2020's when most of these incarnations reached adulthood, a more progressive governance was adopted that eventually would lead to a long awaited loosening of tight religious, moral, artistic and cultural values. Thereafter, the region began a prosperous ascent that was in full swing by the middle of the 21st Century, and though not the center of the Eurasian renaissance per se, Russia's success and regional protection did have an impact on cultivating the possibility of its very emergence. Geopolitical strategy aside, beginning in the mid 21st Century this activity culminated in a period that would become known as the Eurasian (sometimes also referred to as the Byzantine) Enlightenment.

The Eurasian Enlightenment reestablished the concept of humanitarianism, the equality of diversity, freedom of expression and freedom of choice as ideals for mankind (all Fourth Dimensional qualities and values) while also birthing new spiritual, cultural, artistic and philosophical visions for a post world-war planet in disarray. Furthermore, it became clear that almost all outmoded heritage-thinking, including ancient concepts of religion, morality, race, culture and politics, had either been completely annihilated or were now being rejected by world populations that had suffered through its abject failures.

Eurasia (Byzantium) now began to identify itself as the western world's true cradle of democracy. This was widely promoted based on newly discovered archeological findings around and under the Black Sea that confirmed an advanced Eurasian society existed predating even ancient Egyptian civilization (indeed, the area does have direct links to Atlantean civilization, and many references in the Bible actually originate from stories about Byzantium events in the pre-modern era, including stories of the flood, among others). For historians of the time, a quick connection was now made to ancient Greek civilization, democracy and even Alexander the Great, thus allowing claims that positioned Eurasian history as a precursor of fundamental classic western culture. Most were only too happy to condone the world's reinvention of itself and therefore allow such connections to be made even if they seemed a stretch, which they often were. This was particularly true since the links were used as a basis for promoting newly emerging principles and models that needed to be grounded in something tangible but elusive in order to take hold.

In truth, this linkage did not amount to just an imposition of existing old regional philosophies but was instead based on a real universal quest to find new workable ideals and values to assist a world struggling to rebuild itself in ways that could never be identified with the past again. The focal point of that quest just happened to be centered in a peaceable and newly prosperous (by default) Eurasia, which had

Timeline Collapse & Universal Ascension

skirted the most violent upheavals of the war and had now achieved the basis of altruistic intent, free expression and exuberant implementation of the new forms being birthed. This period of endeavor, achievement and enlightenment would set the course for Earth's Third Dimensional continuation into the 23rd Century.

At the onset of the post Great War period most of the world blamed Christian, Christian Orthodox and Islamic religious philosophies and structures as the root cause of the greatest conflict man had ever known. Highly suspect and widely loathed, post war global societies consciously gutted, neutered and turned away from religious dogma or structures of any kind, seeing them as directly linked to the seeds of disaster. This occurred in much the same way humanity had abolished from mainstream discussion or adherence the concept of Nazism following the 20th Century's World War II, or Stalin-style Communism following disintegration of the Soviet Union later that same century.

Though difficult for many to anticipate or accept, the void created in the West caused by the decentralization and collapse of many of the world's great religious dogmas and structures, including Christianity, Islamism and Judaism, heralded a period of new spiritual awakening not based on structured religious organization. Though Hinduism, Buddhism and Eastern Orthodox Christianity, among others, continued on as regional organizations catering to the spiritual interest of some and though small independent religious sects continued to exist locally around the world, the demise of major organized players lessened the overall voice and importance of "religion" in the eyes of humanity considerably. Even those powerful world religious organizations that survived the great conflict, such as the Hindu, Eastern Orthodox or Buddhist orders, became more sectarian, philosophical, historical institutions, disengaged almost entirely from populace governance with virtually no political or social influence.

Seekers who felt the need to follow gurus, dogma or ritual as part of organized religious cults (of any kind) were now generally frowned upon, and those searching for spiritual connection were encouraged to find their own independent means of spirituality and connection to Source. For the most part religious institutions based on historic and outmoded dogmas quickly decentralized and were now content to tend to the spiritual needs of their local flocks, refraining from all political, national or international affiliations as well as any highly organized activities or involvement. This was assisted by first the outlawing, then the mocking and eventually the relegation of all ancient religious literature to the realm of complete fiction and primitive history. These beliefs were enforced by advances in science and physics as well as revelations concerning and originating from verified contacts with interdimensional non-Earth Beings. It became widely known at the time that various alien races had participated with secret factions of some world governments, even interfering with world events, since the late 20th Century. Much of the modern weaponry, particularly advanced scalar technology that allowed for the weaponization of Earth's natural processes, was directly attributable to such alien interventions.

But perhaps the greatest impetus in the dismantling of religious structure was the destruction of the religious centers that had functioned as the epicenters of population control for millennia. This included the fact that there would be no turning back once the collapse of the Roman Catholic Church had taken place, an occurrence directly linked to the nuclear holocaust perpetrated on Rome itself during the conflict. The nuclear devastation felt in Rome and other major centers in Europe was not unlike that felt throughout the Middle East (including its ancient religious centers) just prior to Europe's destruction, and this included much of what was formerly known as Israel, Jordan,

Lebanon, Egypt, Iraq, Syria, Saudi Arabia, parts of Iran, Afghanistan, Pakistan and large portions of Northern India, among others.

Clearly, as these areas vanished from world-importance almost overnight, other less-affiliated regions quickly filled the void. In addition to Russia and Eurasia in the West, China in the East and Pacific together with Southern Africa, Canada and distinct areas in South America became centers of commerce, advancement and trade not to mention economic, geopolitical and philosophic strength. That said however, it was Eurasia, firmly led by a victorious if not unscathed Russia with its attention focused in Moscow, St. Petersburg, Helsinki, Warsaw, Budapest, Kiev and to a lesser extent Constantinople, Prague and Berlin, that would emerge as the new intellectual and social Meccas of the world -- the combined New York, Paris, London and Los Angeles of 22nd Century thought, wisdom and creativity.

From the Soul's perspective this region became the land of "choice" for physical incarnations by Souls in the newly structured world of the late 21st and early 22nd Century. Moreover, while younger Souls still in search of challenging Third Dimensional-type lessons now had ample opportunities worldwide for growth by incarnating in areas devastated by the great conflict, older Souls not quite ready to depart Third Dimensional incarnation but in search of less challenging karmic situations found the Eurasian regions and this period to be the perfect opportunity for physical incarnation. In this manner, prior to the definitive shift of many Souls from Third Dimensional to Fifth Dimensional incarnations, these regions could be said to have Fourth Dimensional qualities with most of those who were incarnated in them readily preparing to cycle-off the continuing Third Dimensional timeline.

Eurasia at this time became linked to higher vibrational frequencies (remembering for a moment the location of our energetic waves that transverse the globe), better guidance and superior qualities of consciousness. This easily translated into more enlightened Human Angelic Souls being born there, with most of them expressing near-Fourth Dimensional values and leaning heavily towards future Fifth Dimensional incarnations. Even though they would not take part in the timeline's continuation or reap the full benefits of their efforts in future lifetimes on Earth, they would nevertheless be the ones to essentially pave the way for those Souls continuing on with the timeline's trajectory. Regardless, these Souls would serve as the heart of the Eurasian Enlightenment, and guided by various incarnations of the Spiritual System Lord this would be the true second coming following the "End Times" or "Armageddon" if you prefer that was anticipated widely. Furthermore, the precepts and mass consciousness established at this time would form the basis of Third Dimensional existence for all Souls committed to Earth-bound incarnations through the 26th Century.

To be sure, it can be noted that the Eurasian Enlightenment and accompanying economic resurgence and leadership of the region did ultimately lead to new imperialistic global and military adventures led by its principal benefactor nation, Russia, and these very events would conspire to bring about final subjugation of Europe and the ultimate disintegration of the United States. However, the period cannot be discounted for its great social, philosophical and economic revival, particularly with regard to the opening of consciousness it permitted in areas previously ultra conservative or, as we prefer to describe them, Third Dimensional regions chosen by younger Souls oriented towards a more fundamentalist Service to Self growth pattern. Indeed, its global impact, particularly in the areas of technology, spiritual thought and artistic endeavor, are directly linked with the European Renaissance period, the Enlightenment period of the 18th Century and the period of great invention, prosperity and creativity of the later 19th and early

20th Century. In an historical context, by the last half of the 22nd Century over a century after its start, the Eurasian Enlightenment, as it would come to be known, would be called one of the most creative and productive periods in all modern history.

It should be realized that as we have said massive destruction and change generally act as a precursor to the arrival of a "Christed" figure (not to infer a connection to any particular religion, but in the sense of an anointed adept, or spiritual master). Such a figure is always an incarnation of the Spiritual System Lord. The arrival of just such a prominent incarnation of the Spiritual System Lord at the time was indeed linked to the one formerly known as the Master Jesus, as well as other incarnations before that entity (see the System Lords and the Twelve Dimensions) and in that sense the many prophecies could be said to have been fulfilled. However, this was not a "resurrection" as expected by fundamentalists per the Christian religious mythology, nor was it a "return" where the historical figure Jesus would take charge of his armies and vanquish his enemies.

Instead it was the mass devastation that had taken place around the world in the Third Great War that ultimately set the stage for an incarnation of the Spiritual System Lord in order to lead a change in consciousness, much as it would be during the Enlightenment period becoming the "second coming" anticipated. This emergence was a far cry from what is currently expected by those awaiting the return of their champion. Instead it would come when the world was ripe for a redress of world spiritual outlook and values, implanting new philosophical, cultural and artistic thoughts to fill the void and pave the way for a new world.

This is in contrast to ancient Roman history, where it might be said that the Master known as Jesus brought about new spiritual insight that *itself* would ultimately lead to the collapse of Rome. In this era however, system collapse, which was led by incarnations of the Physical System Lords, precipitated the emergence of incarnations of the Spiritual System Lord just before and during the Eurasian Enlightenment. The truth then is that the mass devastation that afflicted the world came prior to the Spiritual System Lord's new incarnations of the mid to late 21st Century, and these could only have been undertaken with success following a great turmoil that had swept away all major geopolitical and religious structures that were operating in the world at the time.

Global collapse complete, emergence of the new Spiritual System Lord also brought about a change in the fabric of daily life for all sides and from all perspectives, and it is for this reason that many in your time have already prophesized that a new Christ figure (Spiritual System Lord) would most likely incarnate in Eurasian territories. Thus, the proximity and accessibility of that incarnation to what would become the birthplace of new social, spiritual, cultural and artistic vision and consciousness in the later part of the 21st Century. This is not to be confused with incarnations of the Physical System Lords, whose main incarnations are to alter geopolitical structures and who in this case incarnated in various lifetimes prior to and during the great world conflicts that ensued primarily in the United States, the Middle East and Asia.

In other terms, the third great conflict provided no real victors in the sense you would understand today and left not only a geopolitical and world structural void, it also left a cultural, spiritual and philosophical void in consciousness as well. As we have said, this was particularly true in terms of religious or fundamentalist perspectives, and it is important to note that the utter destruction to fall on all sides of the conflict caused complete dissolution of prior religious, philosophical or cultural differences and beliefs once and for all.

It was no longer possible for those in the western world witnessing such complete devastation to truly believe that a Jesus or any other great Spiritual master, not to mention God himself, was ready to arrive on a white horse to save them. Indeed, how could any existential power exist that would permit such terrible horrors and massive devastation, let alone condone such events from the distant sidelines. Similarly, in the Middle East and throughout the Islamic world, based on particular cultural perspectives in those regions that placed literal interpretation of the world above all other interpretations, such complete and utter defeat of the Prophet's many loyal followers could only mean one thing: the real and definitive defeat -- the actual "literal" death -- of God himself.

Obviously in the aftermath of terrible conflict, particular and peculiar religious views, rituals, rites and all-important daily cultural norms were buried in the face of starvation, the need for shelter and the disintegration of basic common laws of any kind. One could easily see that the loss of geopolitical, cultural and religious structures on such a grand scale naturally heralded the dismantling of all existing geo-political, cultural and religious values. And since there was no victor, as it is known in your terms, neither was there any cultural, religious or geopolitical system to fill the void that devastation had wrought. It was natural therefore that the great conflict of the late 2010s and 2020s would lead directly to the need to create completely new structures based on emerging consciousness and thought. Incarnations of the Spiritual System Lord were present throughout the Eurasian Enlightenment to coax along that very rebirth.

One should not be mislead into believing however, that the experience or plight of the world following the Third Great War was a simple one, sweeping aside the existing establishment to easily formulate a brave new world. In truth, regions of the world that had been devastated by destruction either directly, as in the case of the Middle East and Europe, or indirectly, as in the case of North America, required more than half to three-quarters of a century to revitalize themselves regionally. In many cases, some areas never truly recovered even centuries later.

Still, life continued as best it could even in those areas where nuclear war and massive destruction had taken place. Hardest hit by nuclear devastation were most parts of the Middle East and certain parts of central and southeastern Europe (particularly those areas historically embroiled in religious, sectarian and ethnic fighting in the past), as well as vast areas of Italy, Southern Germany and France. As mentioned, the devastation experienced in Milan and Rome was complicated by the annihilation of the historic entity known as the Roman Catholic Church, and in Paris destruction of the city was no less devastating, traumatizing all western historic, cultural and artistic centers not to mention ending the existence of the nation of France overnight as well.

Nuclear holocaust did not occur widely in Great Britain, Northern Europe or Scandinavia. However, turmoil within these areas caused by terrorist-styled events, population exodus, fallout and fear followed by cosmopolitan disintegration via starvation or severe social, economic and financial hardship, saw these regions turn inward creating what appeared to many as a replay of earlier European Feudal societies. In essence, most of the populations in these regions returned to some form of independent City-State Republic with no real centralized federal authority, each beholding to whatever outside help, intervention or influence they could attract. Those regions where the populations already had vast experience cooperating within and organizing or maintaining comprehensive social structures for the common good of the community faired best in such circumstances, so this was particularly true in the Scandinavian and Nordic lands.

For most of Europe assistance came primarily in the form of Russia, while in other world regions, including Australia, South East Asia, Southern India, Japan, Central and Southern Africa and South America, the role of assistance fell to China. In the post Third Great War era, Russia and China represented the new world regulators and military strength, filling a void left by the bankrupt and now unraveling United States, an emaciated Great Britain and a disemboweled and devastated Europe.

Chapter 6
More About the Unraveling of America on the Third Dimensional Timeline

Total nuclear destruction on such a grand scale did not occur in the United States. However, following the great world conflict, North America was not immune to limited regional nuclear devastation within its own borders. This combined with widespread natural and unnatural Earth disasters in the region that were a result of nuclear fallout and, more importantly, mismanagement of Federal Scalar weaponry and other secret technologies, caused the greatest domestic harm. This was particularly true in areas such as New York, Washington DC, the Western US and specific areas in the Southern US, particularly those areas in and around Atlanta. In addition large areas outside the city of Chicago and portions of Southern Texas suffered from nuclear incidences, all of which were devastating on both a regional and a national level.

These centers never truly revitalized following the attacks, which were perpetrated by terrorist "insider" agents and regional provocateurs looking to promote State rights and once and for all break the back of a US Federal government now unable to defend itself or counter such complete disaster. It was a strategy that would prove overly successful and ultimately defeat any goal of State autonomy as well, leading instead to the long-term disintegration and demise of not only United States Federal authority, but the majority of State governments formerly comprising that Union. It would also open the door to a limited regional second US Civil war and, as a consequence, foreign occupation of a large swath of the former US in order to contain that war.

This was compounded by the fact that although organized religion was shunned by the majority of the world immediately following the end of the Third Great War. This was not necessarily the case in America where mass conversions into one or another fundamentalist-styled religion had silently continued since the dawn of the 21st Century. As discussed already, not only did the polarity related to these opposing religious fundamentalist groups take real hold at this point, in the absence of a definitive victor in the Third Great World War, all factions found themselves disoriented and angered at the outcome.

Fermentation of this anger would have a profound long-term effect on the degeneration of North American unity, as these groups quietly and, in most cases covertly, took up the fallen banners of their respective religious group. Suddenly, historic, social, cultural and racial tensions rose to the surface unchecked and began to display important karmic implications. The surge in the number of Islamic converts in the United States, which for the most part followed racial divides in defiance of centuries of Christian dominance there, spurred renewed calls among American Christians to unify in order to defend themselves, their God and their way of life. As the population divides widened, this would not only serve as a basis for State populations to call for an end to Federal support, it would ultimately seed complete organizational disintegration leading to civil conflict on both sides.

In that regard, it was instigators from the two sides of this particular polarity that would eventually unleash the limited nuclear devastations on US soil and hasten final breakdown of Federal authority and support. In sequence, the demise of Federal Authority would ultimately lead to out and out Civil War among former States and regions of the

US, and this would have even more impact on the whole of North America soon thereafter.

The experience of Souls incarnated and living in the US prior to final collapse of the US Federal authority was one that placed them under a semi-totalitarian regime within a national state of fear, misgiving and ethical bankruptcy. Fear mongering of this sort had long been used as the pretext for foreign involvement and homeland protection, and over time was also used as an excuse for abandoning virtually every democratic and constitutional ideal upon which the US was based. Constitutional protections were blatantly dissolved during World War III and a despised congressional and legislative electorate soon after cancelled elections, declared themselves the de facto regime and imposed marshal law as they barricaded themselves inside the new fortress that was to become the city of Washington, DC.

Bankrupt and seemingly dysfunctional though still operational through military mercenaries (mostly based overseas and would take the lead role in several global nuclear exchanges that would drastically affect the Middle East), this situation soon alienated US State governments and separated the populace from the US Federal government almost entirely. Within a short time, most areas, particularly those under the thumb of religious fundamentalist thought, seceded and declared independence and non-compliance. Only parts of New England (centered around Boston, Providence and New Haven), New York, Chicago, Atlanta and small areas in Denver and Southern California kept loose connections with a failing US Federal government until such time as it could truly no longer be considered a viable entity, a time they would soon discover was not very far away indeed.

Together with Washington DC, federalist regions were eventually targeted by homegrown "insider" terrorists who in reality represented religious fundamentalist and terror groups that had disguised themselves under the cloak of "States' Rights." Up until then a tenuous if unsustainable Federal structure had remained in place managing the day-to-day conflicts of World War III. That came to an abrupt end as soon as conflict in the Middle East had waned. On its heels there were numerous small-scale nuclear incidents that occurred across the US instigated by parties sympathetic with Middle Eastern affiliates that had lost in the Great War and angered at the overall results. It was a devastating nuclear incident delivered by such a group at the doorstep of Washington DC that brought the existence of a US Federal government to a screeching halt.

The enormous fear generated by a virtual police state mindset before and during the war had dominated the national US psyche for decades, and perhaps this could be seen as the single most important factor exhausting the populace psychologically and speeding the country towards national collapse. To the majority of younger Americans, Federal or National collapse now seemed preferable to living life in a continuous state of fear, suspicion and loathing, especially the kind fermented by the last seated Federal government. The institution was mocked widely for being blinded by its own dictatorial controls and endless edicts, which were designed merely to prolong government dominance as long as possible and enrich its leaders via totalitarian and secret tactics. Exasperated from the many years of war and fatigued by the incessant fear mongering and militaristic control, all factions of the US populace, even those most vulnerable to the fears being propagated by the central government, began to see Federal national authority as an intolerable, burdensome and archaic structure, which could only be exorcised through state and regional independence.

Once these limited regional nuclear incidences in the US had occurred, destruction of the Federal leadership obliged former American States to step up to the plate. Many were forced to reinvent themselves, and did so by creating their own banking systems, borders, militias and Federal style governments. In some cases, States joined forces with other States or regions to create unions or leagues to ensure economic, political and military security and stability.

In conjunction with the proliferation in natural disasters, the dramatic changes that occurred with respect to borders and economic regions caused widespread refugee problems, with those caught in devastated, less productive or less prosperous regions, as well as those where the cultural or religious mindset was newly alien to them, were forced to migrate. Borders became vigorously defended, and the refugee problem became so overwhelming so fast for some States and regions that groups were not only turned back at borders, mass tragedies ensued as migrants were systematically exterminated.

It was the mass devastation felt in the South and West of the country combined with the refugee problem and severe economic hardship and starvation that caused the greatest antagonism between those State unions that remained fairly functioning and intact, and those where most systems and laws had collapsed. In some states, totalitarian regimes proliferated with small ruthless ruling groups concentrating economic and political control. In others, so-called "democratic majority" rule left unchecked by constitutional protections meant unforeseen hardship if not outright genocide for many minorities (religious, racial and social) living within those regions.

Shortly following regional reorganization, the struggle between have's and have not's in terms of State and region-hood quickly became the focus of dissatisfaction and conflict. Gang-like militias formed in poverty stricken and economically deprived State regions, and soon regional border incursions and conflicts began to be commonplace with wealthier territories. Eventually these border skirmishes and raids escalated into outright invasions that would ultimately lead to regional (Civil) war.

Forecasting the trouble that was brewing, certain regions bonded together for greater protection. Territories such as the New England Union or the California-Pacific Union successfully unified their member states. Now recognized regionally and internationally as independent nations, these unions were able to gain global recognition, signing treaties for mutual cooperation, trade and defense with foreign governments. As they prospered, weaker regions and former US States began wider incursions into their territories, and this not only seeded localized skirmishes and resentment it now began to trigger military assistance via the newly formed foreign alliances that had been forged.

By the 2040s, push back had devolved into North American regional civil war and conflict. In response and feeling opportunities for advancement existed, areas such as the Texas Union, in conjunction with the Southwestern Alliance, began to push outside of former US territories across Mexican borders. Mexico would see such incursions as an opportunity to avenge the indignities it felt it had experienced over the course of several hundred years, in particular the loss of Texas and large areas of the Southwestern US. In a sense, the karma generated over several centuries was now ripe for balancing.

Simultaneously, territories in the former mid western states of Ohio, Indiana and Eastern Michigan, regions already in conflict with the Chicago-Illinois Union (which included the former US states of Illinois, Wisconsin, Iowa and Minnesota, as well as the upper peninsula of Michigan), began to advance through Michigan into Canada, which was the principal benefactor of its new protectorate, the Chicago-Illinois League. Canada, which had had its fair share of fundamentalist terrorist insider trouble throughout the Great War and had militarized its nation, fortified its borders and fought hard against such activities, looked upon these conflicts with rogue former US States as terrorism pure and simple. It vowed to not only defend its territory at all cost against such violations, it took the added measure of sending well trained and armed troops to defend the Chicago Union, with which it had negotiated economic and military alliances that called on Canada to defend that Union's entire regional territory.

Though seemingly minor in effect and purely opportunistic in nature, the fallout from these incursions by armed elements of former US states was terrible and would bring lasting impact on the former United States as a whole. It required only a handful of incidental defeats at the hands of outlaw US regional militias before a shaken democratic and unified Canada called on its Russian allies for assistance. Once this happened, China, which had made enormous inroads both economically and politically throughout South and Latin America, was proclaimed Mexico's principal benefactor and defender. Within a short span, Mexico formally requested Chinese intervention to stem what it described as the onslaught of Texan terrorists across its borders and into its country.

Once Russian troops descending from the north and Chinese troops advancing from the south and southwest landed in the former American States there would be no turning back. These dramatic actions and subsequent events would ultimately lead to the occupation and final disintegration of what was left of the American States by 2055. Outside of the successful and protected unified regions of New England, California-Pacific, the Chicago-Illinois League, and limited areas of unified Northern Texas (including parts of Oklahoma and Arkansas), all of which prospered in the aftermath of these conflicts and resulting consolidations, the remainder of former American States and regions were quickly relegated to the status of foreign satellites. Invaded former American territories were now declared to be under the protection of China in the South, Southeast and Southwest, or Russia in the Mid Atlantic, Midwest, Central Plaines and Western areas not already part of the California-Pacific Union. Subsequent international immigration and emigration to and from these areas, systematically conducted as part of long term occupation plans implemented primarily by the Russians, would leave the regions with little resemblance to their former American selves by the year 2080.

Following the Great World Conflict and as these events were unfolding in the former United States, China had come to wield an enormous sphere of influence in other parts of the world. This was particularly true in and throughout Asia including Japan and Southeast Asia as well as the Indian continent the Australian territories, South America, Latin America and Mexico. They also economically occupied many portions of the Middle East that remained unaffected or at least manageable following the devastation caused by nuclear conflict. In addition, certain areas of Africa were under their sway and these had long participated with the Chinese through various economic alliances.

The Russian sphere of influence also stretched far and wide. Taking advantage of the devastation brought about by World War III, Russian impact was paramount in Europe, Britain, Scandinavian, all Eurasian countries, the Baltics, all of Eastern Europe and in the Balkans. Russia also had dominant influence in Turkey, Egypt, North Africa and other areas of the Middle East that it had historically been aligned with.

Despite temporary local resistance and a short lived armed popular revolt, the former US Alaskan territories eventually voted to revert to Russian control following the final fall of the Federal United States (a vote many say was strong armed by factions with Russian ties looking to disarm the local militias), and via these ties Russian economic and political influence pushed well into Canada via new alliances with that country. Using its political ties with Cuba as a basis, Russia also held sway over the majority of Caribbean island nations formerly linked to either Britain, Europe or the US, as well as specific areas of Latin and South America. Many of these consolidated and bonded together to become member States in a newly formed independent Caribbean nation, which was placed under Russian protection.

Politically independent, free and relatively unscathed by the vast global conflicts, many Latin and South America nations prospered by forging new economic and other world affiliations following World War III. This was particularly true for Brazil and Argentina, which also led a mid 21st Century movement to establish a South American Union based on the principles of a now disintegrated European Economic Union.

Of all the former US States, only the Hawaiian islands were able to remain fairly intact and autonomous. Hawaii was reestablished as a unique and prosperous independent Republic (despite substantial Earth changes and the loss of territories through earthquakes, volcanic eruption and other natural disasters) by reinforcing its natural isolation during the US turmoil and bolstering its position as an exclusive world-class retreat. It also established itself as a new international banking center, cementing alliances with China, Russia and others via lucrative monetary and tax agreements and setting itself up as a new-styled Monaco and safe haven for the 21st Century.

It is from these spheres of influence that power and world geopolitical structure emerged in the Third Universal Dimension on the continuing Third Dimensional timeline after 2035. And it was the emergence of incarnations of the Spiritual System Lord in Eurasian and Russian territories, China and South America at the time that would herald a renewed emergence of philosophic, spiritual, cultural and social excellence to become known as the Eurasian Enlightenment. This would lead the world, as well as the Third Dimensional timeline, to a much calmer if not better place following the more than 30 years of anarchy it had experienced globally during the trials of the 21st Century.

Chapter 7
A Timeline in Turmoil and Beyond

Nowhere was the devastation of the Third Great World War more profound or more complete than in the Middle East. Karma, as the balancing of energetic forces, had a great deal to do with this and in many ways the conflict's basis held direct links as a continuation of events that had transpired in the Middle Ages through the historic religious crusades (a battle between principal dualities) that pitted Christianity and Islamists. Though the period of the Crusades has perhaps the most direct link with events that would take place in the 21st Century, it must be said that this polarity struggle is also related to the age-old conflict fought throughout the modern era (the time period beginning after the final fall of Atlantis) between the East and the West, whether we are describing the struggle between the Persian and Greek worlds, the Barbarian hordes and Roman Empire or Native residents anywhere in the world defending against European invaders.

Take into consideration also the fact that those who incarnate in these time periods and events do so on many sides of the equation, and rarely do they incarnate exclusively on one side of the polarity or struggle. Thus, it is never a case only about who the winner might happen to be, and this has little significance. Rather, it is always a case of mass conscious opportunities for consciousness growth. This is accompanied by which side within the polarity on the timeline has an increased incarnation from Souls that either have karmic debt to undertake or those that have earned the right to cycle-off further incarnations of this nature, the personal Soul karma being balanced at some point. Because of this, it is incorrect to assume that the "winner" is in the "right" and the loser is in the wrong. On the contrary, generally it is merely a pause in the proceedings until new incarnates are brought together on the timeline again where actions of the System Lords once again permit opportunities to be created in order to generate a balancing of karma for the purposes of consciousness and, hopefully, Soul growth.

As a vortex of extraordinary energetic propagation, a place where thought, desire and will are made manifest more readily and intensely than many other areas on the planet, the Middle East has long served as a magnet and catalyst for the manifestation of great events. In the case of World War III that manifestation, karmic influences aside, was linked to financial and political alliances forged during the 19th and 20th Century that would prove to be devastating not only to the region but to the world. Certainly the culmination of events generated on the Third Dimensional timeline by the on-going duality struggle (we remind you of the clash between entities wishing to continue on in Third Dimensional experiences and those that wish for Fifth Dimensional ones, the struggle between fundamentalist-thought as the flip side of the same coin, and the eternal struggle between Soul orientation based on either Service-to-Self or Service-to-Others) would be amongst the most challenging ever experienced on Earth.

It was not widely known until nearly 75 years after the fact that in the 1960's and 70's, the US government had in fact negotiated to hold the world hostage by forcing it to use its currency, the US dollar, as a basis for global economic purchase. It did so by forcibly tying its currency, banking systems and ultimately, global trade, particularly the procurement of any advanced technology needed to ensure a nation's growth, to the principal world commodity at the time – crude oil. In essence, this placed a wide segment of the world under the US yoke, with the price of prosperity and internal security being use of the US currency for all external purchases. This not only ensured the US dollar's dominance, it acted as an economic stabilizer for the United States, allowing Americans a global advantage that ensured American economic supremacy.

In conjunction with this, most world currencies became tied to the dollar, and wherever it led they were obliged to follow. Thus, the cost of goods anywhere could be easily manipulated by a rising or falling dollar value. While a difficult pill for most countries to swallow, living with the US led strategy ensured that the US would for the most part not interfere in their internal affairs. Those that complied prospered through manipulation of the cost of goods bought and sold to them. Those that did not, including a large segment of the world, remained locked in third world limbo or suffered US interference in the form of ruthless coups, dictatorships and other events meant to disengage the offending parties.

As a devastating side effect, this unilateral strategy kept certain nations virtually enslaved by the US dollar and economy, with citizens in most countries barely able to earn living wages producing cheap goods for consumption by the US and its allies. This would have deep implications for America and Americans karmically, and when analyzed from a higher consciousness it is easy to see that this was in fact a continuation and perhaps even an expansion of America's imbalanced energy related to the enslavement of humans, an obvious Service-to-Self orientation. Indeed, generally America's story beginning with European settlement can be seen as the indenture of one group in order to maintain the lifestyle and privilege of another. In many ways, this linked it directly to the excesses of the Roman Empire, and in fact numerous

US Soul incarnations are derived from those who have also had experiences within that historic timeframe. Suffice to say here that though an opportunity to remedy the karmic imbalance did exist at that time, instead greed ensured that the US orientation towards servitude for the benefit of the privileged was expanded in the latter part of the 20th Century to include the virtual economic enslavement of entire portions of the world. Once this had occurred and the opportunity to balance existing "enslavement" karma had been turned away, the long-term fate of the United States, from a karmic perspective anyway, had been sealed.

If we mention this, it is not to judge or admonish the direction chosen, recalling once again that events serve as opportunities for Soul growth and these events also generate karma in their wake that must be brought into balance by individuals who, either knowingly or not, have participated in the events. In detailing it here we wish only to draw reference to the implications inherent in such situations, particularly for those who in reading this book find it difficult to understand the reasons —karmic and otherwise— behind the eventual failure of the United States on the Third Dimensional timeline.

Thus, in the early to middle part of the 21st Century, the world became more and more aware that the political and economic success of the United States throughout the last half of the 20th Century was based on a strategy that basically had kept it held hostage. The world also had become aware by then that in the late 1960's the US President Nixon devised a global strategy to enforce America's continued world dominance through military might. His administration negotiated and signed numerous secret treaties calling for the defense of certain regions of the globe and the global economy in exchange for continued use of the dollar for the purchase of world oil supplies. These treaties, many of which focused on the protection of oil producing nations in the Middle East, would serve as the basis for US foreign and economic policy until the outbreak of World War III.

The US strategy that was maintained through the 20th Century and into the first quarter of the 21st Century was two-fold in nature. First, it institutionalized the concept of the United States as a world police force, promoting globalization, one world vision and one world culture. Second, it reinforced the use of the dollar in the global economy to continually ensure American economic advantage, while at home, media frenzy and excess promoted an orgy of consumerism in a US populace still able to buy products at artificially low prices. Additionally, while the US outwardly promoted conservation and new energy sources, behind the scenes it worked to ensure that crude oil and the economic structures based on it remain the core of world economies. Industries that used crude in any manner as the basis for manufacturing or creating its products were strengthened and encouraged. By the early 21st Century, the overwhelming increase in the use of plastics and crude-based products in almost every form belied the official "cover-story" related to developing alternative fuel sources. It became clear once 3rd and 4th dimensional printing became the staple of manufacturing operations by the late 2010's that newly developed plastics and resins using crude as a basic component of manufacturing would significantly increase oil's worldwide importance.

Though greatly beneficial to the US and others in the short term, these policies would have far reaching consequences. Nowhere would this be truer than in the Middle East, where unbeknownst to most, though seemingly autonomous established governments remained the pawns of the American economic and military machine until following the great World Conflict that would ensure.

As the US strategy became known and showed signs of faltering in the very early 21st Century, attempts to dismantle it at the global and regional level accelerated. Many of these attempts were led by various incarnations of the Physical System Lords, maneuvering to bring about a collapse of the American controlled order to facilitate new consciousness opportunities and growth for populations living in second and third world regions where, together with their economies, the populations had been enslaved by US economic dominance. The karmic link between a typical uneducated peasant (child or otherwise) in a third world nation earning a few pennies for long hours of demanding forced labor and the average US citizen who might buy the product being made was becoming all too clear. This was true whether the benefit was to the individual purchaser by way of cheaper prices, the global corporation involved by way of higher profits, the government entity by way of revenues from taxes and levies or all of the above. Once the link was established and visible, the energy from that link as well as the energy from its needed karmic rebalancing (which would be demanded by the consciousness of the third world peasant AND the typical US citizen buying the product in question) flowed freely into the global conflict that was brewing. When this occurred, additional turmoil within the polarities or factions themselves surfaced. Thus the Third Dimensional-based Souls with fundament leanings that we have described previously emerged with more and more prominence on either side of the equation. The activity of these Souls not only came into conflict within their own sectors, they became the driving force leading to conflict with Souls of equal but opposite force on the other side of the coin (and in other parts of the world).

It was the fear of the US dollar's collapse as far back as the 1960's, as well as the negative energy generated around that fear, that had originally motivated those involved to work to create the US global strategy. However, rather than choosing a strategy that would serve as a win-win for all and benefit individuals and countries equally on a global basis, the strategy became essentially a policy to de-stabilize and enslave the many for the benefit of the few. As a fear-derived motivation that was based on a Service-to-Self orientation overall, this would become the principal catalyst leading the world, albeit over many decades, to the point of no return.

The scenario we have detailed further demonstrates how karma works in the Third Dimension to balance and correct itself, just as water seeks its own level in order to find balance and harmony.
Events that took place at the turn of the 21st Century therefore, linked with the resentment and decades of inequality propagated by the US strategy would eventually lead to the trials and tribulations that morphed into the greatest conflict the world had ever known. In fact it was not until the fall of the United States and the chaos experienced on the North American continent that the world became aware that the devastating attacks known as the 9-11 tragedy were actually based on an insider project perpetrated in order to provide the motive for further implementation of the on-going US economic and military strategy. In conjunction with that strategy, it also created the path by which an angered US populace would endorse expanded activities in the Middle East with the ultimate goal of retaining US influence and control there, not to mention obliging the region's adherence to the use of the US dollar as the currency of choice.

Few realized at the time it was occurring that the military actions undertaken, which constituted the actual unofficial beginnings of the Great World Conflict known as World War III, would not by any means be limited to simply the invasions of Afghanistan and Iraq. Though a first phase in the overall plan, the broader long-term strategy would call for nothing less than the complete destabilization of almost every country in the Middle East over time. It is the fact that various System Lords, particularly incarnations of the Physical System Lord, were present not only in the US but within the Russian, Syrian, Persian, Iraqi, Turkish, Arab and Chinese worlds at the time that actually served as the greatest deterrent to US strategy and would lead the conflict into continuous global escalation. In fact, those entities controlling the United States power structure showed little to no concern for escalating events, firm in their belief that there was no alternative since the United States would lose any prestige it still had and become a relatively powerless and bankrupt player should they fail.

What these entities did not count on was that they would be countered by their brethren on the opposite side of the equation, meaning that other incarnations of the Physical System Lords located in global spheres that were intent on countering the US strategy. This would promote the very failure that the US factions thought they were trying to avoid. Once it was known widely that the United States had in fact orchestrated these events over time in order to lead allies into an endless destabilization of the Middle East, most distanced themselves from the action in all but name while quietly beginning to seek new alternatives as they privately planned for the eventual failure of the US dollar.

Undaunted, the American contingent at the time continued with its plans to disrupt the majority of Middle Eastern capitals. The resulting so-called "Arab Spring" was a misguided attempt to topple various Middle Eastern governments by promoting democratic proceedings that would open the way for western trained Islamic fundamentalists to sweep in and ruthlessly subjugate the populace. When this failed to materialize widely as planned due to unforeseen circumstances (the actions of forces knowing about and opposing US manipulation, particularly at the Russian and Chinese levels), covert US factions began training a new, more ruthless breed of Islamic fundamentalist that would be able to take full advantage of the chaos already created on the Iraqi, Afghani, Syrian and Pakistani stage.

This was of course in keeping with the karmic bonds that had been generated between the opposing fundamentalist (East and West) factions. In fact it was the nuclear annihilation of the Middle Eastern territories during the Great World Conflict that ensued, in conjunction with the fall of the North American territories, that ended the lifetimes of many of the young Souls involved. This would fulfill the karmic rebalancing and in a sense pave the way for incarnations of the Spiritual System Lord to come forth following World War III in order to create a new level of consciousness that was not religious but, rather, humanistically-based, which rose out of the Eurasian Enlightenment that followed.

However, the conflict that would become known as the Great World Conflict gained its greatest impetus from the covert US-trained Islamic Fundamentalists operating in Syria, Iraq, Afghanistan, Pakistan and Turkey. With the stated purpose of creating a new Islamist Empire, it was the second part of this plan that included the Islamic Fundamentalist invasion of Lebanon, Jordan and Egypt that gave a true indication the tide had now turned and a great world conflict was imminent. These events served as a pretext for movement into the Iranian and Saudi Arabian territories to further destabilize the area and thus discourage any use of a world currency that was not the US dollar.

Resistance to the radical Islamist movement was not only futile once news of the invasions had reached the world it was late in coming as well. At the beginning of the conflict the United States acted almost secretly in its role as hidden police force of the region relying on a perceived coalition of participants. In this way, it felt it could easily control its secret Islamic Fundamentalist progeny who had been created to ferment chaos, disruption and despair. The original plan was to incite revolution to break up any Middle Eastern government flirting with using currencies other than the dollar for oil sales, allow the creation of extreme regimes in the region to control and oppress the local populations and, as usual, allow the US dollar's continued use via newly forged secret agreements to look the other way if Islamic totalitarian regimes agreed to only use US currency as a basis for crude oil sales. Thus, it was expected by handlers that the US could control events in much the same manner it had controlled countless world dictators in the past.

This was in fact the case until the first limited exchanges of nuclear weapons in the region took place. As unexpected as they were extreme, this would end US covert actions once and for all, leaving it instead to scramble and deal with the newly independent nemesis it had created. It would also serve as wake up call to the world announcing the great destruction that was in store. Much of the conflict and strategy to this point had been based on the belief that countries in the region that possessed nuclear weapons would never dare to use them. It quickly became clear however, that once these weapons were in the hands of radicals they would not hesitate to use them even within their own territories. This, combined with the fact that governments and terrorist groups not known to *officially* have such weapons had already obtained them long before, meant that the weapons were well in hand and ready for use as soon as the going got tough on any side.

It was this misstep in judgment that actually unleashed the holocaustic conflict and allowed major cities throughout the Middle East, in Iran, Syria, Lebanon, Israel, Saudi Arabia, Iraq, Pakistan and Egypt, as well as Yemen, parts of Eastern Africa and northern regions of India, to become victims of mass destruction. Worldwide disbelief at what occurred meant that the conflict's escalation would be ill understood in the West. Most felt it to be a regional conflict that had spiraled out of control, and urged a measured hesitant response from the international community. It was not until nuclear terroristic events took place in European centers that Americans, and the world for that matter, realized a point of no return had been crossed.

Third Dimensional Earth and the Third Dimensional timeline can be said to be infinite in terms of how long it will continue. However, there are periods of reset. There is an anomaly on the Third Dimensional timeline that reveals the possibility of just such a period of reset caused by a dire threat to Earth's physical wellbeing occurring in the year 2569. Bear in mind that this does not portend the final end of physical Earth but merely suggests a massive destructive force, not man made in origin, that will alter the world in such a way that essentially Third Dimensional existence begins again at that time.

That said, the civilization you currently know, particularly the one that arises from the ashes after 2050 and forms through 2115 serves as the dominant cultural force in your world up to the point where the complete demise of civilization on Earth is imminent in 2569. The restart that takes place at that time parallels the final fall of Atlantis in that vague remnants of the civilization lingers in mass consciousness but is all but forgotten, along with technologies and other advancements. As you know, the final fall of Atlantis circa 13,000 BCE lead the way to the restart of civilization that would ultimately become your modern era. Though symbolism and remembrance were to be found throughout the disintegrated Atlantean colonies, such as those found in Egypt and the Americas to name of few, these connections were forgotten within several generations by local surviving residents and quickly became the stuff of lore.

So too, mass physical destruction on Earth around 2569 will destroy the last vestiges of the current civilization, and a new era for humanity will then begin requiring millennia to achieve the level of sophistication and technology that you know today. To be sure however, the period of nuclear incident in the Middle East and elsewhere that is part of the Great World Conflict, World War III, that we are referencing does not physically end life on Earth, although it does alter the culture and civilization substantially.

The principal centers of civilization that emerge after World War III can perhaps be best understood by the composition of its inhabitants. For the most part the "civilized" peaceful regions of the world after 2050 were populated by Soul incarnates who wished to transition from third to Fifth Dimensional worlds. These areas were the places of wisdom, compassion and retained knowledge, and those within them had opportunities to maximize their growth through Fourth Dimensional experiences while still incarnating in physically based Third Dimensional lifetimes. The areas where this could be seen were, as we have discussed, Eurasia, in particular Germany and the regions currently known as Central and Eastern Europe, Russian and Scandinavian regions, the Pacific Union of the former United States as well as the New England League, and pockets of Latin and South America retained high learning and prosperity. China and Southeastern Asia in general enjoyed artistic, cultural and technological rebirth, and certain areas of Nepal, Tibet, Mongolia, Myanmar, Cambodia and Thailand will renew themselves as non-denominational centers of spiritual enlightenment and philosophy as well.

It is an incarnation of the Spiritual System Lord who emerges within a region of Northern Turkey around the Black Sea, and who will travel and study widely in the spiritual East that essentially fulfills the Christian prophesies of a second coming. Unlike the expectation however, this entity preached a new humanism that became widely accepted as a basis of new Eurasian Enlightenment philosophies.

His message disseminated throughout the civilized world at the time will be one of a new tolerance and compassion for all. He also addressed and imbued followers with a new understanding of reincarnation, resurrection and reality manifestation. It is in this regard that his philosophies were a readdress of the message originally intended by the entity known as the Master Jesus, whose principles had been neutered after his death in Egypt following the passion events of 33 ACE by a church focused on power and population control.

Not all chose incarnations in centers of civilization for reasons that by now should seem obvious. Those Souls choosing to continue with incarnations on the Third Dimensional timeline, particularly younger Souls seeking growth through Third Dimensional karmic opportunities, will populate any number of regions of the world devastated by either the Great Conflict, great Earth changes or both. First and foremost among these regions were areas in the Middle East, where life would never completely return to even a semblance of normalcy. Although pockets of higher consciousness existed everywhere, wide scale devastation in Northern, Central and Eastern Africa, in Europe and throughout North America made these areas particularly interesting for Souls seeking growth through severe and challenging mass consciousness events and situations.

Most of the Souls in these areas shall incarnate on the heels of the mass destruction we have already documented. Those areas shall have various Physical System Lord incarnations that will work to wreak havoc, stoking the fires meant to allow younger Souls ample scenarios for growth in a continuing Third Dimensional arena.

The emergence of a Spiritual System Lord incarnation in Eurasia was all that was needed to bind the region, and later the civilized world, to the concept of renewal under the auspices of a belief structure that was essentially "Resurrection" based. This allowed heartfelt acceptance by a newly forming free society that itself was emerging from the ashes and becoming more culturally, artistically, socially and environmentally conscious. Death of the physical body and reemergence of the Soul into a new lifetime was easily understood and accepted by those who had witnessed such terrible events and were looking for deliverance and renewal within the current lifetime. The message was one of hope as a better and more compassionate civilization was encouraged to take root.

This message also comes about at a time when the majority of the world, having experienced all manner of chaos and nuclear war, was attempting to rebirth from wounded and dismantled societies. The European arena in particular searched for leadership if not assistance, and this help came willingly from Central Eurasian populations forging a guiding light in a recovering world. This would continue to be the basis for world culture from approximately the 22nd Century to the 26th Century, at which time cosmic influences altered the final course of modern era civilization in the Third Dimension.

What is interesting to note is that world culture in that period will be shaped by those of higher consciousness that are in the process of cycling off Third Dimensional incarnations altogether. These incarnates shall nonetheless pave the way for a world that will serve as the playing field for those younger Souls continuing on in Third Dimensional incarnations up until the actual end of the modern era civilization. In this way, as it has always been, Earth remains a vehicle for reality experienced at different levels and by Souls of different states of consciousness. By the mid 21st century, the vast majority of Earth's inhabitants with Third Dimensional orientation will represent two-thirds of the population, and these will incarnate in regions of the world with challenging living and karmic situations. The remaining one-third of the world's population is split throughout the pockets of higher consciousness that we have detailed, with particular concentration in the Eurasian regions where the Eurasian Enlightenment dawns.

Many of those Soul entities will have already begun to experience incarnations on a Fifth Dimensional Earth known as Terra, which we will describe in the second part of this book. Those Souls that either chose to remain within Third Dimensional lessons or those Young and Baby Souls who were in need of the process of growth offered in a Third Dimensional, karmic-based reality will continue on in lifetimes on Third Dimensional Earth. Of these, there are those that continue on in a Third Dimensional Earth environment even after the cosmic reset indicated that occurred in the mid 26th Century on the Third Dimensional timeline.

In this manner there is a logical and neat progression of those Souls that continue to explore reality in the Third Dimension and those that are cycling off Third Dimensional incarnations and transitioning to higher dimensions in Terra, and perhaps beyond. Until the process is complete however, these Souls come together over the course of the 21st and 22nd Century on Earth, and ultimately, despite a devastating time period in Earth's history, one of the most advanced societies known yet on Earth was created, even though the majority of Earth's inhabitants were still suffering from the devastating blows of global war and destruction.

This society, or rather the pockets where it exists, will provide the world with many of the most futuristic and scientific discoveries projected in your current Science Fiction and futuristic visions.
For example, it is this society that shall accomplish extraordinary feats of healing the human physical body. It is also that society that will

blend perfectly the spiritual and the physical to arrive at new levels and definitions of beautification, with the individual's body and physical state seen as a holographic reflection of a Soul's entire journey.

As we have previously stated, the current western civilization led by the United States has direct links both karmically and historically to the Roman Empire period. This is particularly true in that many Souls currently present in one were also present at that particular point on the Third Dimensional modern era timeline. In fact many of the karmic endeavors and karmic links that are being balanced now and through the 21st Century stem not only from such long term issues as slavery and the civil war period but actually reach back and are connected to Roman karmic imbalances. It is for this reason that many will find any number of parallels between the fall of Rome and the fall of the US Empire, from the invasions of barbarian hordes to the rise of new religious philosophies (both Christian and Muslim) that emerged from the ashes of the destruction of these two great civilizations.

Returning for a moment to our conversation regarding the Eurasian Renaissance, that period will embody many advanced concepts, some of which are even being studied and discovered by a few enlightened scholars today. Then, as now, these brilliant Souls unconsciously participate as a contingent of Souls tasked with creating a world society ideal for Souls that are transitioning from third to Fifth Dimensional existence. For example, the Eurasian Enlightenment will exalt high environmental consciousness, developing and implementing many of the extraordinary innovations currently needed but blocked by powerful economic forces in your world. You should know that technology and know-how currently exist in your world for generating new replenishing forms of energy, using thermal dynamics as well as electromagnetics but fast development of these environmentally friendly methodologies is blocked by governmental and other forces not prepared to relinquish economic power or financial control. Much world hardship is being perpetuated in terms of energy sources and energy application, and this constitutes not only a continual rape of the planet, its resources and its inhabitants it represents a contemptuous usury of the citizens of your world. It is *this* form of usury and not the mere lending of money or charging of interest that is sinful. This is the true meaning of usury that caused it to be included among mankind's greatest sins in the teachings of so many of the world's religions.

The greatest strength of the Eurasian Enlightenment is that it gives rise to completely new forms of cultural freedom, technological innovation and artistic endeavor in those regions able to benefit from its influence. This includes innovations whereby science, healing and health finally meld the spiritual and physical aspects of medical treatment, ultimately reaching an understanding of the relationship between the Soul and the physical Being, or at the least that the physical body is always a reflection of what is spiritual in nature first. Thus after a millennia of divorcing the dual nature of your Being, health and the healing process will come to be understood as spiritual and energetic in origin, and this basis will be used as the principal means of understanding the functioning and dis-functioning of the physical body in the future.

It is interesting that the impact this cultural change will have worldwide is one that essentially alters humanity's perspective towards itself, and through this the goals of the Eurasian Enlightenment have enormous impact on a change in course for Third Dimensional reality after the 21st Century. This can be attributed to the fact that those Souls benefiting the most from higher consciousness initiatives, which are part of the enlightenment period, do so in order to experience the possibilities that will soon become their reality when they finally leave Third Dimensional incarnations and begin to incarnate into lifetimes on Fifth

Dimensional Terra.

The new civilization established in those areas of the world that prosper will incorporate and expose many hidden innovations, advantages and technologies already present in your world. This will be the case whether they be alien-derived as they are now, or formulated independently by the extraordinary scientists incarnated during the period. By the dawn of the 22nd Century mankind discovers that there is no need to rape or destroy Earth in order to reap its natural benefits, and the wise stewardship of Earth's naturally occurring advantages takes precedent over the mindless misuse of resources you currently know.

Though a great deal of the world will continue to struggle with the use and ownership of Earth's resources, fighting over control of those resources throughout the 21st Century, the emergence of Eurasian technologies developed at that time will be empowering to humanity as a whole. Once established and the technological practices are widely known, even Younger Souls in areas not as prosperous become aware that it is no longer necessary to endlessly compete for resources such as water, energy, food and other life-giving necessities. Though it requires time for the Eurasian innovations to circle the globe, similar to earlier in your history when it took many years for electricity to become common place, despite the fact that poverty stricken regions remain dominated by struggle with a 19th Century warlord mentality, the competition for life essentials in most regions decreases substantially by the beginning of the 23rd Century.

Despite these advances, it must be understood that Third Dimensional reality is intended to remain Third Dimensional in nature. Naturally, many new innovations are the result of direct guidance and access to higher levels of consciousness, and the initiatives serve mainly to create an ideal transitional civilization to be used by those Souls that would soon be cycling-off Third Dimensional Earth incarnations. That said however, it is universal intention that a Third Dimensional Earth realm will always remain intact, providing those choosing or needing to remain there with the opportunities for growth required for future Soul evolution and, eventually, Ascension.

When the cosmic climax (perhaps preferable to using cosmic disaster terminology) we have discussed occurs in the 26th Century, pockets of human existence will still remain present on Earth. However, for the most part Earth and its population will revert at that time to a highly primitive state, which will serve as a basis for a complete Third Universal Dimension reset and the creation of a new era. At that time, the majority of Souls incarnated on the Earth plane intending to Ascend will have either done so or will do so then, and post the cataclysm new cadres of Human Angelic Souls will be cast into Third Dimensional evolutionary incarnation. This is generally the process that follows completion of an Ascension period such as the one Earth and all Soul groups in Third Dimensional incarnation are experiencing. It is the unconscious knowledge of just such a reset event that lingers in the consciousness of humanity making it prone to stories of Armageddon and the mythology of cataclysm.

As we said, with respect to the Eurasian Enlightenment that emerges in the last part of the 21st and well into the 22nd Century it must be considered a period that far exceeds the typical scope of Third Dimensional consciousness on Earth, particularly in terms of wisdom, culture, heritage, spirituality, peace and prosperity. In that sense, the regional pockets of awareness and prosperity created via the Enlightenment period should be seen wholly as places within the Third Universal Dimension where Souls who remain on Earth just prior to cycling off to higher dimensions can incarnate and safely experiment with experiences that are essentially Fourth Dimensional in nature. These are best understood when they are seen as the bridge they are to Fifth Dimensional incarnation experiences.

The enlightened regions stand in stark contrast to what will be the norm in much of the world for the majority of Souls remaining in Third Dimensional cycles of incarnation on Earth through the 26th Century. Beginning in the 22nd Century most of the world outside the Eurasian pockets of advanced civilization live in somewhat backwards, totalitarian societies under regimes where technology is mostly used to control human thought, emotion and action. These Souls will be subject to autocratic and terroristic style governmental controls. Even here however, such situations will generate numerous opportunities for Soul growth at a pace more intense than found in many other timeline periods. The majority of such challenging places will be found in the Western hemisphere, and will come about as a result primarily of the severe breakdown in culture and society that takes place over the course of the 21st century. This will be especially true in Western European regions as well as regions directly involved in the catastrophic fall of North America, and to a lesser extent regions affected by the turmoil and tribulation experienced in vast parts of Africa and Southeast Asia.

No discussion of this period however, from its beginning through approximately the year 2250, would be complete without a look into the many natural and, as we have called them in the past, "unnatural" natural disasters of the period. Catastrophic in nature with far reaching global and environmental consequences, these disasters further complicated world affairs at the time and many, if not most, were the direct result of misguided human manipulation of natural Earth phenomena and the weaponization of Nature.

 CHAPTER 8
THE WEAPONIZATION OF NATURE LEADING TO CATASTROPHIC EARTH CHANGES AND OCCURRENCES

Unbeknown to most, it became exceedingly clear by approximately 2025 that governments had in fact reengineered Earth's atmosphere, its oceans and the planet's electromagnetic grid to facilitate the use of scalar and sonic technology in such a way that was harmful and in some cases detrimental globally. This fact combined with a dramatic downturn in solar activity beginning in the mid to late 2020's leading to markedly colder climates and a mini ice age effect, especially in the northern hemisphere, would have enormous impact on world natural phenomena, global economies and Earth populations for nearly a century and a half from the 21st well into the 22nd Century.

Frankly, it was naïve of world residents not to believe or to discount reports that their governments were experimenting with the weaponization of the atmosphere, including tampering with weather and all manner of natural Earth events. By the late 2010's, one needed only to look up at the increasingly greying, hazy and unnatural streaking of usually blue skies, hear about the extraordinary natural occurrences, experience the extreme weather patterns, see the mass disorientation and beachings of Cetaceans, or witness the unprecedented extermination of bird and animal species to know that something profound and unusual was taking place.

This alteration of natural events had begun in the early part of the

20th Century with simple efforts to reengineer weather patterns in order to provide for rain and crop growth in various western countries and regions. The technology proceeded slowly until alien collaborations with secret factions of the US government took place beginning in the early 1980s. Those collaborations were conducted completely without oversight and, in some cases, in plain view under the auspices of developing new weather and space technologies. Before long however, they were being directed full force towards Earth-based atmospheric and inter-planetary weaponization efforts.

These covert operations used the cover of working on routine Earth "weather modification" and atmospheric manipulation as ways to fight environmental deterioration and end global warming. Most scientific participation saw this as a necessary means of curtailing the Sun's intensification and heat blasting effects taking place as a direct result of the natural Ascension period, which had indeed led to a rise in global temperatures beginning in the later 20th Century. This was particularly true when these covert governmental operators enlisted the voluntary cooperation of mainstream industries such as in the jet fuel and aviation industry, working closely with major customers at multinational defense departments to ensure that additives necessary to metalize the atmosphere were included in most fuel products as well as aerosols released by commercial and non commercial flights worldwide.

In the mid 2010's the "chemtrail" phenomenon was openly discussed and movements were born worldwide to uncover the goal of such atmospheric experimentation. Once these metallic and chemical aerosols were perfected and nano-engineered however, they became virtually undetectable to the public at large. For the most part this prevented deeper investigation by those concerned and permitted even wider dissemination of the toxins by aircraft and other means as well as an expansion of almost all atmospheric transformation programs after 2014.

Those truly responsible however, were experimenting with nothing less than complete weaponization of the atmosphere, the oceans, Earth's magnetic fields and the electromagnetic grid system of the planet. These efforts would secretly turn weather patterns into potential weapons of mass destruction, be able to provide continental and even Earth visibility cloaking and, perhaps most destructively, use the Earth itself as a medium for transmitting massive scalar and electromagnetic energy waves that could silently be used for enormously destructive purposes anywhere in the world.

Once the initial technology had been shared with western allies, it quickly spread secretly to major western and eastern world governments, each of which attempted in their own way to take advantage of the metalizing of the atmosphere. By the mid to late 2010's, hardly any region on Earth was free of the newly ionized and metalized atmosphere, or, by virtue of particle fallout, the ionization of the electromagnetic grid system of the planet. Earth itself, and its atmosphere, were now the ideal medium for the transfer of vast waves of scalar energy, which could be used to control weather patterns, control natural phenomena or directed and delivered with near pinpoint accuracy and devastating results.

This technology soon expanded in the first part of the 21st Century into systems for holographic projection and mind control, and unwitting populations in the West were used as guinea pigs by various covert branches of government seeking to experiment uses for the new technologies by targeting locales, individuals and groups using mind bending psychotropic and mood altering technologies. Once initiated, directed scalar microwaves using precise Earth coordinates and common (at that point) positioning technologies could literally ride on invisible energetic patterns through either a weaponized sky or underground via Earth's electromagnetic grid. The wide global push in the late 20th Century to employ GPS technology everywhere, and it's augmented innovations in the 21st Century that virtually made every human Being a walking statistical position and potential target, was far beyond the naïve debates over commercial advertising tracking, which world privacy advocates had all but lost by 2020.

As technology advanced, particularly after the real outbreak of the Great Conflict, almost every member of civilized society was easily identifiable on secret monitoring systems maintained for "national security" purposes by most Western governments. Due to this, much of the vast increase in so-called mood disorders and psychotic behavior in the early 21st Century, not to mention the inordinate increase in migraines, dementia, nervous system disorders, disturbed hormonal balances and other related physical ailments in the populace were in fact mostly related to scalar and electromagnetic psychotropic experimentation and use of the new technologies. These symptoms were equaled only by the deep undertone of a constant "humming" sound that began to be heard continually by large segments of the population in regions where energy resonators were being used (equipment transformer stations placed along specific grids and axis used to magnify and propel energetic currents) or where scalar equipment discharges originated or terminated.

It became widely known by the late 2020s in the midst of World War III that although still not acknowledged by the many perpetrators, these highly advanced technologies had already been used secretly for over a decade, not only for defensive purposes, such as the manipulation and reengineering of global weather patterns, but as weapons of global mass destruction. Indeed, by this time an undeclared, underground war (of sorts) had raged for years between various world governments, using them to control all manner of natural phenomena, including wind, rain, ocean currents, hurricanes, typhoons, tornados, earthquakes and volcanic activity. Rather than troop invasions, enemy attacks now could come in the form of a hurricane or typhoon, an earthquake or a volcanic eruption with the potential to devastate a region or national economy indefinitely, as uninformed populations continued to attribute the disasters to the forces of "Mother Nature." This left perpetrators and victims alike free to retaliate in other parts of the world with little to no consequence, and without sending a single troop or ever formally declaring war. Neither was the technology's use limited to deployment on the enemy, and in some cases it was used on unsuspecting citizens by their own governments for economic or political reasons.

The secondary use of the technology employed during and to an extent after the war was to control the thoughts, movements, emotions and health of the very populations that had unwittingly financed and been a part of its development in the first place. Unofficial acknowledgement of this by virtue of its widening and blatant use during World War III would cause the first great rift between world governments and their internal populations. In the United States this would have far reaching implications and would serve to bolster the notion among State and local governments that the Federal institution and the country's own military were completely out of control. Most agreed that if this technology could be used against its own citizenry without their knowledge, as in fact it had been, what wouldn't the government be capable of doing.

People openly began to debate whether or not the US Federal government had crossed the line of decency and mass demonstrations broke out nationally calling for a new government, an end to all covert government operations and stiff limits on the defense department's virtual autonomy. These demonstrations expanded quickly into anti-war riots calling for immediate isolation and sealing of all US borders based on what citizens perceived as the US government's ethical and moral deprivation, the Federal authority's actual bankruptcy, a collapsed US economy and the devastating results of nuclear holocaust being witnessed in the Middle East.

Despite overtures from the Federal government saying it was willing to negotiate its policies, the national demonstrations were violently put down by homeland defense agencies that had been created in the early 21st Century for the purpose of protecting the US from terroristic plots. The government attempted to frame these demonstrations as being instigated by "terrorists" that had infiltrated the US due to the war, and tens of thousands were arrested or detained nationally. Many of them were tortured and killed by these same national security forces under the guise of protecting US national security interests.

Federal agencies now began widely using those same population control methods that were being protested against by the public on a national basis. Continued regional unrest allowed the President to declare martial law, and a rogue Senate and Congress quickly walled itself up in the newly fortified city of Washington, DC. Now distrust for the Federal government that had been festering since the earliest parts of the 21st Century reached new heights. In time, the resulting infection would have direct links to dismantling the American union, state-by-state and region-by-region, as discussed previously.

Returning to our discussion concerning the weaponization of the planet's atmosphere and electromagnetic grid, it must be understood that Earth itself shares many similarities with the structure of the human energetic and physical body, and in many cases they do not act in isolation of each other. As children of Earth, which is itself a Being that has a Soul, all Beings existing within it are interrelated with the planet, and the planetary systems interface with human genetic, physical and energetic anatomy. This is the reason the current model of western health and healing generally falls short in the long term pursuit of health, since it can be said that the technical approach of attempting to isolate and manage specific symptoms does not take the holistic nature of well being into consideration. Efforts to separate out symptoms that are intrinsically linked together energetically as part of a cosmic system can cause more harm than good. Reengineering the body in accordance with physical symptoms only and in isolation of its energetic centers and holistic nature, or divorced from its natural interface with the planet, can have even more disastrous effects.

This is particularly true with regard to the planet Earth itself. It was little understood by scientists perfecting scalar weather and natural phenomena manipulation that the nature of cause and effect or outright control would have enormous impact on related parts of the system, however invisible or unrelated they may have seemed. Thus, disintegration of a cloud here, the change of the vortex and direction of a wind there, disbanding or substitution of harmonic frequencies in the ocean, addition of an additive here and there in the atmosphere, or slight increases in electromagnetic pulsations pushed through the Earth's grid can have enormous consequence with regard to natural global patterns and well being throughout the system. Indeed, such manipulation causes great stress and not only does weather affect temperature, wind, rain and other phenomena it also has a tremendous effect on the electromagnetic nature of Earth's core. Of most importance, this can cause havoc within the Tectonic plate structure of the entire planet. Severe weather patterns and temperature changes began to develop and these had dire effects with regard to volcanic and earthquake activity, as well as the creation of additional Earth system anomalies. As you may assume, this caused abnormal or even catastrophic events to occur.

While up to this point we have discussed primarily the geopolitical consequences with respect to the Third Dimensional timeline's continuation, it is in great part the reengineering of worldwide weather patterns and planetary ecology, the use of sonic weaponry on land and in the oceans and the wide scale use of scalar technology in the atmosphere, which reached its peak between 2020 and 2035, that perhaps did the most harm to civilization at the time. In fact, this could be said to be the single greatest factor related to the consequences leading directly to the downfall of what you know as western civilization, particularly as it existed in Europe and North America.

The worldwide famine of 2025-2050 not only caused severe hardship for many global regions it also caused severe economic turmoil in most of the western world. Naturally, this was also related to the devastating effect of nuclear fallout during and after the war, but more importantly it was the combination of draught and drastically altered unnatural weather patterns, combined with severe Earth changes in the physical structure of Earth that had been caused, which created the most dramatic consequences. These dire situations allowed ruling classes and parties, as well as independent warlords, to take complete control of territories using the excuse that they were preventing lawlessness and the myriad of problems stemming from ongoing natural catastrophes. Lack of centralized response or assistance meant that populations banded together locally to survive, further isolating regions from their national governments and thereby stressing the system even further.

As this occurred, both at the local and national level, governments, particularly those in Europe, North America and Asia became more conservative enacting totalitarian policies to deal with draught, famine and scarcity situations caused by weather changes and natural Earth disasters. Many agreed with this trend, finding it preferable to starving or existing at the precipice of mass chaos. Some populations willfully discarded liberties and freedoms in exchange for some form of autocratic control in an effort to ameliorate the situation.

It was during two main periods, the late 2010's to 2030's and the middle to last part of the 21st Century that would see the bulk of world catastrophes occur, and these would ultimately change the face of planet Earth forever. We shall attempt to provide some insight into these occurrences for although the great conflict known as World War III and its fallout had much to do with geopolitical alterations in the world, the Earth changes wrought during the period, either natural or unnatural in origins, had the single greatest effect on the demise of existing culture.

In the early years of weather weaponry and control, meaning the period up to 2020, severe manipulation of the atmosphere caused isolated complications with regard to natural weather events, and weather and natural disasters had struck regions of North America, Europe, Hawaii, Mexico, the Philippines, Russia, China and Japan, to name a few. No catastrophe however, was more important than two global events that would occur.

First and foremost among these was the great earthquake in north central Japan in the very late 2010's and early 2020's that would unleash vast tectonic movement off the Japanese coastline. This major earthquake would ultimately sink a great part of the north central territory of Honshu in a definitive manner, and the catastrophe would open the door to a tsunami and flooding in Japan itself as well as from Alaska as far south as the Baja Peninsula. It would also cause severe erosion and flooding up and down the US Pacific coastline well into

Mexico, even reaching into some Pan American areas.

This catastrophe was so enormous and intense that it sent shock waves through western populations even though it could be easily recognized by those aware of the existence of such events as a major "unnatural" natural disaster with significant consequence. We are not here to be sidetracked by the reasons behind this occurrence but it should be understood that it was caused by unnatural scalar and sonic manipulation and exploitation of natural Earth vortexes, interlocking electromagnetic grids, natural geological formations and existing natural phenomenon.

In effect, this great earthquake was a retaliatory "attack" upon the Japanese island for cooperating too closely with China in a secret and underground struggle raging for nearly a decade before between China and the United States and its principal Asian allies (Japan, South Korea and the Philippines). That struggle had originally emerged in approximately 2010 over issues of trade, economic alliance and regional political dominance. In 2011 a major warning shot (retaliation for an earthquake that had been directed at south central China by the West earlier) had been fired by the Chinese via what it expected would be a relatively benign attack on the off shore fault line of central northeast Japan near the Fukushima nuclear power plant. The uncontrollable resulting tsunami and Fukushima disaster this caused aside, that attack was intended by the Chinese merely to threaten Japan into relinquishing disputed territorial water rights, and agree to come into closer Asian (Chinese) cooperation. Most importantly, it was also intended to formally isolate Japan from its 20th Century ally, America.

In fact, much of China's objective in its 2011 scalar attack on Japan was achieved, and Japan soon began, reluctantly at first, to cooperate with the new Asian powerhouse. It was the devastating retaliation for that cooperation however, effectuated by US factions several years later on the Japanese homeland that would escalate the discord unlike any other. That massive event would not only punish Japan for its distancing from the US, but would stress US-Chinese relations even further, just as war was beginning to take hold in the Middle East. Seeing these events, an increasingly opportunistic Russia further cemented ties with China antagonizing the US and Europe in its wake. Natural disaster aside, this major earthquake and tsunami in Japan forever damaged US-Japanese alliances that had been in place since the end of World War II. With this, the US lost its most valuable strategic partner in Asia just as pressure was mounting globally and the world was taking sides in an East versus West style showdown.

Of course, the entire struggle between China, Japan and the US had been completely fought secretly via hidden technologies, with the populations involved ignorant of the fact that this was occurring until many years after it had already wrought unparalleled damage and consequence. This catastrophe was not only devastating in Japan, which lost untold numbers of its population and large segments of its principal island to the disaster, the shift that occurred pushed a wobbly magnetic North Pole even further towards Siberia, where it had already been migrating for some time. It also had the additional impact of knocking the Earth slightly further off its axis and shifting the Arctic Circle so that regions of the planet were pushed either closer to or further from the equator depending upon their location on Earth, further exasperating natural weather patterns and causing additional changes in world temperatures, growing seasons, jet stream patterns, wind, rain amounts and similar factors. Due to the shift as well as the drastic change in trade wind patterns, this created a tendency for the northern and eastern hemispheres, particularly northern Europe and Russia, to slip into what could be called a mini ice age with much colder than average temperatures in the winter and cooler temperatures in the summer, while in regions of the western and southern hemispheres, particularly in the United States, temperatures rose considerably.

As we have said in the past, although humankind's contribution via pollution to increasing temperatures on the planet cannot be discounted, the temperature of the Solar System and all planets contained therein is naturally increased primarily as a result of any Ascension period, such as the one experienced through 2250. Increased energy from the Sun during these periods, intended to increase the vibration and frequency of the Solar System and all Beings within it as the transition is fostered to higher levels of dimensional awareness (see "The System Lords and the Twelve Dimensions"), is a natural evolutionary process.

With regard to our current discussion it was the use of artificial means to alter natural events, including the inadvertent shifting of Earth landmasses and altering of weather patterns and natural occurrences through scalar manipulation at a crucial time (during Ascension energies) that caused drastic consequences. Foremost among these was the enormous and overly swift movement of the magnetic North Pole caused by the great earthquake in Japan, which instigated a terrible and long lasting deficiency in the electromagnetic grid system of Earth making it less efficient than at any time in the past. We remind you that the electromagnetic grid is known by your science to protect you from radiation occurring from the sun and from your solar system. You should know however, that it acts like a mesh to hold the magnetic field around Earth in place, anchors the magnetic poles, and also magnetizes the atmosphere, which were all diminished greatly in scale by the grid's lessened force and energy.

At a time when energies from outside the planet were naturally and increased in magnitude by necessity due to the positioning of the Galactic Center and the solar system's ongoing motion through the

Universe, this was an occurrence that had an enormous impact on the protection from radiation afforded to the planet. Moreover, as we have described previously the electromagnetic grid system of Earth is also the electromagnetic system through which Earth communicates to all Beings, and through which all Beings communicate with their higher dimensional guidance and Soul energies.

When the pole shift lessened the electromagnetic field around the Earth, this had the very important secondary consequence of pushing the Third Dimension into a lower dimensional octave than it would have naturally had at a time of Ascension. This lessened the ability of the grid to act as an energetic linking system that connects incarnated species to their Soul intelligence via their chakra systems and the chakra vortexes and lay lines of Earth. This also hindered greatly Earth's connection to its own Soul energies as well as the connection all Beings physically incarnated on the planet have with higher dimensional resonance, the guidance that comes from their Soul source that is needed by each Being to navigate the Ascension process.

In other words, higher dimensional guidance was curtailed at a crucial time. In this way individual Soul energy coming from higher dimensional realms – the very substance that animates physicality and, in part, manifestation in your dimension – and using Earth's electromagnetic grid as a point of linkage for the chakra system of every incarnated Being, was greatly lessened. When this happened, all Human Angelic Beings together with a vast majority of planetary species were in some way affected.

This loss was not limited to the Soul's ability to communicate with incarnates or the Earth's ability to communicate with it's inhabitants (you) or with higher dimensional levels of itself. At such a moment during the Ascension process, when Ascension energies are at their most intense and necessary to promote the natural evolution of entire planetary systems, curtailing of the grid and the electromagnetic energies it maintains could be seen as a premeditated attack on the evolution of the entire system and all Human Angelic Beings. Indeed, that is exactly what it was.

While this is not the place to detail such implications, which we have already provided you previously, it is important to understand that although the use of scalar weapons on Earth derived from alien technology was being used for singular human political purposes, the alien sponsors of this technology had in fact orchestrated such usage and foreseen the eventuality that it would lessen the planet's potential to evolve. These alien participants, whom we have discussed in some detail (see "The System Lords and the Twelve Dimensions"), provided this technology to their human associates in order to disrupt Earth's protective energy grid system knowing full well that its demise would lessen the degree of guidance and intensity of energies coming from higher dimensional realms. Their intention was to stifle the ability of Human Angelic Souls to perpetuate further incarnations on Third Dimensional Earth in order to provide them with dominance and the potential colonization of this Third Dimensional planetary system in the future. We might even suggest that the catastrophe that ends the current civilization and modern era on Earth in the 26th Century is also linked to these same extraterrestrials, although be assured that only Human Angelic Souls hold the genetic keys and energetic codes necessary to have access to the energetic portals of Third Dimensional Earth.

Of importance to the Third Dimensional timeline under discussion here however, is that the diminishing of Earth's electromagnetic grid structure at the time had far reaching impact with respect to Earth's many faults, the movement of tectonic plates and the integrity of energetic ley lines. Once the interdimensional and communicative aspects of the energetic grid were curtailed, lessening the energy coming into and exiting out of the various realms, existing energy within the planetary system, which was unable to be freely vented through Earth's electromagnetic grid, had no other place to go but deep into the heart of the planet. It is this fact, together with the tendency towards energetic structural changes that take place naturally on Earth at times of Ascension and combined with the *unnatural* natural events being orchestrated by human manipulation, which served as the basis for the most significant, impactful and disastrous Earth changes that would occur.

Fortunately, there was no complete pole reversal on Earth during the time period (an event that would transpire as a result of the great Earth calamity in the 26th Century), but the poles were disoriented and wobbly enough to make their protective power, both in terms of protecting the Earth and its inhabitants as well as the protection received through the information received through the electromagnetic grid, much more difficult and problematic. For example, beginning in approximately the late 2010's and increasing dramatically by the mid 2020s there was great planetary dismay that quickly turned to chaos caused by the significant increase in meteors making their way through the now diminished natural shield usually afforded Earth by it's atmosphere and magnetic field. Meteor showers became more frequent and more visible, while meteorites bordering on the size of asteroids became objects of public fear and, in some cases, veneration (with several world cults forming around the concept of God and meteoric death). Suffice to say that meteorites, as well as asteroids and comets, became the new global boogey man, causing significant damage and destruction on a number of occasions in various regions of the world.

Considerable turmoil erupted in the early 2020s as a series of meteorites landed just off the South American and southern North American coastlines as well as the Gulf of Mexico, causing tsunamis and destructive flooding of coastlines. Such occurrences in combination with the unnatural manipulation of Earth's atmosphere and weather patterns naturally caused severe weather. However, it was the catastrophic weather patterns that had direct impact causing massive Earth changes in the middle of North America after that period that triggered the single most devastating natural disaster America had ever experienced in modern times.

The underpinning of the New Madrid fault in the United States was the first indication that detrimental Earth changes were in store for North America. New Madrid had long been studied and most agreed at the time that it was of insignificant importance in the affect it could have long-term. However, no one had taken into account that shifting landmasses, particularly those caused by the great Japan earthquake in the 2020s, would stack the cards towards massive eruptions of various faults in the United States.

Scientists had known for many years that natural gas pockets existed under much of the North American continent, but no one foresaw the enormous increase in methane bubbles that would be created by the cumulative effect of tectonic movement, new weather patterns, electromagnetic grid slippage, ley line movement and dangerous man made efforts to mine these gases. In fact few realized at the time that the true intention, other than profit, driving the "fracking" craze in the late 2010s was actually government sanctioning of a strategy to relieve the pressure mounting underground from a growing number of massive and dangerous methane bubbles, especially those forming under the North American continent, as well as in England, Europe, Russia and southern China. Symptoms of these pockets included earth trembling experienced in areas that had never before experienced earthquakes,

The Weaponization of Nature Leading to Catastrophic Earth Changes and Occurrences

as well as the mysterious death of flocks of birds and other animals migrating through areas where methane was being naturally released into the atmosphere due to the extraordinary pressure that was building underground.

One such methane bubble, a relatively large-scale pocket, formed under the New Madrid fault and this would end with devastating results. One can debate whether or not this was a natural event, as it had been tampered with for some time in an effort to ignite a disaster. Suffice to say here that it would serve as trigger for an even larger Earth event that would take place in portions of North America well known for super volcano activity, the legendary Yellow Stone Caldera.

The massive New Madrid earthquake of the 2020s had enormous impact on almost every state surrounding it causing wide spread destruction. This included reversal of the Mississippi River for a period as well as substantial flooding of portions of Louisiana, Mississippi, Alabama and Northern Florida. As a result of the event, areas within these States sank below sea level and water from the Gulf of Mexico flooded into the new low-lying regions. Portions of the lower Mississippi River turned into vast lakes as these areas flooded uncontrollably. Together with other Earth and continental plate changes occurring throughout mid America these events would set into motion unexpected consequences that would bring even greater destructive forces to bear on many of the Western, Midwestern and Great Plain States in the United States.

Though it did not lead to the absolute continental destruction predicted and was not as utterly devastating as might have been possible, the triggering of the Yellow Stone Volcanic Caldera in the late 2020s was nevertheless a determining catastrophe in North America. The event caused the demise of not only tens of thousands but ultimately hundreds of thousands, if not millions, of lives. Additionally it caused significant Earth changes continent wide with accompanying land devastation that lasted years from the countryside of Idaho to the Southwestern US, and from North Dakota to Texas.

In conjunction with the expensive geopolitical wars raging in the Middle East and other parts of the world, it is clearly this great disaster that caused the final impact on the future of the United States, pushing the country into utter bankruptcy under the weight of widespread national devastation. It would be only shortly afterwards that the populace revolts and situations we have already discussed were generated from which the US Federal government would never recover. The resulting break up of the United States, the Second American Civil War and ultimate foreign invasion and occupation of areas of the country not already under regional control would end North American culture as it had been known since the founding of the United States in the 18th Century.

Europe at this time did not fare much better than the US in terms of Earth changes and disasters. In addition to the limited nuclear exchanges that would affect it widely, great turmoil was wreaked by virtue of the fact that the jet stream, which historically warmed the coast of Northern Europe, England and other northern European and Scandinavian areas, was impacted by the disasters occurring in the Americas. As the jet stream bringing warmer waters north was greatly diminished and practically destroyed, northeastern areas in America as well as areas in Northern Europe, England, Ireland, Scotland and Scandinavia were subjected to plummeting temperatures, and a mini-ice age took over in most of these regions. Growing seasons in many of these areas vanished, and famine raged causing a mass exodus to the south. Most of these from Europe, England, Scotland, Iceland, Greenland and Scandinavia migrated to Africa, which was experiencing its own population explosion, while those from Northeastern Canada and the Northeastern US migrated to Latin and South America at this time.

This naturally led to an increase in religious and racial strife, as European refugees fleeing the mini-ice age and devastation of the great war that by now had destroyed most of Italy and cities such as Paris and Rome, migrated to growing but still somewhat ill equipped nations that were still intact in central, western and southern Africa. This set off intense fighting, racial conflict and civil unrest between migrating groups and those currently living on the African continent. Many saw this merely as an expansion of the ongoing, though winding down struggles of World War III. Others saw it as a new global conflict, although it contained many of the hallmarks of the Great World Conflict, pitting West against East, religion against religion, culture against culture, race against race, haves against have-nots and fundamentalists against fundamentalists. Each of these were fighting for survival of their way of life, their culture and their race in a seeming winner-take-all showdown.

As decisive as these events were, it would be a mistake to assume that the turmoil accompanying the Third Dimensional timeline through the 21st Century was defined by endless mayhem and destruction. Though we have highlighted the principal events during the time period and they may seem to occur in a nonstop fashion, this actually is an incorrect way of looking at the continuation of the Third Dimensional timeline. In reality, people lived and existed much as they do in your own time, and life continued on a daily basis as it always does. Following the great conflict and turmoil that occurred after approximately 2035 things returned to a somewhat livable pace, albeit with a great shift and tremendous change in the average person's way of life.

We would go as far as to say that the greatest departure of Souls through physical death on a large scale and in significant numbers occurred principally during the first half of the 21st Century. Whether this occurred by virtue of war, pandemic or Earth trauma, it is during this period that society was altered pervasively and important geopolitical, cultural, spiritual and political changes culminated. This happened in conjunction with an initial decrease in Earth's overall human population, but despite the fact that population growth was virtually nonexistent through much of the 21st Century Earth's human population was relatively stable throughout the period. Still, the period is reflected upon as an equalizing period for mankind, as well as an important time of purification on Earth.

What is important is the fact that the vast majority of Earth changes occurring during the period were magnified substantially by the significant interference of various governments and organizations all of which were manipulating the already awesome cleansing forces that were sweeping the planet. It is in fact the unnatural natural events that caused the most imbalance and lasting alterations to the planet's systems and these affected mankind most severely in the long-term. However, it is notable that one of the most significant Earth changes was related to a sharp rise in sea levels worldwide and the subsequent tidal flooding that occurred in the same period. This caused destruction and brought economic loss to vast areas populated by humans. We would add that these occurrences could all be said to be extraterrestrial in origin, since much of it was caused by technologies derived from alien knowledge that was grossly misused by various world governments and secret organizations. It could further be debated as to whether or not they were inflicted with intention on Earth by these alien races collaborating with the covert segments of society with which they had agreement. There is no question that these groups, in conjunction with their human counterparts, were most responsible for chaos that was unleashed using technology for manipulating natural Earth phenomena.

The intervention of higher enlightened Beings protecting Human Angelic guardianship of Earth subdued the wayward influences of these alien races temporarily. Yet these races, acting with the cooperation and in many cases through their counterparts who were incarnated in human physical bodies, caused the most significant environmental damage, detrimental to the planet and the timeline. However, without casting judgment (good, bad, right or wrong) on these Souls or their actions, as we have so often advised, there could be found a higher purpose even within their interference on the timeline. This is because the turmoil caused worldwide during the period directly caused or in some manner permitted the departure of vast numbers of Human Angelic Souls from the lifetime. These Human Angelic Souls would choose to leave their current physical incarnations on the Third Dimensional timeline through death as a direct result of many of these dramatic events.

As we have also said, participation in such mass consciousness events is by Soul choice for purposes of understanding, karma and growth. Those departing Souls therefore were aligned willingly with the choice to cycle off Earth incarnations based on the lower vibrational energies being perpetrated on the Third Dimensional timeline by the alien interference. In a sense, the lower vibrational energies brought into Earth's sphere *inspired* these Souls to Ascension, and this would entice them into incarnations at a higher vibrational level on Fifth Dimensional Terra, which we will discuss shortly. Terra exists at a dimensional frequency significantly removed from any turmoil experienced on Third Universal Dimension Earth.

Following the 22nd Century, incarnations on the planet by Souls destined to depart the Third Universal Dimension of Earth would be far less if not cease. Younger Souls remaining within Third Dimensional incarnations after that time did so with the knowledge that very soon a reset would occur in which they would essentially be starting incarnational cycles on Third Dimensional Earth over again. In a sense, loosing many Human Angelic Souls to higher dimensional frequencies meant that the Third Universal Dimension would quickly become a closed system, spiraling towards its natural conclusion. In fact, those alien (to Earth) races that would continue their interference within the timeline after the 23rd Century would seal its fate and would be partly responsible for the grand event of the 26th Century that would reset Earth's Third Dimensional timeline, ending the modern era on Earth that had begun approximately 13,000BCE following the final destruction of the Atlantean world civilization. In this respect once again, these alien races were (unknowingly) participating in the higher purpose that would reset life on Earth in much the same way life on Earth was drastically changed forever with the extinction of Atlantis, leaving only that empire's distant colonies, such as the Egyptians and Mayans, who forgot their links to this great culture within a few generations.

As we explained, events on the Third Dimensional timeline from the early 21st through to the 26th Century were not comprised only of loss, turmoil and despair, but rather of final opportunities for growth to be participated in by all Souls, particularly those cycling off the timeline forever. Thus, there were significant occurrences and opportunities to be experienced, whether a Soul chose to remain in the Third Universal Dimension or was seeking to begin incarnations on Fifth Dimensional Terra. What is clear is that each Soul would use the remaining time within Third Dimensional incarnation for purposes specific to each, and ultimately, a choice – Ascension and evolution, or not – would have to be made.

Younger Souls preferring authoritarian style (me and other me's) regimes began to predominate the Third Dimensional timeline by the middle of the 21st Century. Since karma, that is to say growth through the experience of energetic balancing, was the basis of their consciousness process they tended to perpetuate many of the fundamentalist disputes as well as the resulting turmoil. Turmoil and desperate times aside, alien interactions brought forth significant progress in the form of new technologies at the time, many of which we have already discussed and foremost among these the advances in weaponry and interplanetary involvement.

As an example of advances in other fields, the greatest advances made in the Third Universal Dimension at the time had to do with healthcare, as well as energy and uses of new energy discoveries globally. Much of this was due to necessity following the near complete breakdown of the global infrastructure that had previously allowed for globalism, free trade between cultures and nations, as well as access to petroleum-based products. The enormous and seemingly endless natural disasters and conflicts, not to mention the Great World Conflict centered around the Middle East, caused a near complete shut down of all infrastructure related to the fossil fuels used not only for energy but for products of all kinds by most humans worldwide.

By the middle of the 21st Century, new alien-derived technology had been introduced, adapted for use by Earth scientists that provided electromagnetic and chemical fuel cell technology that could provide virtually unlimited energy sources, creating, in effect, portable mini power plants that replenished naturally. This was a great boom to local economies, which no longer had to rely on outside sources to be replenished, making it possible for people to be self sufficient and no longer need to look far beyond their local community in order to exist or survive.

This was complimented by new technologies in third and Fourth Dimensional printing processes, whereby anything of any size or complexity could be manufactured locally, even in the home, with simplicity and ease through access to only a digital license. These innovations caused substantial changes in cultural structure, breaking the need for centralized control or massive organized delivery systems. It is in this manner that self-reliant populations in North America began to question intrinsically their need for distant centralized controlling powers.

In connection with this, communication and digital technologies progressed substantially, and new advances in ways to access the Internet and, more importantly, data "Clouds" and other forms of artificial intelligence, allowed populace interface without the need to travel long distances. Holographic communications technologies meant that individuals could virtually interact with others, attend functions or even visit distant places as if they were actually present, without ever leaving a certain locale. Combined with sensory technology, one could *feel* as if one were actually present, emotionally and sensually interacting via communications devises using all principal human senses.

These advances ultimately caused re-isolation of communities and regions similar to the kind of isolation experienced in the timeline's distant past, but with the distinct difference of having the ability to be digitally present anywhere at anytime. Essentially, there would be no need to visit a foreign city when new technology could deliver you there virtually in holographic form as if you were present in body as well. Regions began to become reacquainted with their roots, and residents and neighbors bonded in seemingly old-fashioned ways. Those regions that succeeded in implementing these new digital (sending and receiving) infrastructures quickly began to prosper, while those that refused them fell too far behind to ever catch up again. It is for this reason that certain regions began to prosper while others fell into poverty and despair, particularly in the Unites States.

In North America, this was also the reason that where one found oneself living during and immediately after World War III would become either the greatest asset or the most important deterrent with respect to one's livelihood and day-to-day life. The great alteration of American and in most respects global society from one that had previously moved around widely to one that was fiercely independent and loyal regionally allowed tighter communities and stronger personal bonds.

This form of structure would be one adopted by most towns and areas from the 21st through the 26th Century on the Third Dimensional timeline, and this would serve as a preview for Human Angelic Souls with respect to what they could expect to experience in the societal structures that are prominent on Fifth Dimensional Terra, as you will see shortly. At first glance, many of you might get the impression that this is similar to the 12th or 13th Century world structures of your own timeline, a period when there was forced isolation, limited consciousness, severe hierarchy and local myopathy. However, the higher consciousness available to most incarnates living in the emerging prosperous *localized* areas of the 21st Century combined with the advanced technologies we have discussed allowed this new societal format to expand opportunities for growth rather then diminish them by allowing expansive outlooks, perspectives and consciousness, as well as egalitarian perspectives, while also fostering the development of close interpersonal relationships.

While there would continue to be those individuals who explored and traveled the world, this became the exception rather than the rule. The isolation that ensued, unique though it was based on the fact that these isolationist groups were now more highly advanced and educated than those found in the Middle Ages, turned ruthless and in some cases violent as residents became locality-centric and almost psychopathically opposed to strangers and outsiders. This is perhaps the reason that authoritarian rule became the norm. A new standard of authoritarian isolation was birthed based on protectionism, and this went hand in hand with the development of heavily armed towns and regions that sealed *in* its occupants just as much as it prevented outsiders from entering.

However, the intellectual and inventive exchange that could now be had artificially through a digital and virtual presence meant that ideas and innovation could travel broadly and be implemented quickly without the need for physical intercourse or exchange. Inventions being created in one small region or part of the world could now be immediately accessed then reinvented and employed around the globe by any other local community with the means to do so. Surprisingly, this would foster greater homogenization of culture and thought in a quicker time frame than had ever transpired. Higher knowledge could now infiltrate global communities unhindered by the fear of contamination and without control and domination by some external force, so often the case when physical contact is required for change to be effectuated. As people began to feel protected by authoritarian, closed-off communities they ironically also became more open to global and particularly technological influences, as well as less resistant to change or fearful of the outside world.

For those Souls experiencing Third Dimensional incarnation at the time, this made life measurably better, allowing life to be livable while still permitting opportunities for growth and the lessons that have always dominated Third Universal Dimension Earth. This further provided a sense of protection to people within the context of deteriorating world situations on the timeline. Advances in technology such as the fuel cell revolution freed every community and every household from the dominance exacted by overseers controlling power systems, such as the electric or fuel grids. This was perhaps one of the single most important advances of the age, and in conjunction with new holographic communications techniques and digital cloud storage technologies, was invaluable to the world's emergence from the devastating period it had gone through from the early to mid 21st Century.

In the best of all possible worlds, when a Universal dimension Ascends to a higher dimensional frequency, in essence the lower dimensional vibration evolves into a higher dimensional value. This transition takes place throughout the Solar System and the Universe, up into the highest reaches of vibrational frequency and dimension. In the case of the transitional time period when much of the Third Universal Dimension evolves to a fourth and Fifth Dimensional vibration, we have already discussed with you how the Third Dimensional timeline continues up to the point that it's frequency has unified with Second dimensional wave values, at which point the Second Universal Dimension is ready to Ascend (evolve) into Third Universal Dimension Being. When this occurs without incident, there is a continuation of growth and expansion throughout the entire system, and likewise there is no real drastic or noticeable shift. This is to say, as an example, Second becomes third, third becomes fourth and so on in a seamless fashion without the definitive ending or jolting start of one or the other.

Think of this in terms of your current basic scientific views on evolution. Genes are passed down, altered from one generation to another until one day, without even realizing it, the physical Being has evolved and now has what you would call "mutated" genes. We would prefer that this not be seen as a mutation however, and rather as an evolutionary jump related to the Ascension process, with the point being that its transition takes place without much fanfare and certainly without a definitive beginning or end. In many ways, we would suggest this to be the true origins of the esoteric wisdom contained in your religious and philosophic literature regarding the God source and the creation of your world as being "without beginning and without end."

In the particular case of your solar system and Third Universal Dimension Earth, the First Universal Dimension is poised to expand its frequency and become the Second Universal Dimension, while the Second Universal dimension will evolve and become the new Third Universal Dimension, continuing on its own timeline replacing the existing Third Universal Dimension time wave. Specifically in the case of Earth, the majority of those Human Angelic Souls who are presently incarnated in that realm on that timeline will transition in conjunction with the planet's Third Universal Dimension to fourth and firth dimensional frequency. Thus by the mid 26th Century the vast majority of Human Angelics will have already begun incarnations on a higher vibrational Earth, that is to say on Fifth Dimensional Terra.

This however, presents us with an interesting dilemma, one we have discussed in the past with regard to the fate of Third Dimensional Earth. An explanation is in order. Most Solar Systems in the Universe are "anchored" by the genetic codes of the Soul inhabitants. In fact, most planetary bodies are created as vehicles for specific Soul groups. This includes the Souls of planets and other Beings that are a part of a particular Solar System. These systems are also designed through the genetic and energetic coding of the designated inhabitants to participate in the process of Universal Ascension. The genetic and energetic codes they possess not only anchoring the systems as a whole, they actually provide the keys to the energetic portals and synapses that interface with the barriers separating the Universal dimensions. We would term these codes the "Keys of Ascension" as they are basic to the process of universal evolution known as Ascension whereby the

Universe and all within it continues to expand and grow. The keys also relate to the portals that separate or join, as the case may be, access to other dimensions and time waves, other dimensional cadres of Soul entities, access to other Galaxies and Solar Systems, interface with Seventh to Ninth Dimensional Avatars and even every Being's relationship to the continued evolution of All That Is, the God Source itself.

You should be aware by now that the particular planetary entity known as Earth in the Third Universal Dimension, or by any other name in all dimensions, was in fact created long ago in order to house the development of Souls from the Human Angelic race. Here perhaps here you begin to see the dilemma.

Though the vast majority of Human Angelic Souls might Ascend to Fifth Dimensional Terra, in principle there always will be new Souls cast out from the same cadre ready to populate the planet at lower dimensional frequencies. However, the on-going interference on Third Universal Dimension Earth (see "The System Lords and the Twelve Dimensions"), as it regards an alien presence in your world and its attempt to infiltrate the planet via hybrid physical human bodies that can accommodate their Soul group, changes the fate of Third Dimensional Earth somewhat drastically.

As transformation of the planet's environment by this alien group occurs and the world's energies are curtailed, it becomes more and more difficult for Human Angelics to incarnate into suitable physical bodies that can be energetically sustained. Under normal circumstances, the species would have a chance to evolve in order to accommodate such quick environment changes. But the speed with which environmental alterations are being manipulated and accomplished by this alien race, in conjunction with their human hybrid incarnates now present on Earth, means that Human Angelics have little time to master the physical genetic transformations necessary to continue incarnations on Third Dimensional Earth.

This is not only the precursor to the planetary "reset" we have mentioned in the 26th Century, the degree of success this alien race has in commandeering the planet will be paralleled by the severity of the event when it occurs. Obviously, planet Earth, a Soul entity itself with the mission of providing the ideal vehicle for the nurturing and growth of Human Angelic Souls, will not allow her mission to be thwarted. Neither the Solar System, the other planetary Beings within it or the higher dimensional guardians of this universal sector.

Planets and solar systems are not separate from the Beings that inhabit them anymore than you are separate from the various cells that inhabit and function within your own body. In fact, most Solar Systems and even entire Galaxies are created in conjunction with the Angelic Soul groups that will populate them and use the system, by agreement with each entity, as a vehicle for Soul growth, creation and exploration. In the case of your Solar System, as we have said, its creation was intended, and will continue to exist, for the purposes of incarnation and growth of Human Angelic Souls.

On the Third Dimensional timeline currently under discussion, the infiltration of a Soul race from outside your Solar System and Dimension will force the planetary system to exterminate almost all life forms on your planet in the mid 26th Century. This will occur because at that time a majority of Beings existing on Third Dimensional Earth will no longer be Human Angelic in origin. As a result, they will not have the ability to properly anchor the planet's energetic grid, nor will they possess the genetic coding necessary to organically interface with the dimension's energetic portals and openings.

A planet's energetic transfer is a closed loop system whereby energy coming from Source passes through the system's Sun and is focused and disseminated by the electromagnetic grid of planets to the physical Beings present on that system via their energetic body (chakra system). What may not be clear to you is that the chakra system and the physical body in a sense act as boomerang points where the energy coming from Source enters into the physical system and is then returned through the same electromagnetic grid, making its way back through the system to Source (God, if you prefer). As energy creates matter it is quickly transformed, falling into lower and lower vibrational states until, ultimately, it is magnetized by what you know as anti-matter and this is the method by which Galactic Black Holes absorb and draw back to Source spent energy. Black holes, which act as galactic gravitational fields of a sort, literally suck up spent dimensional energy from the systems and return it to Source following its creative journey through a Galaxy.

When this closed loop system is overly compromised or weakened by whatever means, it becomes difficult for the system to sustain itself. Energy flowing through the system is no longer readily accepted and regenerated by the Soul group or other Beings inhabiting it. In rare cases, this causes closure, a failure of the energy to come from or return to Source. When this occurs, it can be said that a particular Solar System has entered free fall status, which is to say the planetary system has in effect become a run away system no longer connected to its Source. It has lost its ability to accept, absorb or dispel energy and therefore can no longer evolve, or Ascend.

When a Star system experiences such a paralyzing effect, the Sun entity will usually make an attempt to augment the energetic connections emanating from Source and distribute them, until the planetary system regains homeostasis. Such an experience is known in your science as a Nova. When homeostasis is no longer possible and the system has remained in free fall, the Star reaches its conclusion and chooses death. Thus, a Star connected to Source energy will explode or implode in a Supernova. Once this occurs, sadly those Souls incarnated within that dimensional planetary system are lost.

If we are informing you of this it is not to imply that the end of Third Dimensional Earth is imminent. Rather it is to enlighten you as to the reasons behind some of the anomalies we have discussed regarding your timeline and its future. When, within an energetic system, the inhabitants and Beings (human, animal, plant and the planet itself) are no longer genetically coded to the planetary system's energetic signatures (a cautionary tale with regard to genetic modifications in your world as a whole), not only is there a loss of connection to Source, the entire system becomes unstable and unpredictable. In a certain sense what you see happening today with regard to a hotter, brighter Sun and planetary system, extraordinary weather patterns, Earth changes and related atmospheric anomalies - those that are *not* man made or manipulated by mankind - are in fact indications of augmented energy coming from Source via the Sun that is not being grounded in your world and returned.

This creates great additional stress and havoc within the system overall, the result of which you are currently seeing and will see more consistently through the 21st Century. This fact, taken in combination with the human manipulation of weather patterns and the environment that is currently and will continue to occur, shall render many future Earth events nearly immeasurable in scope. Rectification within the system on this timeline is set for the 26th Century. That is not to say that this is completely inevitable, as we have explained early on, but this is the current trajectory of the timeline. What does appear to still be a matter to control is the degree and depth of the devastation necessary in order to reset Human Angelic dominance on the planet in or about 2569.

Nevertheless, the stress and havoc this energetic anomaly causes means that you will find over the course of the coming several hundred years energetic and physical Earth extremes that seem nearly insurmountable. When the system is working the way it should, we liken it to being in a room where the occupant is able to control aspects of the room's amenities through their will. They are able, as an example, to turn the heat up or down, turn the fans on or off, turn appliances on or off and open or close the windows based on their desire and their Soul's intentions. In the same room however, where the energetic grid is turned upside down and they are disconnected from an exchange with their energetic Source, their will is muted and they are unable to consciously impress their goals, wishes and desires on the surroundings. Suddenly our occupant finds the heat rising and falling, the fans going on and off and the windows opening and shutting haphazardly. Such a condition continues to escalate while the occupant sits dismayed in the center of the room unable to fully participate or intercede in what is occurring until ultimately they are no longer able to physically function within the environment at all.

This will be the experience for many Souls incarnated on Third Dimensional Earth from the 22nd to the 26th Century. In a real sense, that extreme volatility will seal the fate of this timeline on Third Universal Dimension Earth. The grand event will culminate in Pole reversal, something that has already begun as the Poles drift more and more based on every Earth occurrence. The ultimate shift will occur following the extraordinary impact caused by a planetary system event meted out on a weakened Earth suffering from an absence of Human Angelic Souls, a dissipated atmosphere and a deteriorated magnetic field, as we have already mentioned.

Pole reversal will signal the final hours of the current world culture and the end of what you know as the modern era of mankind. Once it occurs only small pockets of humankind will remain. These pockets will be of Human Angelic Soul origination, and together these Beings will serve as the proverbial "Adam and Eve" of a new era on a Third Dimensional Earth that emerges after these events.

Again, we do not wish to infer that Third Universal time and space vanishes from existence at this or any other time. For those Souls that have transitioned and those who are now transitioning to Fifth Dimensional incarnations on Terra, none of what we have discussed here needs to be of concern or be feared. Together with those you love, you will at that point most probably be already enjoying rewarding incarnations at higher dimensional values, on Fifth Dimensional Terra or wherever your Soul's journey takes you. To those entities who are not Human Angelic in origin, that is the hybrid physical human Beings (alien Soul originated and incarnated in genetically modified physical human bodies) that are being created by extraterrestrials who plan on usurping Third Universal Dimension Earth, we can say only that continuation will no longer be possible at a given point on the timeline. This is not because of any wrong that has been committed but because these Beings are not genetically, energetically or consciously equipped to anchor Earth in the planetary system where it lives within Third Universal Dimensional reality.

PART TWO

THE FUTURE OF THE FIFTH UNIVERSAL DIMENSION AND PLANET TERRA

 CHAPTER 9
THE NON-LINEAR MOVEMENT OF TIME AND SPACE

As we have said many times in the past, the grandiose demise of the Third Universal Dimension foretold in mythology is a much-distorted story that is being reiterated at this time in order to generate fear amongst those who are susceptible in your world. In truth, the Third Universal Dimension has always and will always exist. It will continue to exist even following the potential reset of Earth in Third Dimensional reality that occurs in the 26th Century.

Despite such a reset, we have gone to great lengths to demonstrate that in many ways the end is the beginning, and a beginning is always birthed from an ending. We could continue such a discussion as reference to the fact that there is in fact no "time" and all time is coincidental and happening simultaneously. In this way, there is great truth in the adage "without beginning and without end." But for the matter of this discussion, let us simply reiterate that there is no ending to the Third Universal Dimension; As the Third Universal Dimension expands to become Fourth and Fifth in nature, the Second Universal Dimension will evolve to become the Third Universal Dimension. This process of evolution continues into eternity and infinity. Therefore, fear mongers can be assured that we in no way are implying the end is near or that the end is at hand, for in truth this is not the case.

However, what is clear is that environments change, planetary systems change and solar systems change and the Universe is ever expanding and ever changing. As such, it is quite possible in the case of Third Dimensional Earth that the great cataclysm to befall it at the end of the designated time period will in effect sharply alter the story of Human Angelic life on the planet known as Earth within the Third Universal Dimension. This by no mean implies the demise of the Human Angelic Soul group, and Human Angelics will continue to evolve, Ascend and incarnate life times in an expanded Universe in most universal dimensions, particularly, at this juncture, the universal dimension where Fifth Dimensional Terra exists.

Fifth Dimensional Earth is known universally as Terra. The vast majority of future Human Angelics will incarnate and inhabit Fifth Dimensional Terra and the process of this evolutionary transference will occur over the course of the coming 250 to 500 Earth years. As we have discussed, at such a turning point, alien Soul groups will no longer incarnate on Third Dimensional Earth, and a new cadre of Human Angelics will incarnate in that dimension, providing a new era of growth that will take millennia to complete via the process of Ascension.

While no generalities can be cited in these formulations, it is usual with respect to Ascension for Soul groups to evolve together with the Universal dimension and the planetary system of which they are a part. Thus, it is natural that Human Angelics, having completed the process of growth in the Third Universal Dimension, would Ascend to lifetimes in higher dimensional versions of their own planetary system in conjunction with the Ascension of the system and the Universal dimension itself. In such a case, this means Human Angelics that have completed cyclical lifetimes on Third Universal Dimension Earth, will now begin incarnations on Fifth Dimension Terra simultaneous with Earth's Third Dimensional evolution into its Fifth Dimensional counterpart, Terra.

Please be aware that our discussion of future Human Angelic incarnations on Terra, or the evolution of one Universal dimension into another is one that may not fit properly into your reasoning and thought processes from where you stand on the Third Dimensional timeline. For example, many will ask why there is not a uniform progression, from Second to third to fourth, and so on. This is due to the fact that certain universal dimensions are so closely linked with others, they are not distinct in themselves and therefore progression is not uniform as one might expect. Again, we use the reference point that, in principle, higher can see lower, but lower cannot see higher.

Thus, in the Third Universal Dimension, you see the First and Second dimensions, but the fourth, fifth and higher are elusive to you. This is not to say these dimensions are not present, but only that they are not perceptible to you. So, in this case the Fourth Universal Dimension is actually present in both the Third and the Fifth Universal Dimensions, serving as a bridge. In the Third Universal Dimension (your own) Fourth Dimensional values are present but not seen by you, whereas in the Fifth Universal Dimension, Fourth Universal Dimensional existence is incorporated into the landscape and the awareness of those inhabiting the Fifth Dimension. The Sixth Universal Dimension is similar in its bridging o f the Fifth and Seventh Universal Dimension, present as it is, albeit in different ways, in both these dimensions.

Human Angelic incarnations may move directly from Third Universal Dimensional awareness to say, a Fifth Universal Dimension world. In the Third Universal Dimension, that part of Fourth Dimension that is incorporated into Third Dimensional awareness is most closely associated to the elements we have discussed concerning your "dreamscape" reality. This requires some explanation.
Fourth Universal Dimension attributes are those that currently exist for you, but that you either ignore or feel are not "real." These attrib-

utes include your level of awareness of and your connection to mass consciousness or the so called one-mind, your ability to consciously access the land of the dreamscape through conscious experimentation, and the psychic abilities inherent in every Human Angelic makeup but neglected, ignored and pushed from your awareness as you age by current societal standards and practices.

Many assumed that when we discussed the dreamscape in our prior books we were discussing the astral planes. In part this is true, but there is a distinct difference. Because you have banished acknowledgment of Fourth Dimensional attributes within yourselves, you currently access Fourth Universal Dimension awareness through the Astral Planes. However, the astral planes, a designation for dimensional regions where disincarnated Soul Beings transition to other higher realities, is not the independent Fourth Universal Dimensional we are discussing.

Remembering that each universal dimension has twelve sub-levels and that you exist within the third sublevel of the greater Third Universal Dimension, the higher sublevels of the dimension (fourth through twelfth) could in fact be collectively called the Astral planes (despite the fact that many consider the Astral Plane to be associated with one level of consciousness superimposed above your present reality). In the higher dimensional sublevels, you have a much closer connection to Fourth Universal Dimensional reality, but the sublevels should NOT be confused with the Fourth Universal Dimension. Therefore, these elements have unity without being conjoined, in much the manner a mountain has unity with your world, but few among you would say that the consciousness and life of the mountain is joined to you (disregarding the idea that all is one throughout the Universe, a universal truth). It is to say that there is enormous overlap in terms of the particulars we are.

In the Fourth Universal Dimension, which we reiterate is a dimension closely linked with the higher sub levels of the Third Universal Dimension sometimes referred to as the Astral Plane, thought-feeling energy is experimented with by incarnated Souls and this is the place from which the raw elements of consciousness take shape and later manifest as reality in your world. In this way, you are already connected to Fourth Dimensional reality in that your thoughts and feelings, including your imagination and your dreams, rise and fall, as the case may be, through the sub levels of the Third Universal Dimension via the Fourth Universal Dimension. It is from here that thought and feeling energy transforms into the probabilities and possibilities of reality. As this consciousness energy oscillates, it magnetizes light energy to form matter, ultimately manifesting as reality in the Third Universal Dimension.

Thus there is an interchange related to possible, as well as probable, manifestation via the Fourth Universal Dimension, and in this way it could be said that the Fourth Universal Dimension serves as an engine of Third Universal Dimension reality manifestation. If we were to provide a simplistic explanation of this mechanism, it would be this: Intense thoughts, desires, feelings, emotions, imagination and dreams are pushed forth from the Third Universal Dimension, through the Astral plane and the Dreamscape (higher sublevels of the Third Universal Dimension). When these elements reach cumulative mass, they are further pushed through Fourth Universal Dimensional awareness into probable future scenarios.

At a critical juncture, the energy related to these originating elements magnetizes light particles to itself and a probable future or past scenario is generated on the time wave. Such a probable future or past seeks out similar energetic waves on the timeline, those usually found in thoughts and emotions related to it, and as the probability reaches critical mass its momentum slows and it is physically materialized in

Third Universal Dimension reality. This occurs for individuals, cultures, groups and mass consciousness generally, and thus a probable reality is made manifest on the timeline.

If we are going to some length to explain this, it is to demonstrate first of all the important association the Fourth Universal Dimension has with Third Universal Dimension manifestation. Secondarily, it is to assist you to understand the vast realm of possibility and the importance of your thoughts, emotions, desires and dreams with regard to the probable reality that you are creating. This means that in the Fourth Universal Dimension, the stuff of life is literally present and malleable, and able to ultimately become part of your world in the form of your Third Dimensional reality. But more importantly, it means that as we have said many times, everything is present and open to you in the manifestation of your reality. From our perspective, this is important because it demonstrates that there are literally thousands upon thousands, potentially even millions of possibilities and probable scenarios already existing in Fourth Universal Dimension awareness related to your existence now. This means there are many futures available to you, speaking for a moment of just the chronological probable future events that you and your world could attract to itself. What is of greatest importance here is the understanding that you have the power to make any of these thousands upon thousands or potentially millions upon millions of possibilities into your probable future. It is a matter of merely shifting the originating energetic elements - thoughts, emotions, desires - and deciding which probable future you will attract into your reality.

Returning to our original discussion, overall we are attempting to explain why Human Angelics and Earth are not evolving in a linear procession into a Fourth Universal Dimensional reality, and will instead incarnate in the Fifth Universal Dimension on a planet holding the presence of Earth in that dimension, which is known as Terra. As we discussed, this is because Fourth Universal Dimensional reality is in fact the essence of potential with respect to what is creatable in the Third Dimensional world.

Here we have hopefully opened up a new concept for you, one that is perhaps difficult to grasp but no less important to understand. That is, universal dimensions are not necessarily equitable and they are not separated in the manner you may think. It is possible for a universal dimension to be closely linked and overlap with either a higher or lower universal dimension, existing (or not existing as the case may be, in both. In this way, Dimensions are cohesive, much the way you and your etheric (energetic) body are independent but also intertwined. Dimensions, like your physical and energetic body, work in tandem to create, balance and adjust each other.

Composite universal dimensionality, where each dimension, though separate, is also unified with every other and assist in the creation of other dimensions, is an important universal truth necessary to understand prior to a world's admittance to knowledge regarding inter dimensional access. Your world is on the doorstep of such knowledge only because it will be prevalent on Fifth Dimensional Terra. Unfortunately, any knowledge Earth currently has regarding inter dimensional travel has been provided by alien technology, and will be lost at the reset of the Third Universal Dimension timeline in the 26th Century.

The movement from Third Universal Dimensional incarnation to Fifth Dimensional incarnation is one that not only raises a Being from one universal dimension to another, but literally from one set of physical, mental and electromagnetic dimensional principles to another. As an example, Fifth Universal Dimension life is closely associated with and has contact with Seventh Universal Dimension Beings. While Sixth and even Seventh Dimensional attributes will be present in the Fifth Universal Dimension and while Beings in higher universal dimensions will be able to see all lower universal dimensions, they will have most contact with those closer in vibrational quality to them. That is not to say that Beings from higher realms and higher universal dimensions are not interceding and working in tandem with all universal dimensions. Case in point would be the Ninth Dimensional Avatars we have termed the System Lords working with the Third Universal Dimension. What is being created on Fifth Dimensional Terra is being derived from the probabilities of the Sixth Universal Dimension and the higher dimensional sublevels of the Fifth Universal Dimension. Just as the Fourth Universal Dimension acts as the plane where reality is staged and originated for manifestation in the Third Universal Dimension and the Sixth Universal Dimension acts as the area where the many possibilities and probabilities are orchestrated that will materialize on Fifth Dimensional Terra.

We have taken the time to assist you in understanding this in order to explain that the linear movement of time and space as you think of it is not necessarily a fact with respect to Universal Ascension and progression. It is also to allow you to understand that in every universal dimension, the timeline is operating closely within a multi-dimensional field of reality that provides the multitude of possibilities and probabilities that can or cannot, as the case may be, be manifested in that dimension's reality. Not only does this allow you a glimpse into why there are literally thousands and thousands of possibilities and directions - paths if you prefer - upon which you may manifest but it demonstrates that because of it there truly is no beginning and no ending in terms of the timeline's creation.

This brings us once again to the fact that while Third Universal Dimension Earth is choosing a path where the vast majority of Human

Angelic Souls will Ascend to Fifth Dimensional incarnations, it is by no means the end of the world. In fact, it could be seen as the probable beginning of a new adventure. That adventure brings us to Fifth Dimensional Terra, a world of momentous difference from the world you currently know. Let us take a glimpse into Fifth Dimensional reality on Terra and show you the timeline that waits in the realm of Fifth Dimensional probability.

# Chapter 10
The Ascension Mechanics of a Universal Dimension

It is a mistake to believe that the Fifth Dimension does not currently exist or is in the process of being created to accommodate you, just as it is a mistake to believe that the Second, third, fourth, fifth, sixth, seventh or any dimension come and go at will. Unfortunately, far too many of those currently in the Third Universal Dimension believe that your present dimension is ending and a new one is about to begin. This is not true.

What is true however, is the fact that Ascension, the evolutionary plan of the Universe, is just that, the evolution of one dimension into the higher oscillation and resonance of the next. This may seem difficult to understand for those using their current position in Third Dimensional reality as a viewpoint. Nevertheless, as we have said Ascension is the evolution of universal dimensionality. As such, all elements of the current universal dimension that are ready to increase vibrational frequency range will evolve to meet the vibrational level of the subsequent higher universal dimension, from lower to higher and higher to even higher, as the case may be.

For example, the existing Fifth Dimension, which has a unique and consistent experiential base that includes certain parameters defined by its frequency and time-space position, will receive evolutionary stimulus (think of them as you do genetic variations, only for an entire dimension) that enables it to augment its nature so that it has the capacity necessary to link with the time-space wave of a higher dimensional frequency. Yet it must be understood that there are vibrational sequences inherent in the Fifth Universal Dimension that remain constantly Fifth Dimensional in nature, what you might describe as an underlying vibrational curve that always remains Fifth Dimensional in essence.

So in this case, there is an "essence" of the Fifth Dimension that always holds the same time and space, and though all the elements (the very dimension itself) within the dimension may be able to evolve to a higher frequency, and indeed does, a place is always reserved for new elements raising awareness from lower resonance and coming into, or "linking" with the existing Fifth Dimensional time and space. This is the same with all universal dimensions, from the First to the ninth, and the law changes only in the Tenth, Eleventh and Twelfth Universal Dimensions (the Trinity related to your some of your religious mythology) where magnitude generates unification of the creative universal force (God) so that the integrity and inter-dimensional quality of these dimensions is expanded but unaltered. Though distinct, these three highest, and we would add magnificent, universal dimensions, described before as the God Source or the realm of All That Is, appear unified in a single dimensional frequency although they retain certain aspects of uniqueness and individuality. It is precisely for this reason that some of your religious and philosophical mythology tells you that there is a unified "Trinity" consisting of a Father, Son and Spirit all of which are unified as one, yet separate. It is also why Eastern esoteric mythology discusses the potential for nine levels of consciousness, with the ninth level equated to "godliness," a dimension we have already stated relates to Ninth Dimensional Avatars -- System Lords – higher dimensional Beings that choose to assist the lower dimensions in their evolutionary process while expanding their consciousness and growth in preparation for their own Ascension into the Tenth Dimension, the realm we have symbolically designated as home of the "Sons of God."

Similarly, other traditions envision twelve or thirteen dimensions, while others only see three (an Earth-centric misinterpretation where Heaven, Earth and Hell represent the unified three dimensions related to the God force). With respect to those traditions that further describe twenty-four or even countless higher dimensions, we would suggest that these interpret the sub-levels of each universal dimension as dimensions that are distinct and separate from the universal dimension of which they are a part. Following this line of thinking, considering that there are 12 universal dimensions and each universal dimension generally has 12 sublevels, recent scientific investigation surmises that there are no less than 144 or more possible dimensions in the Universe. Technically, universal dimension sublevels (most of which are non physical in nature and relate to the upper - sometimes described as under - worlds of each universal dimension) constitute part of the entire universal dimension. Regardless of your perspective or personal belief on this however, suffice to say that the tenth, eleventh and twelfth dimensions carry unique properties not related to the nine dimensional frequencies preceding them.

So what occurs is that aspects of each universal dimension gradually increase vibrational frequency so that its quality and resonance becomes resonant with the next corresponding vibrational level. As the elements of the dimension raise their vibrational oscillation, the entire dimensional space-time wave is raised, and when it reaches maximum oscillation, elements within the dimension are ready to "step-off" as it were onto the next universal dimension. As the Ascension period subsides, the universal dimension's basis normalizes, and it is readied to receive those Ascending frequencies from lower dimensions, if warranted.

Thus, the inherent experiential and physical properties of an Ascending universal dimension do not change. However, select attributes and those facets of the dimension that are ready to proceed have the potential to lift themselves from the dimensional basis, rising to the next dimensional oscillation and linking with it at a certain point. As we said, there always remains a basis of each dimension though most of its attributes have increased vibrational resonance and progressed to become ready and eligible to evolve to the next dimensional experience. Does the dimension Ascend? In a certain aspect one might say it does, since most of the Beings and elements within it do indeed. Does the dimension itself progress, becoming a new dimension? No, not exactly.

Your difficulty in understanding such a mechanism may be hidden first of all in your disbelief that anything other than the human species has the potential to evolve through experience and creative endeavor. This includes you inability to potentially see the Universe, your planet, your Solar System, plants, insects, animals, minerals, mountain ranges, clouds, or even inanimate (to you) objects as spiritual Beings experiencing some facet of a dimensional physical reality within the same time-space wave as you.

On the other hand, if you agree with the premise that all sentient Beings evolve to the next level of experience, then it may be your difficulty in understanding that the dimension itself is not a Being that raises its consciousness along with you. The dimension, not to be confused with the Universe, which for the most part IS a sentient Being, happens to be the time-space wave you are presently riding. It is not generally however, considered an experiential or sentient universal Being, and instead should be seen as an envelope housing the experience of existence. As such, the dimension is actually shaped by its inhabitants according to the particular oscillation, consciousness and resonance they project in the fabrication of their dimensional reality.

Though reason tells you that the Third Universal Dimension becomes fourth or Fifth Dimensional in nature, or that the Fifth Dimension turns into sixth or seventh dimensional reality, in truth what is occurring is an evolutionary mechanic where the potential of every Being within the dimension is realized at a higher vibrational quality. As such, everything that is not part of the basis of third or fourth or fifth and so on dimensional reality transcends to the point that its essence is unified with a higher dimensional frequency, opening the Ascended Being to a new range of dimensional experience. The newly Ascended Being becomes part and parcel of a new dimensional reality, which it has obtained in great part through compatibility.

In this manner you can see that when everything is progressing normally there remains a basis for each universal dimension toward which certain aspects and attributes of the prior universal dimension are constantly evolving or in the process of becoming. An example of this can be best seen with respect to, let us say, the process of geological transference that you see on Third Dimensional Earth. The fact that a mound of rocks wears away or that the wind takes the dust and sand of the broken rocks and creates islands does not mean that the basis of what was the rocks has disappeared. It means that the rocks have evolved to another level of existence. Making this a physically progressive (from your perspective) rather than physically degenerative analogy (although evolution may in fact take place in either direction), what if you take the same mound of rocks, compress it for millennia to form diamonds, and then excavate, cut and polish them to become a particular gem of adoration in your current reality. Now, are the mounds of rocks turned to sand that ultimately create the island or the mounds of rocks transformed into a diamond tiara First dimensional, Second dimensional, Third Dimensional (when finally noticed by you), or all of the above?

If your answer to this is "all of the above -- at some point in its evolution," then you have stumbled across the evolutionary progress of the entity known in our example as the mound of rock. All of this may reinvigorate questions you have asked yourself in the past with respect to the nature of reality, such as, "If a tree falls when no one is in the forest, does it make a sound?" But for our purposes these crude examples are intended to demonstrate that a "basis" of reality remains constant while the elements within that reality experience an evolutionary change in energetic nature and a transfer of that energy to higher and higher fields of dimensional awareness. This is to say that in terms of the positioning of a universal dimension, it is the rise in vibrational frequency of the elements within that universal dimension that cause them to Ascend and evolve to other universal dimensions. The universal dimension, which in essence could also be termed a transference wave, retains its basis and motion. This evolutionary mechanic takes place universally, regardless of the time-space wave that forms its basis and delineates the particular dimension.

If we are taking a moment to explain this, it is mostly to demonstrate that contrary to the belief of those fixated on apocalyptic scenarios for the world, Earth in the Third Universal Dimension, or for that matter the time-space wave known as the Third Universal Dimension, is not destined to be destroyed. And while we could debate the fate of the planet Earth, since there are indeed many planets within dimensions that have been destroyed (although again we would argue that even destruction is merely a transference of energetic nature), the Third Universal Dimension neither vanishes nor changes its basis, suddenly becoming something different or turning into a higher dimension.

However, it is the evolution of elements within that dimension that push towards higher dimensional resonance. Ultimately this is what changes the quality of each and every element as it works towards self-realization and propels itself through the process of Ascension into a new dimensional time-space wave. As the universal dimension dissects aspects of itself (including all Beings, even the solar systems and planets within it – all of which are to be considered evolutionary Beings) the elements within it rise energetically, through an increase in consciousness, until transference occurs and fusion with the preceding universal dimension is achieved. This is the evolutionary mechanism known as Ascension.

To begin at the beginning and return to our discussion of the Fifth Universal Dimension, you should be aware by now that the dimension's basis already exists. However, along with the Ascension that is being experienced within the Third Universal Dimension, elements within the Fifth Dimension are also experiencing transformation. That transformation is being fueled in large part by the incarnation of Human Angelic Souls coming from Third Dimensional reality. These Souls are beginning the process of incarnation on a Fifth Dimensional version of Earth, which exists in a reality that has vague similarities but properties and a future far different from the Earth they have known. As we have said, Fifth Dimensional Earth resonates as the planet known as Terra.

The planet Terra is an extraordinary Being. It has existed since the inception of Earth in the Third Dimension and will continue to evolve in its manner through many million millennia to come, despite the fact that Earth in Third Universal Dimension reality will go through major transformation and the possibility of near complete annihilation that will transform it permanently in the middle to later part of the coming few hundred years on the Third Dimensional timeline. As we have already discussed, planet Earth will continue its evolution without the dominance of its inhabitants for some time to come in Third Dimensional reality going forward. Fifth Dimensional Terra however, will escape much of the lower energetic turmoil that is the destiny of Earth on the Third Dimensional timeline, where the great reset to occur is potentially a positive occurrence necessary to reboot Earth and Human Angelic life in the Third Dimension.

Regarding Fifth Dimensional Terra, it is a planet that is represented in current Third Dimensional mythology as the proverbial "Heaven" or more appropriately perhaps, Valhalla. Although many of your references to heavenly realms are in fact related to references concerning the astral planes, which are non physical sub levels of the Third Universal Dimensional, mythology related to the Garden of Eden or Biblical "heaven" is more apt to be drawn into Third Dimensional consciousness by those sensitive and intuitive Souls who are tasked through their life purpose with relating to you reality as it exists on Fifth Dimensional Terra.

It should be understood that like Third Dimensional Earth, Fifth Dimensional Terra has always hosted Human Angelics, albeit of a somewhat higher consciousness and awareness. Similar to Earth, Terra is designated as an originating experiential home for the Human Angelic Soul race. This is to explain that the current Ascension period does not represent the beginning of Human Angelic incarnation on Terra, and neither will it be the last. What is clear however is that the bulk of Human Angelic Soul matrices currently incarnating on Third Dimensional Earth have begun the process of cycling off Third Dimensional incarnations, and, having reached a level of consciousness and resonance compatible with Fifth Dimensional reality will now incarnate in lifetimes on the planet Terra.

In fact, an interesting fact is that Human Angelics that have already been incarnating on Terra for some time now view the coming migration of Human Angelic Souls with trepidation. Remember that those who incarnate within a certain universal dimension are able to do so because they have reached a resonance that allows them the compatible consciousness and availability to do so. It is for this reason that those who have either not reached specific consciousness levels or who prefer the karmic endeavors and opportunities allotted through lower dimensional vibration will choose to keep having incarnations on Third Dimensional Earth for however long that is possible.

Those Souls that have not reach resonance will not automatically Ascend to Fifth Dimensional Terra. Rather, they will continue within lifetimes, albeit ones different than those found in physical form at the third sublevel of the dimension, in the astral planes and sub levels of the Third Universal Dimension. That is to say that once the physical components of Earth are no longer hospitable to human physical incarnation and the environment has transformed, many Third Dimensional Soul inhabitants will remain in the higher sublevels of the Third Universal Dimension until the time that physical life is once again hospitable and possible on Third Dimensional Earth. At that point, these Souls will begin over in Third Dimensional incarnations, incarnating on the new timeline that will be created and starting from the planet's new origins. These younger Souls will progress and evolve via many millennia of physical incarnations until their resonance and consciousness has prepared them for transcendence during a new Ascension period sometime in the distant future.

For those who have already reached a higher vibrational quality and are poised to Ascend during the current Ascension period, such a fate would be terrible in that it would require them to relinquish the vibrational consciousness they have worked so hard to achieve. This could be seen as equivalent to an older student who, having graduated college, was suddenly required to begin their education over again starting with Kindergarten. In the process, all they had worked so hard to achieve up until then would seem for naught, ultimately forgotten through either apathy or disinterest as they attempted to find ways to fit in with the rigors and routines now presented to them. It is for this reason that almost all Human Angelic Souls that have reached a certain level of consciousness and understanding will choose the transition and Ascension afforded them during the current and coming period and will seek to evolve to incarnations on Fifth Dimensional Terra.

Many of the current inhabitants of Terra, realizing the full effect of what takes place in a universal dimension at the time of Ascension, have been wary of such a mass influx of younger Souls. This is not to be misinterpreted as the fear you experience, but rather a sense of consternation and trepidation due to the fact that many of the Souls that will now be incarnating on Fifth Dimensional Terra along side them are perhaps not well prepared for the demands of existence in a realm of higher consciousness and awareness. While we cannot provide you with an answer concerning the end result of their consternation, we can tell you that unlike Third Dimensional reality, each Soul on Fifth Dimensional Terra experiences the creation of what they fear or emote almost immediately, without the delay you know on Third Dimensional Earth. Due to this, there was in fact a focused effort by Fifth Dimensional Terrans to slow down and in some cases delay the pending incarnations of certain Human Angelic Soul matrices into their realm.

It is unfortunate that they chose to do so, since it did have an impact on the ability of some Souls to raise their consciousness to the levels needed in order to meet the demands of the Ascension period and the timely energetic convergences happening that are necessary for dimensional Ascension to take place. To their credit, it must be understood that the current Fifth Dimensional Terrans did so with concern and respect, and not out of malice. Nor did they do so using methods as insidious as many of the extraterrestrial visitors we have detailed for you in our book "The System Lords and the Twelve Dimensions."

Fifth and Sixth Dimensional Beings focused instead on providing technology in the Third Dimension that would distract younger Souls from their Ascension mission, making Fifth Dimensional reality seem less urgent or attractive. Much of the entertainment and communications technology introduced since the 20th Century relates to innovations and techniques meant to mesmerize young Souls, isolating and hindering them from developing their inner spiritual abilities and thus delay without completely short circuiting their Ascension.

While this has not been done maliciously, its true intent was to merely provide "toys" that would become the focus of these younger Souls, most of whom are profoundly attracted to the notion of "Me, and anyone just like me." Thus innovative communications technology that promotes everyone to the status of indifferent voyeur renders everyone a critic and promotes an egocentric point of view that fosters the subjective perspective younger Souls prefer (a preference for Me and those like me). This makes the attainment of objective ideals essential for higher consciousness, like compassion, unconditional acceptance and live-and-let-live attitudes, more difficult to nurture and harvest.

This has the effect of virtually hypnotizing those truly not prepared to Ascend, if you will, distracting them from the work of consciousness growth and Ascension. In effect, this also delineates desires and separates the Souls that are more prone to Ascend from those not ready for Ascended consciousness. Similarly, this increases the likelihood that those ready to incarnate on Fifth Dimensional Terra will do so quickly in order to flee the chaos they witness around them, while those who are not ready for Ascension might make the choice to remain and spend more time exploring Third Dimensional reality. Little do they realize however, that much of the technology in which they revel is obsolete on Fifth Dimensional Terra. Instead, many of these aspects exist in the Fifth Dimensional realm as natural extra sensory aspects of the Human Angelic experience provided to them through the expanded senses of higher consciousness and not as external technological devices necessary to achieve these talents.

As an example, in Fifth and Sixth Dimensional reality it is not necessary to constantly relate your personal experiences, emotional states or desires via artificial intelligence since it is a world where everyone you come into contact with has the innate ability to accurately "sense" your desires and experiences simply by naturally tuning into your energetic signature. Imagine if you will a world where you only need to think of someone in order to impress upon them your views, perspective, wishes and experiences, as well as your life purpose and intentions. And imagine that they need only think of you, wherever they may be, to impress upon you why they are doing so and to what purpose. In such a world, texting, emailing and posting would be highly ineffective, if not misleading and utterly superfluous.

For those ready to Ascend however, such technologies in the Third Universal Dimension are vehicles of practice for what will become standards of consciousness and inherent personal awareness on Fifth Dimensional Terra. Learning to utilize virtual technologies in a Third Dimensional world acts as a means for training virtual extra sensory talents that are natural to Fifth Dimensional Human Angelics. This is not to suggest that technology is frowned upon or not a part of Fifth

Dimensional existence, which is absolutely not the case. But as it regards usage of technology on Earth, in a manner of speaking it is like providing a child with a certain toy to test its ability to benefit rather than be consumed by it. In the process, such culling allows each individual to determine their own fate as they choose to either remain distracted and hypnotized by the myriad of toys using them to feverishly avoid connection, control others and hinder evolution, or to gingerly explore their own talents for connection, inclusion and compassion. These distinctions become more important as the progression towards higher consciousness and Ascension become more relevant.

One cannot argue that with any influx of "immigrants" into a world, it is preferable that those arriving possess a higher level of consciousness and understanding, providing them the ability to assimilate and enrich their new world so it can be used as a depository for building and melding their personal traits and talents. One would also prefer that such immigration not represent a "takeover," but rather a positive and fruitful contribution to the existing structure. In much the same way Terrans are working in a non-malicious and supportive manner while attempting to protect themselves from an influx of young Souls not ready for the finer points of Fifth Dimensional existence, whose inability to understand the link between desire, emotion and reality could cause havoc in a realm where these things are manifested almost instantaneously.

Why would all this be true? In order to understand this, one must understand that Fifth Dimensional existence is an existence where several personal attributes and structures not common in the Third Universal Dimension are highly prominent. Included first and foremost in this is the innate ability each has on Fifth Dimensional Terra to recognize and understand the life mission and purpose, at a Soul level, of themselves as well as every living Being with whom they share reality. Secondarily is the ability, through thought, conscious intention and desire to manifest the reality of your choosing almost instantaneously. In the Fifth Dimension, these are additional higher "senses" with which each person is born, and these two important factors become the starting point for our next discussion concerning life inhabited by Human Angelic Beings in a Fifth Dimensional world.

 ## Chapter 11
Terra: Earth at a Higher Oscillation in a Fifth Dimensional Time-Space Wave

Let us begin by stating that there has always been a Fifth Dimensional Earth known as Terra. That is to say, in your sector of the Universe there have been Human Angelic Terrans and a place known as Terra oscillating at a Fifth Dimensional frequency since the beginning of time. In fact, it should also be clear that the Universe is not that different universal dimension to universal dimension as it regards structure positioning and, to an extent, organization. Therefore, there is a First, Second, Third, Fourth, Fifth and so forth Universal Dimension with Solar Systems and planetary alignments that have structures, if not the same properties of physics, that you would recognize as consistent from plane to plane.

Thus as we have mentioned numerous times, the Universe is multi-dimensional in nature, and universal dimensions, together with the sub-level dimensions that comprise them, overlap each other. While there is only infinitesimal difference in physical location based on time-space wave coordinates, the real differences are vibrational in nature and have to do with oscillating frequencies. This difference in frequency is important however, as it controls the properties of a dimensional time-space wave. It is also the reason why levels of a dimension can be superimposed one on the other, all existing simultaneously inside the same relative space.

Fifth Dimensional Terra therefore, is located in very close proximity to your neck of the universal woods, so to speak, and there are not eons of distance between dimensions. We are also not describing a Fifth Dimensional planet that exists somewhere in a far off Galaxy or some other part of the known Universe. Instead, Terra is a planet closely related to your current locale, albeit one you are not able to perceive or render real because you are not attuned to its particular frequency. This, naturally, is based on the laws of Third Dimensional physics, as well as your innate vibrational resonance as it relates to your own consciousness, which generally is in relationship with the time-space position of your current incarnation.

We have discussed the concept of multi-dimensionality in the past using as an example the medium you call radio or television. There are many radio or TV stations that propagate the same space. If you do not hear or see them all, it is because you are not necessarily tuned into one or the other, but this does not mean they are not present and coexisting side by side at all times. To encounter them, you need only tune to that particular frequency to actually witness or experience it. In much the same manner, Earth is a "show" oscillating at a certain frequency to which you are currently tuned. Terra on the other hand is being broadcast on a different frequency, one you will tune into as your consciousness rises and you Ascend, factors that provide you with the logistical ability to do so.

We have stated many times that this also serves as the basis for our statement regarding the fact that what occurs in one universal dimension does have significance and, to an extent, impact on the other universal dimensions. This is particularly true with respect to the spheres and sectors related to each other that reside within a specific dimensional vibration. It is for this reason that what transpires on a Third Universal Dimensional Earth has an impact on what transpires on its overlapping point in the Fifth Universal Dimensional Terra.

It should never be assumed however, that there is a traversing of the proverbial lines or a blurring of vibrational separation. What can be understood is the fact that those Human Angelic Soul matrices that have achieved a certain level of consciousness, finishing and accomplishing life lessons on Third Dimensional Earth, would quite naturally decide when they are ready to delve into life incarnations in Fifth Dimensional Terra. This has been the case for eons, and contrary to some belief there is not a continuous never ending cycle of incarnations for Human Angelics on Third Dimensional Earth lasting forever. Instead, Third Dimensional Earth is a place where many incarnations of a Soul are possible until such time as that particular Soul has graduated from the opportunities afforded them through Third Dimensional karmic lessons. At such a point, most Souls will choose to Ascend to higher dimensional values, the result of which is incarnation in higher dimensional realms.

While this statement should not be written in stone, since this occurs on an independent Soul-by- Soul basis, it can be generalized that many individuals from Earth's past linear, particularly what you know as the modern era from approximately 13,000BCE to now, have begun incarnating in higher universal dimensions. While there may in fact remain those individuals, particularly related to karmic endeavors, that continue to incarnate on Third Dimensional Earth and who have had lifetimes in pre-Atlantean eras, for the most part we would suggest that the current Ascension period will see a majority of older Soul matrices graduate to incarnations in higher dimensional frequencies. In fact, those who have balanced the energetic bonds created in Third Dimensional density via karma have for sometime now been incarnating on Fifth Dimensional Terra. Some have even graduated beyond the need for Fifth Dimensional incarnations on Terra, and have gone on to to higher dimensional existences, sixth or seventh dimensional existences, levels of incarnation that you would have difficulty understanding due to the extreme absence of physicality in those realms.

Having said all this, it is important to also understand that in addition to specific physics and physical properties, each universal dimension has a particular energetic focus in terms of the kind of lessons that are met and the manner in which they are experienced. Experiences on Third Dimensional Earth tend to be karmically generated, as related to duality and interactions with each other to understand that duality as well as the need to balance karmic energies within yourselves and with each other. This is ultimately related to understanding the nature of physical reality and the power of creation inherent in thoughts, thought forms, emotions, desires and intentions. These energetic lessons tend to reflect the more densely physical realm of the Third Dimension, and thus the lessons are more physical in nature. This can be seen in older understandings of karma, particularly the philosophy of karma as "an eye for an eye and a tooth for a tooth."

Fifth Dimensional Terra, however, opens up the Human Angelic to new types of experiences focused around what could be termed the "heart" chakra. Lessons are centered around enabling Human Angelic Souls to simultaneously understand compassion and unconditional love while also, due to that compassion, understand the responsibilities and importance of what is manifested in reality through the control of one's emotional and psychological state. Fifth Dimensional Terra provides opportunities for growth based on creative manifestation, teaching Human Angelic incarnates how to streamline those abilities through love, compassion and determination. Reality manifestation principles are based on understanding that thought is real action in motion that has real and definite impact in one's world.

Whereas Human Angelics in Third Dimensional density learn how to balance energetically interactions with others through discovery of the importance of polarity and understanding the commonality of energetic bonds, in fifth density Terra, the Human Angelic learns compassion, neutrality and love as the basis for creating mass consciousness and reality. It is for this reason that Fifth Dimensional Terra can be a place of extraordinary peace and harmony. It is also for this reason that many on Third Dimensional Earth, at least those who have elevated their consciousness and their vibrational resonance, have begun turning towards becoming non-judgmental, objective and neutral, using love and compassion as a starting point for achieving personal peace. This message was in fact delivered by several different incarnations of the Spiritual System Lords, whose objective over the course of the past two thousand years was to introduce into your modern era the idea that Heaven, Nirvana and peace are obtained through neutrality, and release from this world is achieved through unconditional love of self and of others. These messages were meant as an unconscious conditioning in preparation of the reality you will face on Fifth Dimensional Terra, rather than an actual edict on how to behave within the confines of your current world reality.

If we are emphasizing this, it is simply to inform you that Fifth Dimensional Terrans are a highly focused race of entities working to align the heart chakra. Because of this they emanate light and are interested primarily in achieving peaceful coexistence through reality creation. Thus they have worked to ensure that Human Angelics incarnating in Fifth Dimension are truly prepared to do so, as a protective measure both for newer Souls that may be unprepared as well as those Souls already existing within their world.

Fifth Dimensional reality is highly suited to those individuals with a greater understanding of the creative force that all Human Angelics exhibit. Fifth density Souls have a facility for being non-judgmental and compassionate, while readily knowing that what they think, desire and feel has the potential to be immediately thrust into reality. Those ready to graduate to higher levels of dimensional incarnations but not necessarily ready to achieve full-time lives in fifth density are, in a word, quarantined. They exist in what we would describe as a quasi Third Dimensional existence within Fifth Dimensional confines, and once they have proven a measure of maturity they are quickly transitioned into Fifth Dimensional incarnation. Sometimes this occurs seamlessly within the actual span of a current lifetime.

Unfortunately, most Fifth Dimensional Terrans do not see their world as the paradise it will seem from your current perspective. Focused on peacefulness of heart, to them neutrality and compassionate-control of thought and feeling are the ideals that are to be nurtured. This tends to make them seem aloof at best, and perhaps (to you) somewhat apathetic since they are not prone to emotional likes or dislikes. Nevertheless, when comparing life on Fifth Dimensional Terra to life on Third Dimensional Earth many of you will see life on Terra as representative of what paradise on Earth would be like. Let us explore the ways in which this is true.

Chapter 12
The Tertiary Pole Structure of Fifth Dimensional Terra

As we have expressed in the past, dimensional mechanics do not supersede each other. That is to say that higher dimensional values, as well as higher substrates of a dimension, do not necessarily negate lower dimensional values or premise. Multiplicity in the form of polarity (of some sort) is a prime basic motivational mechanism that inspires creation throughout many, if not all, universal dimensions everywhere in the known Universe. Expanding upon this concept however, it needs to be understood that polarity, which we will call duality for the purposes of our discussion here, is the starting point of Third Universal Dimension structure.

In truth, some form of duality remains intact at all levels of universal dimensional existence. It is however, expanded upon with each rise in dimensional level. An increase in vibrational frequency and consciousness builds upon duality as you rise through the dimensional values, augmenting the nature of each reality. Thus a dimension's resonance is augmented naturally and changes, along with its physics and properties, as you go. So as an example, the value and mechanical structure of say the First and Second dimensions are present within the Third Universal Dimensional. Similarly, value and mechanical structure related to the First, Second, third and Fourth Dimensions exists within the Fifth Universal Dimensional level, and so on and so forth as you rise from dimension to dimension. Higher dimensional mechanics do not supersede or negate lower dimensional values and mechanics, but simply incorporate, build upon and relegate them together with all prior dimensional mechanisms into the universal dimension level in question.

In the case of your current position within the Third Universal Dimensional Earth, we have described previously how polarity, meaning duality, is a central theme in lower dimensional levels (up to and including the Third Dimension). For the most part, in the First Universal Dimension there is singularity in terms of this dimension's energetic expression. Similarity and conformity reign. In the Second Universal Dimension, bi-polarity and duality is created.

Now in general, and this is an important distinction to understand, those positioned within a specific universal dimension not only deal with issues related to the confines of the physics of their current dimension, they are highly focused on exploring the issues and lessons mastered in the mechanics of the previous dimension. Thus, in Third Dimensional density, you would find that individuals and Souls, by virtue of their incarnations, tend to focus upon bi-polar issues and the duality of reality, in other words, lessons concerning Second dimensional mechanics. This is due to the fact that higher can always see lower since it is contained within the dimensional scenery, but lower is not generally aware of higher since it is not part of the perceivable landscape, so to speak. In this manner, Third Dimensional lessons focus on both third and Second dimensional lessons, whereas fourth and Fifth Dimensional lessons are unseen in the Third Dimension, if not completely transparent. This augmented approach would be equivalent to learning how to write sentences using the letters of the alphabet that you have just learned and mastered in a prior level class.

Of course, in addition to duality, a Second dimensional value, there are also First Dimensional mechanics present in the Third Dimension and you are well aware that there is a myriad of single cell organisms or single pole mechanics that exist in your world. Essentially this demonstrates the notion that lower dimensional existences are clearly present, active and included within higher dimensions. But what we would like to focus on here is that in Third Dimensional reality, most Souls will tend to focus on Second Dimensional issues, and certainly their perspective will be based on this. Case in point, the concept of duality.

As you know, duality (polarity) is a major focus in your world, from the North and South Poles to the opposite sides of the brain, to the function of your circulatory system and its scalar nature, to Yin and Yang, up to and including the concept of opposing forces in your world in the form of God and Satan - good versus evil. All of these represent polarity and duality mechanics, seen from a two dimensional perspective. Your world tends to be focused on this duality and it is precisely for this reason, at least in terms of consciousness, that you tend to see things as subjective representations of polar opposites: love or hate, good or bad, right or wrong. In fact, this is the basis of your current level of conscious perception, and it is tailored to help you master and learn from reality experiences related to the tension between polarity and, more specifically, the energetic creative force generated by the electromagnetic or scalar dynamic of opposites; the fundamentals of duality that we are discussing.

In terms of karma and energetic balancing of relationships, in third density you are forever focused on those Beings aligning themselves with one type of energetic expression and those Beings that are aligning themselves with its counterpart, the polar opposite or dual energetic expression. We have described in the past how this energetic competition in your world and your dimension, which is scalar (energetic) in nature, also applies to Soul origination.

Indeed, we have explained that Soul origination in several dimensions is related to the duality struggle between those Souls oriented towards "Service-to-Self" and those Souls oriented towards "Service-to-Others." It is in the Second and Third (and to an extent the Fourth) Universal Dimensions that most Soul groups find their truest vehicle for exploring Soul orientation through energetic and karmic experiences that definitively define them as originating from either one direction or the other.

If we are taking the time and effort to explain this, it is in order to introduce you to the fact that Fifth Dimensional consciousness experienced on Terra takes an exponential leap in its mechanics despite the fact that it focuses in great part on experiencing Third and Fourth Dimensional mechanics. Fifth Dimensional Terrans see the world through Fourth Dimensional eyes in much the same way you for the most part see your world through Second Dimensional eyes.

We have not focused on Fourth Dimensional reality in this book since it serves as a base level of Fifth Dimensional existence in much the same way the First Dimension acts as a basis of Third Dimensional reality for you. The particular ways in which dimensions geometrically group together and interface, especially with regards to dimensional physics and mechanics, is a broad and complicated topic that we will save for another time. Suffice to say here that although universal dimensions can be said to overlap in a multi-dimensional manner and all have links of one kind or another, though they are distinct they have certain commonality and links. The most important commonality is the fact that certain among them can also be grouped into what we shall call Triad formations.

In truth, such a grouping is as metaphorical as real, helping to better describe universal structure, but the description does have roots in the fact that dimensional Triad formations exists in general because their structure and mechanics are similar enough to allow for triangularization and, of a sort, conjunction. This further provides a tendency towards comprehension and perception. In other words, physical properties and physics are closely related within certain Triads, and these trilogies support each other's existence and geometry structurally. Looking in from outside a particular Triad however, perception and understanding is problematic at best, since the fundamentals of reality from Triad to Triad can be so vastly different. Again, this does not negate the fact that there is dimensional sharing throughout the system in a truly multi-dimensional manner, but it does imply that certain groupings and structures are more akin to one another than some might be.

We would be remiss here if we did not mention that this is the very reason it is so important for you to take into awareness and consideration the lives of Beings different than you, particularly those you might deem beneath you, which they may well be dimensionally speaking. You have little in common with a rock, and aside from studying or admiring it you do not participate in its experience. But as a First Dimensional Being, represented by the Mineral Kingdom, that rock has as much validity and purpose within its own dimension as you do despite the fact that you are not privy to its life mission or experiences. You can see it, touch it, hold it, break it or throw it, but for the most part, you cannot say that you are aware of the rock or, for that matter, that the rock is aware of you or your purpose. In much the same manner, Fifth Dimensional Beings know you are present though they are not aware of you. They do not interact with you or participate in your experience and they are not generally conscious of your life purpose. Without offending you, we would suggest that to a Being of higher consciousness and vibratory rate, say one residing in the Fifth or Seventh dimension, you are like that rock. Even in the absence of such awareness, you are interconnected and it would behoove you to not only be aware of the rock but respect its Beingness, purpose and life. The same can be said of that Second Dimensional plant life, as well as that insect or that animal, and so forth. In much the same manner, we would hope that higher dimensional Beings are aware of the validity in your lower dimensional presence, respecting and nurturing you via intention and consideration without ever having any real relationship, understanding or interaction.

Now as we said, the First Universal Dimension is the basis of the Triad consisting of the First, Second and Third Universal Dimension, just as the Fourth Universal Dimension serves as the departure point, in terms of mechanics and reality physics, of the Fourth, Fifth and Sixth Universal Triad. Each base dimension of a Triad generates an exponential departure geometrically and mechanically from the prior dimensional Triad. Thus the Fourth Universal Dimension is the door to a new Triad and a major departure geometrically and mechanically from the Triad that consist of the First, Second and Third Dimension. It is for this reason that until now you have had mostly hypothetical and limited tangible experience with higher dimensional mechanics, and again this also is representative of the fact that higher can see lower but lower cannot see higher. The same is true of the Seventh Dimension as the basis of the Seventh, Eight and Ninth Dimensional Triad, as well as the Tenth Universal Dimension, which is the door to the Triad of the Trinity, the "God" experience relevant to the Tenth, Eleventh and Twelfth Dimensions, which are also referred to as the realm of God.

What is important to our discussion is the understanding that Fifth Dimensional awareness and perception occur via a Fourth Dimensional perspective, and Fourth Dimensional mechanics are a radical departure from Third Dimensional physics. The Fourth Dimension acts as boundary and definitive departure point from Third Dimensional reality, and as a consequence it follows that the dimensional mechanics, and manifest reality, are exponentially different in the Fourth, Fifth and Sixth Universal Dimensions, which is a Triad substantially more complex than the Triad of the Third, Second and First Dimensions.

In keeping with this augmented complexity as it regards polarity, Fourth, Fifth and Sixth dimensional awareness achieves the introduction of a third energetic pole. These three polarities add substantial difference to the bi-polar duality with which you are currently familiar. Third energetic polarity generates vastly different experiential potential in the Fourth and particularly the Fifth and Sixth Universal Dimension, and this becomes the basis of the manifest reality known to Terrans. The concept of a third polar structure might be difficult for those focused in Third Dimensional density to truly understand, since polarity in your world is consistent with duality, usually meaning "two," north and south, east and west, good and bad, as we have explained. The introduction of a third polarity is quite naturally a result of the increased consciousness older Souls resonating with within Fourth, Fifth and Sixth Dimensional reality, demonstrate and experience.

Duality does not necessarily change in Fifth Dimensional reality and the added third polarity is best described as being the pole of "neutrality." But do not mistakenly think that neutrality is synonymous with nothing-ness, as you may think or have been taught. Neutrality is in fact an energetic charge that is as vital and important, if not more important, than what you know as positive and negative. What is important to understand is that having a third polar position means that entities in such a world are able to position themselves within a third pole, or choice, providing them with the potential of neutrality. In a sense, this added polar reality takes precedence over the other two polar positions found in a world of duality, and it also has a real and transforming effect on the Fifth Dimensional time-space wave. Because of that fact, it should be highlighted as one of most distinguishing experiential features of the Fifth Dimension.

So let's take a moment to summarize what this all means. Within Third Dimensional existence, life is generally based upon duality; Positive and negative, Yin and Yang form an eternal state of primitive spin, and this generates the scalar energy that ultimately creates life and the magnetic reality that you know. Within Third Dimensional life, this spin of energy most readily expresses itself through polar and scalar opposites, thus conflict is generated and acts perpetual. It is for this precise reason that Third Dimensional existence seems, in a way, based on the conflict between two halves. Here is the basis of why in your world positions form around this side or that, why conflict originates and never seems to resolve, why the flow of energy we mentioned early on is East to West, and why reality appears to be a series of never-ending dances between two opposing poles.

For Fifth Dimensional incarnates, this is no longer the case. The third or tertiary pole added to the dual positions so prominent in your world creates a new perspective and generating force with which every other element in existence can be viewed. When one has a neutral position from which to perceive reality, one realizes that not only is it no longer necessary to be either good or bad, right or wrong, one discovers that subjective positions such as these are, in a way, obsolete. When the choice of neutrality is made, through its availability, one hovers above the duality in a state of neutrality able to perceive both sides equally, landing on neither side. Karma, as it is known in Third Dimensional existence, is no longer necessary or viable when neutrality is achieved.

For many, especially those incarnating for the first few times in Fifth Dimensional density, looking back on duality can seem like the equivalent of living many lifetimes wandering through a labyrinth, not knowing where you stand, constantly going back then turning around and trying again from the opposite pole (karma). Suddenly, when neutrality is possible, the same entity is able to pick itself up and rise above the labyrinth to see where it is going, where it wants to go, where it was and where, ultimately, it needs to be. Such a new perspective makes it impossible to hate the life you are in, or, using our labyrinth metaphor, hit the wall in front you, turn around, repeat yourself or punch the wall behind you. No longer is one saddened, depressed or sullen for fear of not finding your way out of the maze. The neutral perspective allows you to see where you are, what's happening and why, all within the context of daily experience within the labyrinth of reality. This in turn pushes you towards a higher level of consciousness and allows you to banish fear, anxiety, lack or any sides of the duality you no longer wish to be present in your world.

Now Terrans are people like you who exhibit slightly less physical density based on a higher vibrational resonance, and subsequently a consciousness that maintains knowledge of the Soul's higher purpose and intent even within the lifetime. They focus their abilities on mastery of experiences you would describe as being related to the (your) heart chakra. In a certain sense, the chakra system you know is aligned in perfect harmony symbolically with the structural and symbolic expressions that are found and experienced in each universal dimension. Looking at this in more depth, you would see that the first three dimensions are perfectly aligned with the base three Chakras of the Third Dimensional human body. The first three chakras and the corresponding dimensions are aligned in purpose with fundamental basics of reality and existence, the pure mechanics of creation, root living and physical wellbeing. Rising to the fourth and fifth chakras, the solar plexus and the heart, one begins to experience the energy of the heart-connection. Thus, in the Fourth and Fifth Dimension life is focused on lessons of compassion, the interface of physical and emotional content and heart-based caring.

This is accomplished via the tertiary pole we are discussing. The third pole of neutrality is the realm of compassion, the dominion of the Heart, and in the Fifth Dimension it is the heart, through higher consciousness, that creates experience. For the most part, Terrans exhibit true heart-felt compassion and love for each other, for other Beings and for each and every element of their world. They do so through compassionate disengagement, which for them is the ability to allow one to have one's experience without interference or emotional intercession so as not to interfere with a Soul's higher mission and purpose. It is their individual and group mission to bring others to the same heart-felt compassion, assisting each to find themselves through understanding, compassion, peace, harmony and – (non judgmental) neutrality. To explore how this works further, let us take a look at how the tertiary pole effects the space-time wave of the Fifth Universal Dimension, and specifically, the effect this has on reality manifestation and the structure of life on Terra.

Chapter 13
Reality Manifestation on Fifth Dimensional Terra and Terran Societal Structure

For a real understanding of how Terran reality in the Fifth Universal Dimension is created, one must first understand the basics concerning reality manifestation in third density. In the Third Universal Dimension, thought and belief originate from the mental body based in large part on the directives of your Soul purpose as formulated within you through your environment, your upbringing and the specific personality features and karmic endeavors you chose to incorporate within the lifetime. When combined with energetic output, such as your emotions, desires, intent and wholeheartedness, many of these thoughts and beliefs, which may or may not be consciously known to you, are driven as vibrational waves through the energetic body and delivered into the field of electromagnetic potential.

Once this pump is primed and the electromagnetic field has reached full term and availability, energetic particles that form mass slow down and reality is literally attracted and magnetized to your thoughts and beliefs, altered as the case may be by mass consciousness, availability and the consistencies or inconsistencies of your emotional discharge and (conscious and/or unconscious) focus. As the time-space wave of the Third Dimension unfolds around you it allows the trajectory with the most energetic potential to manifest physically and create a reality based on your inner impetus. These reality manifestations can be desirable and what is wanted, but they can also be seemingly undesirable when met by you in day-to-day life if their origins are unconsciously or "karmically" manifested. Based on the properties of the space-time continuum in which you are focused you experience this as a processional linear creation, which you call life.

Secondarily, Third Dimensional reality has a time lag in terms of its structural and time-space wave elements, which allows the potential of thought, desire, intention and deed to come together and be built in conjunction with existing reality mass consciousness, environment and energetic experiences. This means simply that reality in the Third Dimension is materialized rather slowly (from your viewpoint) relying on energetic and physical components to come into position and reach a tipping point in order to manifest the intention or desire in physical experience. It is for this reason that what is manifested may not always be exactly as consciously intended or envisioned by you, and in many cases on an energetic level, manifestation will magnetize and form around "similar" energetic particles or events that are already present in the environment rather than manifest identical to your prevailing focus or thought form.

Moreover, this built-in Third Dimension mechanical safeguard allows thought forms, as well as what is desired by the Soul and individual, to be waylaid, reinforced energetically and in many ways tempered by you so that you and the world around you are not faced with an endless barrage of unwanted realities and experiences. If not, most of these would be made manifest instantaneously before your eyes in exactly the same construct as originated by your mental body. Indeed, dealing with the inconsistencies and inadequacies of your physical creations and experiencing them as "watered-down," time deferred versions is challenging enough without adding to the mix a reality filled with exact and immediate representations of every thought form and energetic desire you propel into your world. Were it not for the physics and mechanical properties afforded by this lag in the time continuum, and without such an energetic braking system in place, reality manifestation by entities not possessing a certain level of experience and consciousness could prove daunting to even the well intended "Co-Creator" in the Third Dimension.

The structure of reality creation and time continuum in the Fifth Dimension is quite different than what you experience in Third Dimensional reality. First of all, the Fifth density is devoid of a truly moment-by-moment linear time progression. Instead it is experienced more fully in a much more multidimensional way. This means that in the Fifth Dimension what you know as "time" is experienced more comprehensively, or as if one were able to experience a unit of present, past and future moments in their entirety and as a whole. From your perspective, this would appear as if the present, the immediate past and the immediate future were all happening simultaneously within the same timeframe and locale, with the observer able to comprehend these distinct elements as a whole unit of measure.

For this reason, time and therefore the creation of reality in the Fifth Dimension would seem instantaneous in nature to you. In the Fifth Dimension, and this is a trait shared at all universal dimensions above the Fifth Dimension, the concept of past, present and future is fuller, less distinguishable, more abstract and more massive. Naturally, its comprehension is geared towards a more developed consciousness, and time progression in Fifth density is not moment-to-moment with only the current moment available to perception as you now experience in Third Density. Instead time is experienced as what we would call a supersized "Now," which includes everything that has just transpired, everything that is currently taking place and everything potentially possible from your present trajectory moving immediately forward.

With respect to reality manifestation, this becomes a sizeable distinction since because of this manifestation of one's reality in the Fifth Dimension can appear to take place instantaneously. Moreover, the possibility of a continuous Now where the immediate past, present and future is unified, tangible and seemingly real you are taxed with the need to control your emotional output, and you have full responsibility for your intention and your awareness. For this reason, the degree of mastery you have over your intentions, emotions and creative force is a hallmark of your consciousness.

It should be understood that basically this is a natural energetic signature of the Universe and even in the Third Universal Dimension, it could be said that there is a series of continuous Now's that lead to a myriad of potential futures. However, what is very different is the fact that within Third Dimensional reality, only the actual linear Now appears to be real. In the Fifth Dimension, not only does the Now appear to be present and real, so does the immediate past and even more importantly, something not necessarily a factor in the Third Dimension, you experience immediate future probabilities and possibilities as present, actual and real within the present moment.

This is far different from imagining various possibilities or potentialities as you do in Third Dimensional reality even though they may exist somewhere, including in the dreamscape, in your thoughts or your imagination. In Fifth Dimensional reality, one is automatically present within the future potentiality that is based on one's current trajectory. It is in this manner that one has significant power, originating in the Now, to choose the potential and the course that one's existence might take.

This can certainly be of great advantage to Souls with an elevated level of consciousness and awareness that are taking action through the heart chakra and are able to transport themselves via the Now to future probability. In fact, centering in the heart chakra is precisely what gives Fifth Dimensional Terrans the ability to perceive and experience the time wave in such a way. We would suggest that heart centering by someone in the Third Dimension could in certain circumstances achieve access to a similar "Super Now" perception. However, this would only be to a limited degree and would prove to be fleeting awareness for all but true masters due to the energetic and physical limitations of Third Density reality. Yet it can be said that those with the ability to experience such perception in the Third Dimension would describe it as being akin to time travel, where the past and thus the present and future are available and in many ways mutable.

What is of most importance to understand here however, is that in the Fifth Dimension this time-space wave perspective provides the Soul with a greater ability to actually change the immediate past through action and intention taken in the Now. Such ability further alters that same "Now" as well as the future potentiality that is inherent in the present. Think of this as playing chess on a multi-dimensional chess board where the boards are clear acrylic allowing you to see through them and play simultaneously on the board above, in the middle and below. Each time a chess piece is moved on the middle board, which is the present, a change occurs on the lower board, the past, as well as the higher board, the future. You are present in all three chess games at the same time, and each time a position is moved on one board, a corresponding move is made on the others, allowing you to immediately experience and alter your course, or in this case, experience your immediate past, present and immediate future as though they were one in the same. This makes Fifth Dimensional reality far more controllable and less disorganized, though it requires a level of consciousness ample to manage focus, maintain intention and execute choice within three simultaneously occurring trajectories of reality, which when combined into one perspective represent a super Now.

In a certain sense, Human Angelics within the Fifth Dimension have the ability to implicitly guide their future, as well as their past, through the emotions, focus, action and intention taken in this expanded Now. With a myriad of options available to them through their heart-focused intention they are free to follow a path that represents the path of highest resonance to them. This is naturally different than the current Third Dimensional reality where you are haphazardly striving to find your path, imagining it endlessly in an attempt to attract the many possibilities, which for the most part you are unable to experience fully because unconscious intention and emotional constructs block you. In a reality such as your current one, the future all too often seems intangible, uncontrollable and abstract.

Mainly because of this feature, Fifth Dimensional Terrans have the possibility of creating and experiencing reality in a manner that is uniquely different from the way in which you experience reality. They have the possibility of manifesting quickly what they intend and what they desire. More importantly, because their emotional content and intention is heart based and guided through the energy of the heart chakra, in a sense they are able to intuitively foresee the immediate cause and effect of their creations.

In this way Terrans can be said to be automatically at one with the reality they manifest. Beings in the Third Dimension, on the other hand, do not have this potential and struggle endlessly with manifesting within the learning gap of creation (time lag) defined by your particular time-space wave structures. This makes Third Dimensional reality creation a causal system of trial and error where what is thought in one moment may or may not transpire or manifest itself either quickly or in a distant future, all of which are subject to mass consciousness settings, emotional content, desire, intention and the Soul's purpose for that incarnation.

Life in Fifth Dimensional reality however, is far more orderly since almost all are able to understand on an intuitive basis what they are about and what they are learning within the lifetime. Additionally, they are able to immediately project themselves via the super Now into a manifestation of the future or, otherwise said, bring a future moment that they experience in the Now into their reality spontaneously. As that future moment is brought into reality spontaneously, Terrans have the ability to experience it immediately, waylay it, test it, change it or alter it as they go. This means that there is far less interface with what we shall call the "mass consciousness" background or environment.

We have described many times in the past how Third Dimensional reality is orchestrated against a backdrop of mass consciousness and mass spontaneity that you know as specific time periods or historic eras and events. These backdrops become the basis for lessons that each individual Soul has the opportunity to experience, if they choose, in that particular reality. Life in Third Dimensional reality is based largely on a Soul's organization of lifetimes within events, situations and environments that provide the mass consciousness backdrop for optimal Soul growth. A Soul will incarnate in lifetimes within these scenarios (past, present or future time periods simultaneously) in order to afford itself of certain possibilities and probabilities or experience lessons that may be inherent in living through the events of such a backdrop. This is particularly true when the opportunities available within it are applicable to that Soul's journey of consciousness.

In a manner of speaking, Third Dimensional reality from the Soul's perspective is the same multi dimensional chess game we have described already. But instead of being experienced in a Super Now, the game is played out via various lifetimes that are implanted within different segments of the Third Density timeline. As one lifetime takes action or experiences events and lessons of growth, all other lifetimes within that cycle that are related to that particular Soul respond energetically (karmically), and events within corresponding lifetimes (played out on different levels of the acrylic chess board simultaneously) will balance out the experiences of each other lifetime as they occur.

On the contrary, in Fifth Dimensional reality mass consciousness and the idea of a continuous timeline exist primarily as a foundational meme for easy reference, as well as group gathering and society forming. For the most part Terrans are less concerned with each individual's interface within a time frame, and are also not particularly interested in growth via interaction with their fellow Beings or through experiencing opportunities in conjunction with the prevalent mass consciousness background. Fifth Dimensional Terrans are much more concerned with reality manifestations that they originate for themselves independently. Their manifestations, which they delve into personally and privately for the most part, are merely placed against the context of the prevailing backdrop as a matter of societal agreement, uniformity and easy communal reference.

This is a subtle but important difference. The bulk of learning a Soul accomplishes in the Third Dimension originates from opportunities based on its interface and energetic exchange with others and the environment (Karma or energy balancing). The bulk of learning in a Fifth Dimensional reality however, is done via a Soul's own created opportunities (Self Karma) that it explores within itself, and these self perpetuating opportunities merely occur against, but not as a result, of the prevailing mass consciousness backdrop. In such a world, mass consciousness and the general reality is more the décor of a generic room that the Soul happens to be in at the time as it preoccupies itself with some personalized endeavor. In contrast, Third Dimensional mass consciousness provides the Soul with a background that generates opportunities that it must explore and with which it must interact. The Soul then gains life lessons by opportunities that come from experiences external to itself, in a sense via its interface with the room décor, as well as with others in the room and through events taking place in that room.

So the difference is that in Third Dimensional reality one builds one's life through references from the mass consciousness background and interfaces with that background in order to fund opportunities for growth. However, in Fifth Dimensional reality, one builds one's life first then picks and chooses what is available in the mass consciousness background in order to add to, fill in or augment its experiences. In truth, a Fifth Dimensional Terran does not necessarily ever need to interact with society or with the events of the mass consciousness background should the entity choose, though most do so through love and compassion that lead naturally to the desire for cooperation in the growth of others.

As you can well understand this means that Fifth Dimensional reality, and in particular Terran society, is far more amenable and less judgmental in terms of its participation as well as in terms of its acceptance of the entities external to self or one's "tribe" since each tends to be more independent and self sustaining with respect to personal growth and more tolerant with respect to the growth of its fellow Beings. Because of this they are not only far less prone to correcting lingering energetic imbalances (Karma) with others, they are much less prone to generating new imbalances, and they tend to participate only in lessons that are seen as self-fulfilling or self-actualizing.

This does not however, mean Terrans are selfish, narcissistic or aloof, attributes that are more applicable to such an individual in Third Density. On the contrary, it makes them less judgmental, more accepting and more cooperative. Fifth Dimensional life on Terra is more about self-karma (self love), meaning opportunities one creates for oneself in terms of growth as opposed to opportunities generated through interaction and relationship with others or society, as is the case in the Third Dimension. When you combine this fact with the secondary understanding that Fifth Dimensional life is focused through the Fourth Dimensional heart chakra, you begin to see why selfishness and egocentric behavior is not their concern. Instead, you have two vital elements necessary for peaceful co-existence. First is the ability to perceive one's full potential. Second is the ability to experience and alter that potential through a perception that combines the present, past and future moments into a super Now. And all of this is then focused and seen through the love and compassion of the Fourth Chakra, one's heart center.

We do not wish to confuse you, and it would be incorrect to think of Fifth Dimensional Terra as a place where mass confusion and chaos reign with entities selfishly pursuing their own agendas endlessly, coming and going at will without taking an interest in their world. In fact the Fifth Dimensional system of reality and its mechanisms in general make organized societies such as Terra far more beneficial and enlightened than anything you can imagine in the Third Dimension. And while this is not necessarily the case for all cultures or civilizations within the totality of Fifth Density, Fifth Dimensional Human Angelics are known galaxy wide as an evolved group. In fact, Terra their home planet and system has close ties to the highly advanced Arcturian civilization. That civilization heads up the principal Galactic organization responsible for maintaining both Third Dimensional Earth and Fifth Dimensional Terra as protected zones of free will where overt off-world interference and oppression is not permitted. In this context, Terra is known for its civilized advantages and freedoms of expression, particularly as it regards the growth of individual or universal consciousness.

For the most part, Fifth Dimensional Terra is not organized according to national, racial, religious or cultural group as you would understand them. Though such distinctions may be highly prized by younger Souls in lower dimensional realities looking to interface with such groups, they have little to no bearing on the organizational and structural units favored by Souls of higher consciousness or older Soul age in higher densities. Instead, Terran communities are based principally and primarily on units comprised of entities that have Soul relationships with each other forged from being cast out of the same or related Soul group. They also may be based on entities that have associations with each other from previous lifetimes or that have established relationships over time based on newly identified principles and lessons they wish to explore in a Fifth Dimensional manner. To be clear, these can also form the basis of Third Dimensional relationships, but Fifth Dimensional communities are more closely aligned to Soul group and cadre associations. In most cases there is a deep understanding that if one is associated by virtue of community in the Fifth Dimension it is because there is a profound Soul group association or Soul purpose.

Thus communities and units in the Fifth Dimension are more spontaneously loving and familial in nature without the deep karmic energetic imbalances that you think of when you hear the term "family." In addition, there is little to no competition or judgment within the group because in many cases there is a profound understanding of each individual's life purpose and the fundamentals of their association. In some cases even the past or future memories of those Soul relationships are known, and individuals therefore tend to be satisfied to live harmoniously within their "family" Soul community adhering primarily to their personal goals and purpose. Although naturally there is interchange with outside groups and communities, even that of an off-world nature, there is less individual or group searching for the stimuli inherent in outside or distant relationships since these are usually viewed as superfluous and unnecessary to personal growth the way they may be sought out in the Third Dimension.

Therefore, whereas in the Third Dimension you might have cities inside of states inside of countries that are organized by cultural, ethnic, religious or geographic proximity offering a vast amount of specialties and experiences from A to Z, Fifth Dimensional Terra is not organized in such a manner. Rather, it is organized into highly efficient and evolved Soul group communities based on Soul age, Soul purpose, common desire, Cadre affinities, Soul camaraderie and genuine affection. In a certain sense, you would be correct in comparing this to the structures found in very basic primitive societies, communities, nations and civilizations on Third Dimensional Earth where an entire town might originate from one family unit (tribe), or similarly be based on one type of occupation or work specialty functioning independently within the greater context of the nation or organized state.

The important difference here however, is that in the distant past on Third Dimensional Earth each family member was not necessarily a Soul family member and generally there was no connection between the entities relating to Soul group or Cadre. Instead, biological family members most likely were connected by the desire to experience karma and energetic balancing (through competition, events and personal longing) with the other incarnated entities in question, and while there may have been loose Soul connections between them, these were generally more rare than you might think.

On Terra you have communities based on long established Soul alliances and casting (the birthing of new Souls within a group or cadre) that are not karmically generated. Since such incarnations are related more to love and devotion than "duty," entire communities can be established that are purpose-based, and each individual is exploring the aspects of a specialty within themselves that is applicable to the entire Soul group from which they originate.

Thus cosmic specialties inherent deep within a Soul Cadre psyche may be formed and explored individually but with commonality. Think of this as a town in your own world that decides unanimously, based on every citizen's innermost desire, to specialize in, as an example easy to grasp, the "production of toys." Then further imagine that each person explores within the production of toys every necessary aspect of that production, from design to the manufacturing to the marketing, sales and all aspects in between. Now bear in mind that the interest or specialty of the group is not something "ordained" or mandated, but is quite natural and intrinsic to the Soul group, each individual in the Soul group and thus each community comprised of Soul group members.

Some of the large-scale organizational business models you see emerging on Earth presently are a precursor to such arrangements. It is not a coincidence that some large scale Internet companies, as an example, are becoming all encompassing in the lives of their employees, with individuals working, eating, playing and living within a consolidated, focused campus (town) environment 24/7. The difference however, as we have said, is the fact that presently on Earth such arrangements are constructed for the benefit of the organization and each individual is molded or forced to fit into a desired need or function of the organization. This stifles individual creativity in the long term and presents a system that if abused becomes a model for a new form of forced labor and slavery.

The complete reverse is true on Terra where the organization or community (work/leisure/living environment) is constructed to fulfill the desires and goals of the individual first and above all else, while also creating a vehicle for each individual to explore their own creativity and freedom with concern for the organization a completely secondary and independent matter. We would suggest that such organizations in the Third Dimension, when operated in the positive polarity, provide workers with the freedom to explore their nature and be who they truly are, and these are being created unconsciously at the present time to accustom incarnates to the potential on Terra. Multinational initiatives on Earth operating in the positive polarity will slowly evolve into similar structures where the company's benefit, bottom-line and outcome become secondary or even obsolete compared to the individual or worker's enrichment and ability to explore their creative acumen and talents.

Those organizations not operating from the positive polarity on Earth (freedom of expression and creativity versus individuals forced into the organizational mold and subject to a working environment 24/7) will become harbingers of forced labor and economic slavery. In those environments, the individual will not be aware that through economic bribery and blissful ignorance, they have actually become enslaved. Again, there will be those individuals that resonate to both the positive and negative polarities of these situations depending on their life missions and personal attributes. We would suggest however, that those who are attracted to the negative polarity situations are those that are destined to remain in Third Density incarnations while those who find themselves exploring the positive polarities where their personal fulfillment and freedom takes precedent 24/7 are being primed for future incarnations on Terra.

Returning to our prior example, take it one step further and realize that on Terra a particular Soul group might specialize in "toy production" as we have highlighted, but that another might just as easily be expert at assisting individuals within the dream state, or quite possibly at mastery of the principles of reality manifestation or the rigueur of manifesting perfection in the Fifth Dimensional physical Being (healing), all of which you will find are actual group and community specialties that exist on Terra.

Again, remember that Terra is generally a place where Human Angelics work on self-karma utilizing the mass consciousness backdrop to support whatever is needed for such endeavors as they relate to basic physics and the mechanics of Fifth Dimension existence. Fifth Dimensional Terra organized to obtain optimal efficiencies based on these physics in conjunction with the desire of each Soul to generate realities and experiences centered on issues pertaining to love and compassion – the Heart Chakra. Because Terrans are more concerned with self-karma and less concerned with the mores and interactions of society within the broader landscape of mass consciousness (since they have little to gain from such interactions other than support of their own endeavors), they are able to be heart-focused and compassionate while also being reserved in their action and introspective, as well as non-judgmental, in their outlook. This translates into a world and reality generated by them that for the most part permits them to live in communities and groups in a society that is fundamentally well organized and peaceful in nature.

Such communities are generally able to exist without the constant monitoring of overseers or invasive ruling bodies, and this also makes obsolete the massive number of laws, rules, regulations and oversight that younger Souls living in Third Density are accustom to navigating. Terrans are able to create their reality in a manner that is harmonic, with each focused on their own inventions and by Soul agreement are able to self-police and unobtrusively manage their interactions with the group or prevailing mass consciousness. This is not to say that rules within the Terran society do not exists, but only to say that society functions by virtue of that fact that policing public interaction is not necessary since individuals are able to adhere to functions and participations that are natural to them and are not used as karmic opportunities for growth as they are within Earth's Third Dimensional realm.

This is further emphasized by the fact that within the Third Dimension current policing of the laws you enact is accomplished via forces that are external to the individual. Third Dimensional reality is in many ways focused on the enforcement of societal rules and standards, since guarding the fabric of that which you interface with in order to gain growth is an important aspect of life. For the most part, external force obliges compliance of the laws throughout the population. This is not the case on Terra where there is little to no real need for compulsory adherence to what most inhabitants consider completely natural rules regarding their engagement with society. Instead, since the rules of societal organization are non judgmental, they are created for the common good while in pursuit of one's personal initiatives and in no way impede an individual's right to self-generated karma. Terrans have no trouble peacefully adhering to whatever natural laws of societal governance have been accepted at a Soul level by all incarnates. Add to this the fact that the individual has no need or real desire to interact (or act out) with society or other individuals in order to generate karmic opportunities for growth as well as the fact that societal organization is principally focused on amply providing the needs (economic and sustenance wise) of each and every Being so they are completely free to pursue their inner Soul growth. Terrans have a society that in many ways is as stable as it is ideal.

All of this is possible because Terrans, and Fifth Dimensional Beings in general, have a higher level of consciousness and a deeper Soul connection that permits them to understand the reasons why things are being created, or why and how events are happening in the context of their reality. There is no need for them to interface with or enforce rules and regulations that are understood to be a natural standard of their Soul level and they commonly wish to participate in and adhere to whatever rules might exist by nature of their higher understanding, compassion and consciousness that is focused primarily through the perspective of their hearts.

This is not to say that all Fifth Dimensional societies are identical or free of the manner of enforcement of reality known within the Third Universal Dimension, but they are more rare. From a Third Dimensional perspective, the only downside to societal structures in the Fifth Dimension like Terra, if a downside could be identified, would be the fact that because each individual is focused on their own growth scenario, there is little need to "advance" society or societal structures generally as a whole.

This serves as an important distinction, since there are in fact a few Fifth Dimensional societies that believe in the advancement of their societal structure as a necessary adjunct to assisting the individual in the society to advance their own growth. We preface this with the fact that this varies according to Soul group purpose and especially to the genre and orientation of the Soul matrix in question. It is possible to see Fifth Dimensional societies outside of Terra and outside Human Angelics matrices that are far different in their approach to reality and Soul growth. There is an important distinction made in the Fifth Dimension that is related to Soul polarity that we have described as Souls originating from Service-to-Self and Service-to-Others Soul matrices.

You would probably assume that because Fifth Dimensional Human Angelics are focused principally on self-karma they are "Service-to-Self" oriented, but this is incorrect. In truth, Human Angelic Soul matrices (to be distinguished from Third Dimensional human Beings, which can also be extraterrestrial Soul groups incarnating in human form) are "Service-to-Others" oriented. Though the Fifth Dimensional models of incarnation revolve around Self-karma, they are no less focused on compassion and love of fellow Human Angelics and other Beings as a whole. In fact, their Fifth Dimensional Soul growth is based on loving compassion for all Beings, expressed as heart centered and completely non-judgmental cooperation with others (Human Angelic and extraterrian in nature).

Human Angelic Soul matrices tend to be individually focused because they have a fundamental understanding and love of all others, and cooperation by them within the community has already been perfected by the time they reach Fifth Dimensional experience. Essentially, perfection of issues related to cooperation within society is what allows them to be able to focus on self-karmic endeavors, and this same loving cooperation has been forged through a Soul's long journey of incarnations in Third Dimensional worlds. This is where interaction with the community and others in the form of karma and energetic balancing experiences has assisted them to raise their consciousness in order to be able to fully grasp Fifth Dimensional structures and opportunities for Soul growth.

In the Third or Fifth Universal Dimension, individuals who are incarnated from Soul matrices that are derived from Service-to-Self orientation have a far different outlook. They tend to be much more unified in the notion that their particular race or species is more vibrant and more vital than all others. It is for this reason that you have, as we have mentioned previously in, The System Lords and the Twelve Dimensions, races and species such as the Zeta race or the commonly known Grays that are derived from Service-to-Self Soul orientations. These races, even in the Fifth Dimension, tend to be much more aggressive in terms of their energetic exchanges with each other as well as other galactic races and societies. Because these races are focused on their group's advancement by whatever means, they do not as a whole have compassion or understanding of what it means to have a common good or care for others Beings. They usually tend to be more focused on promoting themselves and their race or species within the prevailing reality at any cost. This is far different than being focused on self- karma and experimenting with growth that allows you inner wisdom within the context of compassion for self and others.

In fact, this means that the individuals in Fifth Dimensional reality derived from Service-to-Self Soul matrices are more intent on domination and control of the reality. On the other hand, Service-to-Others Beings are content to allow the unfolding of community consciousness without superimposing their own individual purposes or agendas via control or domination of the community reality.

It needs to be understood therefore, that in speaking of Fifth Dimensional Terra we are speaking of a reality that is essentially based on individuals originated from Service-to-Others Soul matrices. Such Souls have reached a level of "Service-to-Others" consciousness where they are able to be in a society but not necessarily of it. This is a precept that was well explained as a goal by the entity known as the Master Jesus. In fact, it was a prediction with respect to what one could ultimately expect in the realm of "Heaven." In this case, the entity known as the Master Jesus was referring to Human Angelic society on Fifth Dimensional Terra.

Returning to our conversation with respect to how society is organized on Terra, it is perhaps a world slightly difficult for those still focused within Third Dimensional Earth to fully grasp or understand. In a certain sense, Fifth Dimensional Terra reflects the ideals associated with a Third Density view of Utopian societies, particularly as it relates to how the basic fundamental needs of life are organized and meted out equally for common good by society consensus. Such a system means that each individual is no longer obliged or burdened with the worry about how their existence and survival will be secured, or how they will provide for themselves and their closest alliances, albeit in a physical body that is much lighter and less dense than the one your are accustom to in Third Density.

On Third Dimensional Earth, the struggle to survive within the mass consciousness societal form is paramount, and many entities become overwhelmed by that struggle. Of course on Third Dimensional Earth, this creates all manner of interesting growth opportunities for the entity, since their growth is derived from such an interaction. However, Fifth Dimensional Terra differs from this substantially since the survival needs of the individual are lessened and growth opportunities stemming from such social struggle is not as a rule sought out. Fifth Dimensional society prefers to be based on organizing and maintain the common good precisely so an individual is free to encounter and explore their own growth opportunities rather than those thrust upon them by mass consciousness. In addition, Service-to-Others orientation as a basis of Soul origin makes them far more apt at ensuring the common good as a means of fostering free individual expression. Basic requirements of life on Terra are met instantaneously and are provided each to the other without question in the knowledge that doing so ensures their own freedom and Soul growth, and Terrans exist without the worry about where one's next sustenance will come from or if shelter and other basic needs will be available to them. Thus you have a truly unified social structure that in many ways could be viewed as idealistically communistic in the sense that it provides every member with whatever basic needs they require with little or no obliged participation but rather a willing participation that is voluntary, limited and never coerced or forced since every member also seeks to maintain the system in order to keep their own pursuits, which are sponsored and promoted, viable.

This frees all individuals in the society to pursue their inner most desires, talents, wishes and dreams. This is possible due to the fact that on Fifth Dimensional Terra all individuals are heart and compassion-centric. The populace is able to provide basic needs common to each and everyone while also allowing each and everyone to live in the manner in which they choose, exploring the growth opportunities intrinsic to them based on their Soul group or cadre. This creates a unique societal structure that allows each individual their own freedom of expression while ultimately also ensuring that each individual has basic needs met, while also giving a common goal for the society at large. This powerful combination and balance of individual and societal needs allows Terran society to function smoothly and beneficially without enforcement or obligation.

Society and communities on Terra are peaceful and there is little need to create vast organizational structures, governments, institutions and the like that would horde power of some, as often is the case on Third Dimensional Earth. This further implies, as we have said, that all basic needs can be provided without the need of force or the creation of super imposed systems tasked with allocating what it deems should be available to this group or that, or this or that individual. This then completely disengages and makes the need for the enforcement of laws, as exists in Third Density, obsolete.

As a result, Fifth Dimensional Terra is a more localized and community-focused society. This does not however mean that they are primitive. You have the mistaken notion that localized or community-focused societies are backwards or countrified or have no sophistication, which may be the case on Third Density Earth but is far from the case on Fifth Density Terra. On Terra, you have a society that has an innately high consciousness, highly educated with respect to the physical principles of its world, sophisticated in terms of Soul awareness and talented with regard to manifestation of reality. Highly structured organizations and systems for managing and organizing groups of individuals, via social, racial, religious or other vehicles, is unwarranted and unnecessary.

Fifth Dimensional Terra is also as technologically sophisticated as any of the highest civilizations in the Fifth Density Universe, far exceeding your own technological advances. Terrans choose to use technology in whatever manner they prefer for the benefit of their own communities and social groups. Therefore, though there is no real centralized federal governmental structure in the way in which you know it, Terrans instead rely on self-governing local and regional communities under democratic oversight that is supervised by (community) Soul elders.

Terran communities are highly advanced technologically and specialize in specific avenues, specific technologies or cadre talents. When traveling on Terra, as an example, you might enter perhaps the zones or geographic regions focused on artistic and creative endeavors; or perhaps you will travel to the regions and communities proficient in healing and beautification as well as techniques related to healing physical, emotional and spiritual structures; or perhaps you will travel to regions where the communities and residents specialize in experimenting with new techniques and technologies for Galactic communication; or a zone where the communities and inhabitants excel in discussing, studying and teaching other communities about the spiritual and structural nature of the known Universe.

What you would perhaps identify as cultures or countries are in fact regions and communities of Souls on Fifth Dimensional Terra living their lives doing what they love to do and are talented at doing primarily and offering the fruit of those talents secondarily. Imagine if you can a world where not only is there a built in community that supports your inner most expressions, but where the civilization as a whole is geared around allowing you to create and market that talent easily, without competition or worry about cost, profit or receipts and on a global as well as a galactic basis.

It must further be understood that because of the high connection that Fifth Dimensional Terrans have with their Soul purpose and energetic expression, Souls choose to incarnate not necessarily with biological or "karmic" family members as you might in the Third Dimension but with family members that are more relevant at a Soul level. This is important because as we have described in the past, it should be understood by now, that almost all Souls specialize in a specific focus or area intrinsic to their inner most nature. Not only does a Soul have a specific energetic vibrational pattern that it seeks to express through its various incarnations, a Soul can in fact be a specialist in a certain field of endeavor.

While this is not the place to discuss the many and varied skills and specialties that a Soul matrix or cadre can have, it is important to understand that a Souls' specialty can enable each lifetime originating from that particular Soul matrix to exhibit specific talents that are innate and inherent in its very "Beingness." Naturally, while this is always present and highly probable, an individual incarnation will still have free will, and thus it can choose, through circumstance or environment, to ignore this innate specialty if it chooses. Think of this as having a particular interest, talent or skill, such as for music or some other field of interest where it seems like you are a "natural," yet although you may dabble in it during your spare time you never truly make it a focus of the lifetime.

Thus, while incarnated on Third Dimensional Earth you might, through time or happenstance, discover what your main talent or interest is, whereas on Fifth Dimensional Terra you are born into a community of like-minded Souls that already specialize in the skills and areas of interest that are the same as your own, at a Soul level. More importantly, you are incarnated into a lifetime with others from the same Soul matrix and cadre of which you are a part. Third Dimensional Earth on the other hand is most likely comprised of family, community and societal units from different Soul cadres so that even close family or community members will have very different talents and areas of interest. Fifth Dimensional Terrans retain the concept of biological family unit, but these units are comprised of members known to each other at a Soul level with a common area of interest and focus.

You can see that from a Soul perspective, such a societal structure is less concerned with growth originating from the individual's interface with society and discovery of where its talents are, and, having crossed that bridge already, more concerned with how the individual develops innate talents within its field of experience. From the standpoint of the Soul matrices this means that one is far better placed to obtain maximum exposure and inner growth by already being placed within a particular communal group that has at its core a particular Soul's specialty. This allows the individual to prosper metaphysically speaking and expand its abilities further through community support and without struggling against family, community or societal preconceptions or prejudgments.

Imagine if Third Dimensional Earth was a place where each individual not only was fully aware of their Soul's energetic purpose but also aware of the skills, talents and interests of their Soul overall. Further imagine what it would be like on Third Dimensional Earth if all individuals were able to automatically accessed the situations to help them develop those skills, as well as the very people who would support and assist them in every possible way to reach fulfillment. In such a case Third Dimensional Earth would prove to be a very different place as you can imagine.

You do in fact see references to this in those individuals in Third Dimensional who demonstrate very strong predilections beginning at a young age towards specific talents, interests or careers. Nurtured within a particular avenue that fits their natural talents and interests, their lives expand and flourish in ways that the majority only dream of in your world. On the other hand, those in Third Density who never find such talents or true interests flounder, submerged by the daily quest for survival in a world where they are most often obliged to participate in a manner that is alien to their true inner self (which in itself might be a Soul's chosen growth endeavor, using Third Dimensional environments and societal formations to achieve energetic growth for some purpose known only to a particular Soul or incarnation).

On Terra this cannot happen, and each Soul incarnates where they will not only prosper but where they will find their place in the world and, as a result, a true sense of belonging. Because of this, Terran perspective is not only one of specialization but also one of heart-felt intention. As we explained, there is no need as there is in a Third Dimensional incarnation to worry extensively about one's existence with respect to the gratification of one's physical, emotional or spiritual needs. In addition, Terrans in the Fifth Dimension are able to experiment with possible and probable future scenarios so you have the opportunity to manifest a lifetime far less stressful than the ones you know in lower dimensions.

This becomes important in terms of the mass consciousness background on Fifth Dimensional Terra. Recall that Fifth Dimensional Terra is less concerned with mass conscious backgrounds and is far more focused on the specialization and individualization of existence. This does not however mean to imply that there is no commonality or common ground for reality creation. In fact, this renders more common ground and mass consciousness scenarios that are fixed and concrete. It is important that the background precepts of existence be concretized and firm in order for real experimentation with probable and possible future scenarios to take place.

What we mean by this is that it is far easier to live in a reality where any number of probable futures is possible for an individual if the mass conscious background is cemented in such a way that it is unfaltering and not as changeable as it is in say Third Dimensional life. Relying on the fact that something in your reality can be truly counted upon and unswaying enables individuals to experiment more freely with their personal existence, something relatively complicated in a realm such as your current reality where mass consciousness is constantly rebooting and altering the environment. Because of this, the occurrences that happen in Third Density life are more geared towards fielding and reacting to the mass consciousness background rather than planned according to individual desire based upon a mass consciousness background that is more or less static and fixed in place.

It is far less likely on Fifth Dimensional Terra to find Fear in the degree that it is found in Third Dimensional existence. This is because Fear is usually identified as a reactive state where the entity is defending or placed in a defensive role vis-à-vis the mass consciousness background or the reality that is ensuing. Faith (not the religious variety but a compassionate belief in oneself and the creative omnipotence of the Universe) is positive action that is the polar opposite of Fear in the creation of one's reality. So, having Faith that a certain premise is locked in place, strategically, makes it far easier to resonate with the powerful oscillation of Faith, creating more probability and possibility in terms of one's life events. Thus, Fifth Dimensional Terrans are less preoccupied with the changing mores and standards around them, and this stability allows them to be much more involved with personal edification as well as their personal direction with respect to possible and probable futures.

To be sure there are comparisons that can be made in both realities. Whether you are in a Third Dimensional or Fifth Dimensional existence, you are essentially creating your reality for the purposes defined by your Soul matrix. The difference is the expanded inner insight that is allotted to Fifth Dimensional lives so that those incarnated on Terra are able to precisely judge from where and why their reality creations are being generated. This allows them to better direct as well as learn from the experiences that happen to them personally.

Again, it must be understood that we are speaking in generalities here because there are always situations created on a mass consciousness scale that oblige entities incarnated within those parameters to deal with and explore the new opportunities of life and creation that are being generated. However, there is a distinct difference between lifetimes that are generated or created because of what is occurring because of the mass consciousness background as happens in the Third Density and those that take place in the Fifth Density, which are created as a result of personal desire and are placed against a fixed and non-permeable background that is intended to foster the purpose of individualized growth. This creates not only a more peaceful society but also one where each individual, fully aware of the learning process and the inner growth desires of others, demonstrates respect and leniency in the process of reality creation.

The prerequisite on Fifth Dimensional Terra is the achievement of a level of higher consciousness by each Soul, and this tends to be a model for measuring the success of an individual in Fifth Dimensional life. This is quite different from Third Dimensional life's measure of success, which usually is seen in terms of an individual's position within social mass consciousness structures, be they financial, power based, cultural, racial, religious or such a nature.

Fifth Dimensional Terra measures the success of an individual based on the level of consciousness they have achieved and the wisdom and neutrality this has provided them. This allows Terrans a greater understanding of themselves, their society, their planet and their Universe. In fact, there is a direct correlation with the understanding and balancing of not only philosophical wisdom, but also spiritual as well as mathematical and geometrical principles (the substructure and foundation of Universal precept), all of which are basic to the fundamental thought processes and a Terran's higher nature.

Terrans tend to see their world and their Universe in a more open and freeing way. Whereas Third Dimensional incarnates are forever attempting to cajole or convince others that their position and perspectives are the right position or perspectives, Terrans have no need to prove right or wrong, good or bad. Instead they tend to be much more allowing and accepting of all life styles, considerations and other entities existing within their realm with one caveat: Terrans demand that all life styles and all entities retain the consciousness level that best permits their society to remain strongly aligned with each member's ability to grow and reach higher levels of consciousness independently and individually. Terrans are not to be considered conformists, and their unwillingness to judge each other with their ability to remain neutral and see all sides of an issue makes them prefer to remain aloof. In fact, were a Third Dimensional Being to visit Terra, their most notable observation (perhaps consternation) would be the detachment and seeming aloofness that individuals in Fifth Density project, though naturally their heart centeredness grounds them in love and compassion as well. A Third Density visitor to Terra would liken Terrans to wise and highly educated Monks who remain grounded, aloof and silent, demonstrating no need to participate in any fray and preferring instead to watch what transpires, bemused and with loving understanding (as one might watch children play) from afar.

This brings us to an important consideration. Terrans are fully aware of the prospect and mechanics of Ascension, and they recognize that at prescribed times when the Universe experiences this evolutionary shift there is a substantial influx in their world of younger Souls, that is to say Souls who Ascend and will begin experiencing their first incarnations on Fifth Dimensional Terra. This influx of Souls, via the Universal evolutionary process we have discussed known as Ascension, is presently taking place.

Entities that have finished with Universal Third Dimension incarnations and that have raised their vibrational frequency to the point of possessing the ability to incarnate physically within higher realms have already begun incarnating in much greater numbers than any of the past 260,000 year cycles within the Terran landscape. Aware that this is occurring, Terrans did in fact become concerned at the prospect of such a large influx of Souls ready to incarnate in Fifth Dimensional existence but perhaps not truly ready in terms of their levels of consciousness.

In fact at this moment of universal transformation and evolution, it should be known that a majority of Fifth Dimensional Terrans of higher vibrational quality have themselves Ascended and are in fact already in the process of evolving to higher dimensional levels. Many have or will begin incarnating shortly in Seventh of other Densities depending on the individual Soul. It should be noted however, that this is precisely what cause some trepidation among Fifth Dimensional Terrans. Just as is the case the Third Dimension, as we have discussed, there will be Terrans not willing or ready to incarnate at higher dimensional levels. These Terrans will remain within incarnations in the Fifth Dimension until the next cycle of Ascension is possible.

The trepidation arises due to the realization that suddenly Fifth Dimensional Terra will be inhabited, for the most part, by much younger Souls of a slightly lower levels of consciousness and vibrational quality than has been the case prior to this. Because Fifth Dimensional Terra is based on the concept of individualized freedom and pursuit of experience and happiness, and the fact that higher levels of consciousness are required in order to sustain a society focused in heart chakra expression, this means that in effect Fifth Dimensional Terra, similar to Earth in the Third Dimension, will be starting anew in terms of its historic or chronological progression.

While the majority of Soul matrices now incarnating on Third Dimensional Earth and graduating as we speak to Fifth Dimensional Terra are ready and prepared for this transition, it is nonetheless clear to current Terrans that the entities incarnating on a future Terra will require some significant shift in understanding and perspective in order for them to retain a Fifth Dimensional society that has developed over the past tens of thousands of years. For this reason, the Terrans have actually closely monitored the emerging situations on Third Dimensional Earth (as we have said, higher can see lower, but lower may not be consciously aware of the higher presence). Terrans have been in discussion with various Soul matrices at their levels of consciousness and higher with respect to exactly how incarnations of Third Dimensional Earth entities on Terra will be organized and how they will unfold.

This becomes another discussion completely with respect to Soul purpose and potential, since Terrans are specialized according to individual Soul nature and the inherent talents of a particular Soul based on its origins and cadre. Thus, Terrans are working to minimize the impact upon their world by Souls with slightly lower levels of consciousness, particularly those that might be currently incarnated on a pre-Ascended Earth. There is therefore a good deal of effort taking place behind the scenes to insure that those entities incarnating for the first time in Fifth Density are not "fallen" and in fact are aligned with their Soul matrices and there inner most origins, nature, talents and desires.

Moreover, a unique problem also exists in that many of the Soul matrices incarnated on Earth at this time are of a slightly unique specialization in terms of their Soul specialties, and in a few cases these specialties have not been established as communities on Terra as yet. One begins to see the dilemma when one understands that in a world based upon communities consisting of Souls that specialize in specific areas of interest, the influx of a large number of new Souls where communities of a particular specialization have not, as yet, been developed is problematic for the society as a whole. Without the communities that will nurture and care for their needs, where in fact would they incarnate? Who would be their support, that is to say their parents, friends, families and brethren?

This is important in that it adds a new and emerging aspect to Fifth Dimensional Terra in terms of opportunities and growth for the planet and realm as a whole. Whereas in the past Fifth Dimensional Terra thrived via communities that specialized in the work of the Soul cadre, it now has the potential to continue as it has the same way or to alter the very structure of its existence in an as yet untried manner. This is not to say that a Third Dimensional Earth-like existence where people group together in a loose and uneven manner with respect to their talents, or via cultural, racial, national, religious or other designation will ever occur on Fifth Dimensional Terra. However, it is to say that now the possibility exists for new forms of societal and community structure (still individually focused) to potentially evolve on Terra over the course of the coming 260,000 year evolutionary cycle.

This is precisely the way that the Universe and each universal dimension within it continually evolves in terms of its make up, the way in which its societies function and the growth potential made available to each incarnate at a certain level of consciousness. This is no less true in higher dimensions than it is in those that are lower by nature of their frequency, sacred geometric structures and vibrational patterns.

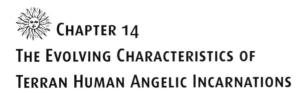
Chapter 14
The Evolving Characteristics of Terran Human Angelic Incarnations

Dimensional Overlap

Your vision of dimensional overlap may be an erroneous one derived from your current perspective and reality. As an example, you probably envision a great expanse between each dimension, because you may envision that each dimension is comprised of the same substance from which your Third Dimensional reality is constructed. You may also tend to imagine dimensions that run parallel to each other, or even at a distance from each other. Unfortunately, none of this is an accurate depiction of dimensional overlap. In truth, dimensional overlap is exactly what the appellation implies. It is an overlapping of dimensional layers, one onto the other, and could more aptly be understood by envisioning dimensional overlap as an invisible onion like structure.

For this reason, all dimensional realities are in a sense superimposed one upon the other if they are applicable to a particular location in time and space within a specific region of the Universe. What we mean to say is that while there is indeed a vastness of space as you envision it, the vastness you envision comes from your perspective and is Third Dimensional in nature. Fifth Dimensional Terra is in effect located in close proximity to Third Dimensional Earth. In fact, we would go as far as to say that Fifth Dimensional Terra is in close proximity via the overlapping of dimensions and, in a sense, is an unseen (to you) layer of Third Dimensional Earth.

Though you cannot see or experience Fifth Dimensional Terra, it is nonetheless built around many core fundamentals that create Third Dimensional Earth, and it is located in approximately the same physical space, but in a different time space wave or dimensional frequency (realm). It exists however, within the same "physical" space in which First, Second and Third Dimensional Earth is created. In a sense, another way to picture this is as you would the many broadcasting stations available to you on your television or radio. All of these reside and are available through one primary vehicle, but a specific apparatus is required in order to "tune in" one or the other. This does not in any way negate any station not presently available to you, but only suggests that your awareness must be of a particular focus in order for you to perceive that particular broadcast. Similarly, you must be situated in or have a particular vision or ability (vibrational awareness or consciousness) in order to tune into higher or, for that matter, lower dimensional activities and truths.

This can become confusing in that, as we have said in the past, each universal dimension is further segmented into sub levels that reside within their own dimensional oscillations. Similarly, the sub levels also overlap and connect to the dimension at large. Thus, one might picture a sphere within which Third Dimensional Earth is at a certain wave frequency and then the Third Dimensional layer is further segmented, via a related but slightly different wave frequency or vibrational oscillation that is up or down on the scale, into twelve minor oscillations. They would then exist just prior to crossing into the next layer of the "onion," which would lead you to the Fourth Universal Dimension, also with its twelve sub segments. The same is true progressing into higher dimensional realms.

In some sense, it could be said that there is in fact an Eighth, Ninth, Tenth, Eleventh and even, in a certain sense, a Universal Twelfth Dimensional version of Earth. These dimensional versions of the Third Dimensional Earth exist simultaneously and are superimposed and overlapping one with the other. Similarly, if you looked at the Universe from an exalted position, you would see that the Seventh or say Eighth Dimensional version of Earth, as an example, is situated in approximately the same essential space as Third Dimensional Earth, existing within the same space but in its own dimensional oscillation speaking in terms of the overall Universe at large.

If we are describing this for you, it is to assist in your understanding that Fifth Dimensional Terra has many of the same attributes physically and spatially as Third Dimensional Earth. However, these attributes are different and are altered depending upon the vibrational time space wave within which they exists. Thus, these "twins" if you will do not necessarily meet each other, though they are perhaps genetically related one to the other. An individual coming to or incarnating on Terra from Third Dimensional Earth might vaguely recognize certain aspects of Terra. But they would quickly see that this Fifth Dimensional version of Earth is rendered and perceived by them at a different oscillation and wave frequency exhibiting lighter density and mass as well as a brighter and greater range of light and color as well as expanded sound qualities. Perhaps of most importance, they would quickly realize the difference in time space and what this means in terms of the manifestation of creation and reality.

Reality on Terra

To be sure, there are many important differences between how reality is created in the Third Universal Dimension and how reality is rendered in the Fifth Universal Dimension. We have described many of these already. To recap quickly, principal among these is the fact that Fifth Dimensional Terra enjoys a lighter density, more availability to light frequencies and higher consciousness levels, all of which we shall call the building blocks of creation. Because of this, and because of fundamental differences in time wave perception, reality on Fifth Dimensional Terra is more readily available and more easily manifested without the interference of an enormous time lag preventing you from materializing your every thought and whim, as is experienced in Third Density.

As we have said, Fifth Dimensional Terra is more connected to higher levels of consciousness and this, in terms of oscillation, allows for the ability to create real events or bring matter into form. The link between one's desires, intentions and thoughts and what is created in one's sphere is relatively immediate. Not only is the pace of creation quickened, there is also a lessening of the veil between the probable futures available to an individual, which allows each to be perceived and acted upon.

Nonetheless, as we have stated many physical characteristics and landscapes you perceive on Third Dimensional Earth, particularly those forms that are the basis of the First and Second Dimensional constructs you find in Nature are recognizable and available on Fifth Dimensional Terra. For this reason, Fifth Dimensional Terra may not necessarily present itself as an alien world to most of those who have incarnated previously on Third Dimensional Earth.

However, this is perhaps where similarities end. Though you might recognize to some extent the trees and rocks, oceans and landmasses you find on Fifth Dimensional Terra, in truth the sub structure of Earth and Terra are different not only in terms of physics and genetics but in terms of the actual organization of those structures. Therefore, the

Continents you might know on Earth, as well as the mountain ranges, seas, rivers and other geographic features are quite different on Terra. Terra, as an overlap to Third Dimensional Earth, does have continents and does have seas and magnetic Poles but they are quite different in terms of their arrangement, position, physical composition and mechanical properties from what you know on Earth.

As an example then, it is quite possible for a Fourth or Fifth Dimensional Atlantis to reside on a continent that is invisible on Third Dimensional Earth. We would go as far as to say that many of the mythological tales of Atlantis, particularly those detailing geographic locations and attributes, provide you with glimpses of this Fourth Dimensional civilization prior to it's "fall" into Third Dimensional reality.

Similarly the continents that you currently inhabit on Third Dimensional Earth may be significantly altered if not completely different, or even non-existent, on Fifth Dimensional Terra. Thus while the physical makeup of landmasses on Terra would be vaguely understandable to you, the actual position of these landmasses and the physical attributes within it would be vastly different from anything you know. If we state this, it is simply to point out to you that on Fifth Dimensional Terra there are no North American, South American, European or Asian continents, although there are continents and landmasses with familiarity albeit far different features, structures, composition and climates.

The Visual and Audio Senses of Fifth Dimensional Terrans

Terran topography might be recognizable to many of you now incarnated on Third Dimensional Earth, but light, color, sound and the genetic perceptive abilities of Terrans is vastly different. Because of the different range of vibrational frequency that is available to Terrans they have the ability to see and hear as you do but with a much wider range of perception. This is due to the nature of the Fifth Dimensional environment as well as their expanded and augmented DNA and genetic structure, which provides them with additional and considerably greater perceptive abilities.

As an example, colors would not be wholly recognizable to you and the nature of light and color are vastly augmented on Terra. Colors appear far more saturated and their range from light to dark is much more pronounced. Whether you are talking about First, Second, Third or even Fourth Dimensional Beings, such as topography, rocks, vegetation or the seas, you would notice an extraordinary range of colors not available on Third Dimensional Earth that exist throughout Terran topography and landscapes. This range of color, related to higher frequencies of light as well as the higher perceptive range of the inhabitants, allows for a stunning and beautiful environment, one that is difficult to imagine on Third Dimensional Earth. This is true despite the fact that Earth has its own natural beauty and qualities that should be quite apparent as perceived by its current inhabitants.

Because of the higher and wider range of electromagnetic waves available on Terra, it offers a far broader spectrum of color than is available on Earth. We would add that whereas the current visible spectrum of light on Third Dimensional Terra is essentially comprised of approximately seven to eight components, on Terra that visible spectrum is increased to over twelve components, and thus the range of intonation visible to the eye is greatly increased. This increases the number of color options available, including all spectrum combinations, and offers an intense and resounding palette on the Terran landscape that frankly, you would find overwhelming or possibly gaudy, to say the least.

In addition to this, a Terran's perception of sound is wider ranging and much more pitch-profound than currently available on Third Dimensional Earth. In fact, expanded sound wave availability and sound perception makes the use of sound vibration for all manner of mechanics a science that has long been employed and even perfected on Terra. Sound waves and resonant vibration are principal methods used by Terrans in a wide range of technical activities, including using sound waves for energy creation, propulsion and other engineering purposes, such as the movement or transport of large objects and equipment. Sound vibration is also used to regulate physical properties in the Fifth Dimensional environment and sound as well as light frequency are the principal methods used for all genre of physical healing on Terra.

The Intuitive Abilities of Terrans and Their Connection to Higher Dimensional Wisdom

Perhaps no attribute is as pronounced as the discovery, elevation and use of intuitive, imaginative and perceptive abilities by Fifth Dimensional Terrans. We have already explained that Terrans by their nature have the ability to foresee possible and probable futures through an expanded "Now" time wave perception, but we have not truly explored the fact that via an established, prominent and useable sixth sense Terrans also have the ability to see, hear and "perceive" a wider range of dimensional wavelengths. This gives them partial access not only to expanded sensory perception within their own world, but access to what you would consider "other-worldy" sensitivity.

This includes awareness of life purpose for themselves as well as the Soul life purpose for their fellow Beings when desired. For the most part, the manner in which Terrans recognize each other is based on this, and Terrans tend to categorize and acknowledge each other based on their Soul connections and Soul intention rather than on their physical kinship, appearance or endeavors. Fifth Dimensional Terrans have an inner understanding of Soul purpose and a conscious understanding of the higher, unseen objectives and opportunities inherent in life events and choices. Access to these facts via higher consciousness and guidance is only dreamed of and rarely discovered casually by incarnates in Third Dimensional existence.

Through a much greater understanding of each individual's ultimate life purpose Terrans also derive a stronger connection to Source. This provides each Terran with a better understanding of the purpose of all life and existence, and this empathy makes them more open, accepting and non- judgmental. In turn this increases their energetic resonance so they are in harmony with their dimensional wavelength, and that higher resonance gives them what would be referred to in the Third Universal Dimension as a "connection to God" (not to imply religious, formal or superficial connections as might be the case on Third Dimensional Earth, but rather Beings who have a true one-on-one connection with their Source via an ultimate life experience based on Soul intention).

This is no small matter. What it means in real terms is a natural and direct connection to one's higher consciousness, particularly one's Truth, on an immediate and constant basis. This is in sharp contrast to the relentless seeking, searching, vetting and battle to prove one's righteousness that incarnates experience on Third Dimensional Earth hampered by the veils of lower density.

Imagine if you will, a world where nearly every thought is made manifest if desired and where you receive immediate feedback from your Soul and higher guides telling you if the choices you have made are aligned with your purpose or not as well as what eventuality the free will expression of those choices will bring into your reality. By no means do we suggest that this connection or feedback is esoteric or vague as it is in your world where most are forever guessing whether or not they have received the correct guidance or are merely being tossed willy-nilly into adventures via a lifetime hijacked by the survival mechanisms of one's Ego.

Via the direct connection to their Souls matrices, Terrans receive constant guidance and feedback with respect to their free will choices. Understand however, that free will is not diminished or negated by such guidance but merely assisted with respect to purpose and promise. This feedback is honest and truthful, and in some cases can be quite literal and vocal providing the recipient with no doubt as to exactly where they are in the process of creating, although each continues to have the creative power inherent in free will and choice. That said, imagine for a moment a world where each Being's actions are instantly measureable and each Being is given direct feedback in real terms within their mind's eye as to precisely what the consequences of their actions will be and the probable future that it creates. Such insight would provide your own world with a very different way of being, and if every entity in your world knew the consequences of their actions in advance, particularly as it applied to their own purpose in that lifetime, we would suggest that you would live in quite a different world. This must be identified as truly one of the most significant differences between Third Dimensional existence and Fifth Dimensional existence, other obvious perceptive, vibrational and physical characteristics aside.

The nature of the Universe is that when one recedes from "All-ness," one's expression represents a limitation or a diminished portion of the wholeness found at the God Source. Similarly, one's vibrational quality is diminished in conjunction with this, and the same holds true for the particular dimension that one finds oneself incarnated within. This is pertinent to any discussion one has regarding the physical features of Beings incarnated in different levels of dimensional reality and it is also highly visible in the sensitivities and the attributes that those Beings possess. Moreover, this can also be applicable to the physical and mechanical properties of a dimensional reality itself.

As you evolve through the universal dimensions you add to your genetic and vibrational make up in such a way that your talents, experiences, physical attributes and non-physical attributes are also uniformly expanded. As one rises in terms of vibrational quality in a universal dimension, one essentially rediscovers their birthright and makes strides, however slight, towards recapturing the original wholeness of Source. This is true in terms of Human Angelic progression as well, and this precept represents perhaps the greatest commonality or link found in the nature of life from one universal dimension to another.

This said Fifth Dimensional and Third Dimensional Human Angelic Souls exhibit many consistencies in terms of appearance and traits, visible or not, even if their actual physicality differs based on the physical rules of the dimensional time-space wave where they are incarnated. As per our discussion of the general topography and landscape, there are several important distinctions afforded Beings in higher dimensional awareness and many of these may not be known nor particularly understood by you.

In much the same way that there are various colors and sound wave ranges in Fifth Dimensional awareness not available to or, more accurately, able to be registered by you in the Third Dimension, there are several specific features inherent in the makeup of Fifth Dimensional Beings not necessarily a part of Third Dimensional Beings. Fifth Dimensional Human Angelics have highly tuned intuitive awareness that you would consider extraordinary but that are in fact commonplace and integral to a Fifth Dimensional Being. Whereas Third Dimensional Beings might consider "messages," guidance or thoughts they are receiving from their Soul matrix or associated higher beings a fantasy or mental disorder, Fifth Dimensional Beings having honed this natural ability to include far ranging telepathic abilities. They are not only able to understand and distinguish a message or thought flashed across their perception from their own thoughts, they are also able to recognize its originating source, whether it comes from their higher self, from a disincarnated loved one residing in a higher sub level of the Fifth Universal Dimension, or from a simultaneously living neighbor, relative or friend communicating with them from the other side of town or the other side of the planet.

Not only does this assist the individual with guidance in their day to day existence, it also negates the need for certain technologies that have newly emerged on Third Dimensional Earth, rendering many of the technologies you now hold dear completely obsolete and irrelevant in a Fifth Dimensional world. In a place where the intuitive and mindful person is able to communicate effectively by telepathy simply by focusing on the particular vibrational signature of a fellow Being, telephone equipment and the myriad of communication services necessary to make such a system function are redundant.

Moreover, whereas Third Dimensional Beings are forever seeking new methods of identifying each other (by name, family name, number or affiliation) Terrans are able to skillfully acknowledge and register the vibrational signature of other Beings, incarnate and not. A vibrational signature holds the essence of every Being and is distinctive at all dimensional levels. It could be said to be the basis for identifying each individual in much the same way fingerprints or retina impressions are used as a means of distinctive physical identification currently in Third Dimensional reality.

Instead, Terrans use the vibrational signature of each Being, readily available to them, to not only identify each other but to communicate by means of tuning into the distinctive vibrational resonance of an individual. In your world, this would be akin to being able to locate someone by simply holding their vibrational fingerprint in your mind's eye and beginning a telepathic conversation with them, all without the means of any technological devices.

This frees Terrans from most of the clumsy apparatus for communicating that you consider so important. It must be understood that Terrans do not learn these abilities, but discover them just as a child discovers they can walk or talk in your world. Once discovery is accomplished it becomes a skill that can be honed and mastered, and how to do so effectively is taught to Terrans from an early age in much the same way humans in Third Density are taught how to master any skill.

As an extra sense inherent in their expanded DNA, Terrans are then taught to master telepathy while also being instructed in the correct use of their individual instincts and particular attunements. They are also taught how to use the "Super Now" and particular Fifth Dimensional time wave properties to best benefit themselves, their life purpose and the life purpose of others. Unlike your world, Terrans are never instructed via dogma, doctrine or the memorization of facts and figures. Knowledge and Truth become naturally available to them and are easily accessed (in a kind of spontaneous download available via intention and focus as needed) once they have mastered their own natural and innate perceptive, focusing and telepathic abilities.

The Physical Appearance of Terrans
& Basis for Terran Societal Structure

In terms of physical features, Terrans could be said to have a blended genetic resemblance to a wide range of races and Beings on Third Dimensional Earth. This creates a homogenization so there is essentially one race but with vastly different individual appearances that combine the best attributes of many races and cultures. This could be said to be similar to current day countries on Third Dimensional Earth where over centuries various races and cultures have blended together in the nation's off spring to create a new, unique and vastly diversified race through wide inter- breeding. What makes one unique on Terra has nothing to do with race but rather is related to one's Soul matrix and life purpose.

In terms of Terran physical bodies, Terrans have cellular structures that are expanded in nature in keeping with Fifth Dimensional biology and physics. It could be said that Terrans are more luminescent in appearance and this is based on the fact that their physical cellular structure is less dense, more etheric and more absorbent in terms of light energy. Since their energetic bodies, the energetic vehicle associated with physical structure through which life force is absorbed (aura or energy field if you prefer), resonates at much higher frequencies, not only does this ensure a greater and more direct association with their energetic field it serves to provide the greater connection they have to their environment and Soul (Higher Self) as we have described. On Terra it is not uncommon to recognize the important aspects of a Being through their energetic makeup rather than through their physical appearance. This is so even though their physical appearance is quite closely connected to their energetic appearance in a much more significant way than is common in the Third Universal Dimension you know.

As an example of this, on Terra it's possible to recognize one's Soul Matrix association first, in much the same way one recognizes someone's name, racial or physical characteristics on Earth. While differences in physical appearance definitely exist, these differences are inconsequential to Terrans and are only considered secondarily as a visible off-shoot of the Being's Soul purpose.

Lack of the need to judge others or of interest in physical appearance as a primary identifier makes the Terran sense of equality and uniformity even more innate and natural to them. It is not one's genetic make up that makes one different on Terra, but one's Soul associations, linked inextricably as they are to one's life purpose and energetic. It is for this reason that on Terra one finds a wide range of vastly different looking people, in terms of appearance, working harmoniously together side by side as brothers and sisters. This is in contrast to present day Earth where one is often judged solely on cultural associations or racial differences. Since diversity on Terra is more energetic in nature, and Soul purpose is accepted as a legitimate primary feature to be encouraged, diversity in terms of physical appearance has no real bearing. This creates vast physical differences in Terrans with a diversified and extremely harmonic society. Seen from your world Terrans would appear to be a beautiful race of blended multi-ethnic people, each with refined but pronounced diversified features capped with an etheric and almost luminous glow.

Terran political structures and organizations lack perceived differences, competition or threats and Terra has no important struggles with regard to culture, race, country or locale. There is some hesitation with respect to the interface with extraterrians, particularly those groups that are hostile to Human Angelics, but for the most part Terran groups do not compete with each other since their objective, based on their heart focus, is to support the life purpose of themselves and each other. Because of this, there is little real political intrigue or infighting with respect to Terran internal governing affairs (again making a distinction from extraterrian affairs).

In certain ways, if there is a form of competition it is not of the aggressive nature you are familiar with on Earth. Competition for Terrans is generally with themselves or other individuals with a similar Soul purpose. Even then it is a friendly competition meant only to help improve the competitors and perfect their goals. On Third Dimensional Earth this would remind you of great Olympian athletic heroes who work tirelessly to improve themselves and their own skills while supporting those in the same field or on the same team to achieve their goals as well.

This returns us to our conversation regarding self-karmic energetics, and in this way some of the karmic life lessons known to you on Third Dimensional Earth, such as the learning of "Pride" or "Leadership," can be part of one's life purpose experience on Terra. Naturally, these are expanded to include a Fifth Dimensional expression, which means that on Terra such lessons would be individually or self generated (self karmic). In comparison, on Earth such lessons would be originated and generally experienced only through karmic associations agreed upon beforehand with others, including families, friends, lovers, working environments, groups, culture or race, as you no doubt realize by now.

Terrans are a proud and ancient people represented by those Human Angelic Souls that have Ascended and raised their consciousness to the point of incarnation on a Fifth Dimensional plane of existence. Because Fifth Dimensional Terra is at a dimensional wavelength that allows its structure and its physical Beings to absorb more light than it is currently capable of doing at a cellular and physical level on Earth, Terrans would appear less dense and almost luminous or ghost-like. But this does not negate the fact that Beings residing at higher universal consciousness are physically considerably taller and more imposing than you would be accustomed to. You see glimpses of this on Earth where as consciousness evolves over historical time Beings gain in stature and height. It is also prevalent in your world culturally where more sophisticated societies begin to present populations that increase in actual stature and physical size, including height, weight and mass.

It is ironic that in your world those who exhibit greater size or girth are often frowned upon or considered less intelligent, when in fact the increase in societal girth in human populations is related to the physical body and cellular structure compensating physically for an increased sensitivity and connection to higher consciousness. This is true whether or not it includes an augmentation of intellect, and is a factor of connection and cultivation of the intuitive centers of the brain effecting related body glands and organs. It is quite probable that the increase you see in physical obesity in many modern world societies at this time (that increase not related to nutritionally depleted and highly processed foods or their over consumption) is in fact related to the physical body of individuals attempting to "ground" itself as the individual begins to receive and absorb more light during the present Ascension period.

The average adult Terran is anywhere from approximately 7 to 8 ½ feet tall, and in some instances Terrans can reach a height of 9 feet tall. Their girth or mass is generally proportionate to height, which would, in your eyes, present a race of near giants. As time and space bends at higher dimensional wavelengths, Beings that are able to hold more light energy at a cellular level become more elongated and their structure increases as a result in order to "ground" their physical presence. Stature is therefore a feature of most higher dimensional Beings and worlds, which generally allows them to physically compensate for their "larger" energetic structures manifested at higher frequencies.

We would also suggest that this is partly the reason why past Earth civilizations and historic periods have demonstrated a preference for depicting higher echelons of society, both aesthetically and artistically, as taller in stature with sometimes grossly elongated physical body features. In addition, we would say that archeological discoveries of larger than normal human-like skeletons (so-called "giants") belong to Beings that are directly descended from the Atlantean era, either just before or immediately following that empire's fall from Fourth into Third Dimensional physicality.

For many ancient cultures on Earth, physical stature remains a powerful if not symbolic representation associated with higher dimensional status and connection. This includes the primordial symbolic connection most human Beings automatically make between height and the potential for augmented consciousness. Although height and mass are not at all an indication or feature of greater or higher consciousness in your "modern" world, generally human evolution in the Third Dimension includes at the least increases in height and mass. As we have said, this accompanies an inner knowing among Human Angelics and, to an extent, alien Souls that there is potential for greater height and stature within incarnations belonging to higher dimensional worlds.

Terran Healing Abilities

Let us recap our description of Terra and the Terrans. First we remind you that wholeness is available at all dimensional levels, controlled only by the principles of matter composition and dimensional physics present. At lower dimensional levels, many attributes are hidden since they are in a sense "whittled" down from the existing wholeness. As one rises through the universal dimensions, there is an expansion of possible attributes, as well as the genetic make-up that can be accessed, generated or perceived.

Secondly, due to their expanded vibration and augmentation of the DNA, Terrans possess self-healing abilities that are more concordant and efficient, and they understand implicitly the connection they have to their Soul, their world and their fellow Terrans. As a result, Terrans have a natural understanding, perception and affinity for the energies around them.

Terran understanding and recognition of each Being's vibrational signature means they have a unique understanding of their own vibrational signature. This becomes quite important in terms of healing abilities. Because Terrans are able to tune into their vibrational signature, which originates at the Soul level, by doing so they are able to maintain health by merely refocusing on their personal vibrational resonance. This is done whenever a Terran loses its connection with Source, a state that portends and is a precursor to physical dis-ease.

Thus a Terran's principal healing method of choice, in terms of actual "medicinal" practices you would know, is using a method that restores and restructures one's vibrational signature. Whenever there is disconnection or lessening of the vibrational signature coming from Source to the physical structure on Fifth Dimensional Terra, one reprograms oneself by reconnecting to the original harmonics of one's Soul.

While this may sound lofty, and indeed it is important, it is akin to how the healing process is best accomplished even now on Earth. Illness that is not karmic in nature or chosen for specific purposes of growth in the Third Dimension are, similar to on Terra, a result of a disconnection from Source and one's energetic or vibrational signature. Unfortunately, such blockages create havoc and are not easily overcome in some cases on Earth, since the innate ability to recapture and reprogram one's energetic signature is not prevalent as it is on Terra.

However, we would suggest that this means of healing is nonetheless available in the Third Dimension, and in fact is an ancient method of healing used, albeit used clumsily and for the most part hidden on "modern" Earth. The use of energetics, harmonics, light and sound to "reprogram" one's vibrational and cellular resonance is an area that will become significant over the course of the coming century and will offer great promise on Third Dimensional Earth.

Your current medicines merely address the myriad of discomforts and problems caused by physical disengagement and disconnect from the vibratory essence found in your Soul's vibrational signature. Terrans wisely understand this, particularly because they are tuned into multi-dimensional frequencies, and must be in order to communicate effectively with each other. Thus Terran healing is related mainly to addressing blockages related to energetic impairment caused by a diminishing of the vibratory signature coming from Source.

This leads to a unique understanding of how one heals the physical structure, not only for the Self but also for one's sphere of influence, one's environment and even one's dimensional reality. Terrans are highly connected to their planet, and they understand that the physical Being known as the planet Terra requires energetic corrections from time to time that express and manifest as anomalies within the physical body.

It must be remembered in discussing this that Fifth Dimensional Terra exists, in essence, in an overlapped, superimposed dimensionally upon Third Dimensional Earth. Thus, many Third Dimensional attributes bleed through and are present on Fifth Dimensional Terra, just as First and Second Dimensional attributes are visible in your world, even if they are misunderstood. Fifth Dimensional Terrans are well equipped at grounding Fifth Dimensional reality based on their connection to

Source and understanding of life purpose, even as it includes the body of the planet as a whole.

In Third Dimensional reality you are fortunate to benefit from this because Terran's intimate connection to Terra allows them to effectuate healing on the planet that in many cases transcends dimensional overlap. As a result, Earth benefits from Terran efforts to assist Terra, and Earth tends to be healed in conjunction with Terra. However, be aware that there is a point at which Fifth Dimensional Terrans cannot effectuate resonant change or alleviate blockages emanating from disruptions at the Third Dimensional level. At moments like these, havoc can take place in the Third, Second and First Dimensional realms, and sometimes these can resonate through to higher realms although generally disruption follows higher to lower dimensional levels. This is the reason what you do to the planet at the Third Dimensional level has profound impact and can be seen by you at the First and Second Dimensional levels (mountains, oceans and sky as an example), which exist alongside you and will show disorientation and dis-ease based on the actions brought upon it from inhabitants of Third Dimensional Earth.

Part of the genetic predisposition and make-up of Terrans is the knowledge that they are one with their planet and their solar system, a consequence of their true and direct connection to Soul and God source. This is to say that through higher guidance and a unique connection to their world and the life purpose of their planet, Terrans are privy to valuable information that fosters respect and a longing to care for Terra, allowing it to grow, prosper and experience its own cycles of awareness and Ascension.

Unfortunately, this is rarely the case on Third Dimensional Earth, where modern societies prefer to think that Earth, an individual Being with a Soul and life purpose like its inhabitants, is mankind's dependent or that by virtue of its technical advances humankind is somehow permitted to exploit and exhaust Earth's abundance. Please understand that much of what is being experimented with and used technologically in the Third Dimension at the current time is increasingly dangerous to the planet and the consequence for its use will not only have impact on the Third Dimension, but may one day come home to roost on Fifth Dimensional Terra as you yourselves begin incarnations in that reality.

That being said, know also that while you enjoy using all of your newly imagined toys and communication methods -- your cell phones, digital pads, televisions, computers and social mediums – these are merely glimpses into the augmented future probability you will experience on Fifth Dimensional Terra. All the technologies and devices currently used in your world will be part of your inherent genetics and DNA on Terra, available to you at will through intention, focus and connection to your Higher Self. Hopefully, those abilities will be used for the benefit of your life purpose and the world as a productive member of Terran society.

Chapter 15
The Current and Future Direction of Terran Civilization

The Current and Future Direction of Terran Civilization

In some ways, Terran history could be said to mirror the history of Third Dimensional Earth in as much as it is influenced by the cyclical nature of Ascension. In your particular region of the galaxy, Ascension, which we have called the evolutionary process of Souls and all universal Beings including Souls, galaxies, solar systems and planets, occurs approximately every 260,000 years. This "grand cycle" of Ascension, which is the time at which universal dimensions Ascend, is peppered with lesser Ascension periods permitting dimensional sublevel Ascension by Souls and Beings within a universal dimension. In your sector of the galaxy your solar system evolves through the minor cycles approximately every 26,000 years.

During the Grand Cycle-Ascension currently underway, individual Beings have the potential to Ascend from Third Dimensional to Fifth Dimensional incarnations. Those that Ascend from the Third Dimension will do so at the same time the majority of Beings finishing incarnations on Terra are ready to begin their own Ascension to higher dimensional levels. In most cases, the majority of Human Angelic Terrans will migrate and evolve to lifetimes expressed in the Seventh Universal Dimension.

Understanding that Beings Ascend at their own rate throughout an Ascension period, the transition of Souls from Fifth Dimensional Terra to Seventh Dimensional lifetimes on Gaia (Earth and Terra's Seventh Dimensional counterpart) will occur over the course of the coming 500 to 2000 of your Earth years. Because of this seemingly lengthy window of transition (actually equivalent in terms of the period length for Earth, but seemingly longer because dimensional time wave properties), many Terrans will continue to exist in present incarnations on Fifth Dimensional Terra as Third Dimensional Human Angelics begin their migration to Fifth Dimensional lifetimes. The Terrans, who it can be said possess a substantially higher consciousness after millennia of lifetimes on Terra, the very essence of what qualifies them for Ascension themselves, will be the ones that initially "greet" new initiates arriving from Earth incarnations to begin their incarnations on Fifth Dimensional Terra (we stress that we mean this metaphorically only, and do not wish to imply new incarnates will be met by literal throngs of greeting Terrans).

It is foreseen that this large influx of new "immigrants" will cause substantial turmoil to Fifth Dimensional Terra, the impact of which will be felt there for the coming 10 to 20,000 years. This is always the case at the beginning of a major Ascension period as incarnates plan, decipher and birth into physical incarnations on a new universal dimensional plane. In this case, they bring to Terra new Soul attributes, skills, missions, goals and life plans, all designed in conjunction with their Soul matrices for the purpose of growth and consciousness expansion in a Fifth Dimensional world.

Life on Terra is substantially different from life in a Third Dimensional reality, as we have already described. One of the principal differences from the perspective of the Soul is that physical lifetimes on Terra are far longer than lifetimes on Earth. This is due to the ethereal nature of the physical reality there, as well as Terrans' propensity for self-healing and their understanding of the fundamentals of healing and energy. This permits them physical lives that are much longer, and in most cases Terrans are known to live to anywhere from 1,500 to even 2,500 years of age, in Earth years. Because of this, Terrans do not have the same number of incarnations that a Soul might experience on Earth. This has to do with the innate genetic healing abilities we have discussed, as well as Terrans' ability to have a closer union with their Soul energy, which is housed in a more manageable and less dense physical presence and permits longer physical life.

As we have said previously, there was a time on Third Dimensional Earth when there was also a closer association and connection to the Fourth and Fifth Dimensions. This enabled Beings on Earth to carry a closer connection to their Soul resonance and, in part, receive greater energetic pass- through into the physical body, which permitted humans to live lifetimes of approximately 500 to even 800 or 1,000 years of age. This, however, was during that extraordinary period of elevation in early Lemurian times over 500,000 Earth years ago, when incarnate Human Angelics on Earth had forged such a close union with the Fourth and Fifth Dimensions that the reality was in essence Fourth Dimensional in nature and the Third Dimension could be said to have for a time Ascended to Fourth Dimensional Awareness.

This was right before what has become known in your religious mythology as the "Fall" of the angels. That is, it was the descent of the realm at that time from Fourth Dimensional experience to Third Dimensional awareness and reality. When the Fall occurred during that Grand Cycle Ascension period great cataclysm was felt on Terra, since at that time it existed in very close dimensional proximity to Earth. From the standpoint of the Beings that experienced it, the Fall from Fourth to Third Dimensional reality was devastating and, in a sense, energy was sucked through from the Fifth Dimensional physical plane into the void caused by the Fourth Dimensional cataclysm. This caused great havoc and physical changes not only on Earth but also, through energetic multi-dimensional transference, on Fourth and Fifth Dimensional Terra.

If we make note of this it is to give you the understanding that while Terrans are in fact an ancient race and Human Angelics have incarnated on Terra for a long period of time, the current Terran civilization can trace its roots to that tumultuous Ascension period. Though long forgotten on Earth, Terran mythology remembers the "Fall" as a period understood to have caused severe turmoil and physical changes to the Terran landscape. As a result, Terrans continue to be wary and are very cautious during all Ascension periods.

Although Terran civilization has its roots beginning 500,000 years ago, the current societal structure of Terra emerged principally following the most recent Grand Cycle Ascension of 260,000 Earth years ago. Terra successfully navigated that Ascension, which coincided with the start of the decline of the Third Dimensional Atlantean civilization on Earth. Atlantis was at that time a fully globalized, technologically advanced civilization that declined into ruin over approximately the next 260,000 year period, until it finally disintegrated, self destructed and was wiped out in a series of devastations by around 13,000 BCE.

During the Grand Cycle Ascension of 260,000 years ago, Terra assimilated a majority of Ascending Human Angelic Soul populations coming to Terra from lifetimes in Atlantis. Those that did not Ascend at that time remained in Earth incarnations for the next 260,000 years, and many are presently incarnated. Others awaited the current Grand Cycle Ascension at higher sublevels (the high Astral planes) of the Third Universal Dimension. Thus, one might conclude that Terran civilization truly emerges shortly after the last Ascension period of 260,000 years ago, and it has advanced more or less from that time until now into what it is currently.

This is somewhat different from what has been experienced on Third Dimensional Earth where civilization appears to you to be no more than 10,000 to 15,000 years old. In fact, because the time space wave is weightier and denser on Third Dimensional Earth it does appear shorter in terms of its cyclical nature. In a way, a 260,000-year time period on Terra could be said to have an equal impact to a 10,000 to 15,000-year period on Earth, especially in terms of what a civilization might achieve. But in this case it has less to do with time wave properties and more to do with the peaceful nature of Terrans in the Fifth Dimension, as well as their ability to heal trauma within their dimensional sector. It also reflects the fact that Terrans as a species live lifetimes substantially longer and more intent on fulfillment of a metaphysical mission than is the case for Human Angelics incarnated in Third Dimensional reality.

As a side effect, this provides more continuity in terms of history, longevity and advancement so that there is a greater link from past to present and into the future than there is on Third Dimensional Earth. Thus, while it certainly can be considered technologically advanced, Terran civilization has in fact maintained and improved upon its technological advancement through tens and even hundreds of thousands of years, whereas Third Dimensional Earth has lost almost all its technological advances many times over the course of the past 260,000 year cycle. Perhaps more importantly, Terra's link to the spiritual and unphysical nature of existence goes hand in hand with its ability to ensure the long-term continuation of societal technology, reducing the need for increasing progress and invention (since all needed technology is already available to them).

This is not the case on Earth where technology has been lost many times over to the entire planet, and civilization has been forced to start from scratch, if you will. Whether you choose to believe it or not, your modern civilization does not as yet possess the high level of technological advancement that has existed on your planet at more than one time in the very distant past. As it regards Terra however, the maintenance of historical data combined with the continuation of advanced technology available for use by all ensures the population's ability to maintain a different focus and this factor provides a consistent basis for the people and culture of Terra.

The Current and Future Direction of Terran Civilization

We have described for you already the make up of Terran society and the fact that the current Terran population is expecting an infusion of new Human Angelic Souls incarnating on Fifth Dimensional Terra. If it happens to be a concern to the Terrans at all, it is due to the fact that in the Fifth Dimension, Terrans are also in the process of progressing to higher states of dimensional evolution but will be transitioning slowly into those higher states over the coming one thousand to two thousand Earth year period. This is due mostly to the fact that as we have explained the collapse of time transpiring in the Third Dimension is not exactly the same as within Fifth Dimensional mechanics. Thus, whereas the Ascension of the majority of Human Angelics from Earth will take place over the course of the coming 200-250 Earth years, on Terra the same transition will take approximately a thousand to two thousand equivalent Earth years to complete.

In addition to this, as we have said, Terrans enjoy a longevity that far exceeds the life span of humans incarnated on the Earth plane. Because of this Terrans may not be exiting to higher dimensions as quickly as entities from the Third Universal Dimension do. Thus, the truth is that while the influx of Third Dimensional Human Angelics via incarnation by their Souls will take place and has already begun on Terra, this will manifest temporarily as a kind of population explosion on Terra that has already begun.

In terms of Terran civilization, this actually provides a notable success story for the Terran population. Your historians on Earth, as an example, would probably see such a period of population growth as being related to social advancement and an era of prosperity being experienced worldwide. While this is certainly possible on rare occasions, this is not usually the case. An example would be the current explosion of population taking place on Earth, which over the past century has disproportionately and abruptly changed much of the make up of your world. We would say that the current global population growth you have experienced on Earth over the course of the past one hundred years is related to an influx of Ascending Souls from lower dimensions into Third Dimensional lifetimes. These Souls are essentially Human Angelic in nature, although not exclusively Human Angelic at this particular point for reasons we described in Chapter Ten of The System Lords and the Twelve Dimensions. They are however, quickly incarnating in Third Dimensional worlds in much the same manner that Third Dimensional Human Angelics that have reached higher resonance and are harvestable have begun or will begin to incarnate on Terra.

We would add that this is not only in preparation for what is essentially happening in terms of Ascension but is also consistent with the continuation of that particular realm through new entities and new learning situations related to the emerging of new universal parameters. Though confusing to you no doubt and difficult to describe in a manner that is understandable to you, it is important to note that, as with all evolution, there is not an abrupt cut off, transformation or merger from one world into another. Rather, there is a slow progression and the evolution of one physical realm into another. It is during these key portal (Ascension) periods that First and Second Dimensional reality is transformed, evolved and grown so that the dimensions eventually resonate with and become Third Dimensional in nature and form. Likewise, Third Dimensional form evolves until it resonates at higher frequencies and becomes compatible with Fourth and Fifth Dimensional resonance. Eventually, as an example, what was the Second Universal Dimension evolves into and emerges as the new Third Dimensional realm. This process continues for all universal dimensions, which is why the Ascension cycles are in fact the evolutionary process of the entire Universe, from Souls and planets to time-space waves and beyond.

Returning to our story of Terra, however, this process presents a slight dilemma for the current populace and because of their awareness and consciousness Terrans are presented with a unique issue related to overpopulation. Current Terrans, it must be understood, will initially be your "parents" as you incarnate into those higher realms for the first time. An important thing to add is that it is precisely through this kind of evolutionary association that Souls become known to each other and Souls of higher consciousness become the mentors and "spirit" guides of Souls who may not have a parallel consciousness within the realm they are incarnating within.

Terrans foresee a time on Terra over approximately the coming thousand to two thousand years that will be quite intense in terms of supply and demand, causing particular strain on the civilization because of the manner in which Terrans have organized their society for the past 200,000-plus years. Because Terran society is highly focused on each entity's involvement with the aspect of True Self and the divine as it relates to the mission of one's Soul, it is important that populations are manageable in order to allow incoming Souls to have the opportunities and environment that will best support their experiences and expression. In times of great overburden, such as times of overpopulation, this becomes problematic to say the least. It is this influx of Beings on Terra combined with the knowing of their true and divine nature and subsequently their wish to incarnate within specific communities, areas and regions that will become most difficult.

Though Terra is of a higher consciousness, it is nonetheless subject to specific Fifth Dimensional principles of manifestation and reality construction. Many of those principles are no less physical than in the Third Dimension, even if they are different from the physics and relativity with which you are familiar. Of most concern, as we have said, is the challenge of supply and demand. On Terra, it does no good to create something that is not usable or desired by others. In fact, we would say that within a society primarily based on the principles of Service-to-Others, this is a guiding factor since Service-to-Others cannot be actualized or expressed without others being able to enjoy and benefit from the fruits of one's offer. In this respect, Terrans foresee a long period of dissatisfaction and possible neglect, which ultimately could lead to societal challenges. Naturally, this also portends enormous long-term growth opportunities for all Terran society, which we would suggest is always the basis of challenges that are made manifest around a given world's social structures at all.

Regardless of this, as we have said in the past most Human Angelic Terrans will soon be graduating to and beginning new incarnations on Seventh Dimensional Gaia. Seventh Dimensional Gaia is not currently our subject and will perhaps be explored further in another book at a different time. Suffice to say for now that all realms evolve and grow through opportunities that are created by the entities within that particular dimension. By entities, we remind you that we not only referring to Human Angelics but to all sentient Souls, and that includes alien (to you) life forms, the galaxies and the planetary systems and Solar Systems, all of which have life and a Soul as well.

It is through the evolution of the dimensions during Ascension that all Beings transform and move into higher consciousness, but evolution is not without its particular challenges. This is why Third Dimensional Earth as well as Fifth Dimensional Terra will face a myriad of challenges --opportunities for growth -- over the coming several hundred years in the case of Earth, and several thousand years in the case of Terra. These challenges can cause great internal and physical stress within the system that affects every entity, the society as a whole and the planet. The energetics that come into play can also produce great geographic upheaval creating changes in the physical mechanics, structure and function of entire planetary bodies, Solar Systems and Galaxies.

Despite this, many of you may feel that Terra is the ideal world and Terran culture represents the best of civilizations with one of the most advanced and rewarding realities you could ever know. Considering your current perspective as a resident of Third Dimensional Earth, this would be very close to true. However, it needs to be understood that while higher dimensional reality may seem perfect to you, in the eyes of that reality or from the perspective of realities beyond it, each dimensional reality is subject to change, growth and the continuation of its own evolutionary process. In other words, the view is relative and each has its benefits as well as its challenges and issues.

This is as much the case on Terra as it is on Third Dimensional Earth, residing as it does in the Solar System you currently know. The difference here however, is that Terrans have innate attributes and senses that are far different from those you know, which makes them far better equipped to understand and manifest the needs and desires of their Souls, the Souls with whom they reside and their planet. Issues and challenges in any dimensional realm are always opportunities for growth to be experienced by each and every Being in the dimension, and this is an important thing to understand before definitively condemning the inadequacies you find evident on Third Dimensional Earth.

While you sense that you have a connection to Earth in the Third Dimension, you probably do not comprehend the complexity and intimacy of that connection. First and foremost it should be accepted that the Earth itself is a Soul that is evolving, Ascending and progressing just as you are. In that respect everything on the planet and within the Solar System has relationship, and each Being has its mission, its goals, its foibles and its evolutionary process occurring within the context of the whole. You would look at your Solar System or your Galaxy differently if you realized that these planetary and celestial bodies have Soul purpose and are siblings working together and creating specific opportunities for each other, in a manner of speaking.

In much the same way there is a unified relationship between yourselves and your planet, and it is not far off to acknowledge that while incarnate physically in that plane of reality you are indeed the children of Earth. We remind you that we are not just talking about Human Angelics or Human Beings generally, but every living creature, every geological attribute, every blade of grass, every stone, every mountain, every stream, every tree and every cloud that passes overhead. While not of the same dimensional value as you, they are nonetheless Beings that are interacting with you and contributing to your experiences as entities with independent powers to manifest and co-create in your world. This is no less true on Terra where this connection is not only understood but where each Being revels and shares in it.

Take this a step further and you have situations in Fifth Dimensional reality where it is quite possible that entities not necessarily living next to you on the same planet might have awareness of you as well as your life purpose. Naturally, this would only be true if they focus on obtaining this information and desire to know it. Of course, on Terra you would also have an understanding of their life purpose and intentions.

Now this becomes important, and we begin explaining it by reminding you that there is also the factor of polarity, which comes into play at every dimensional level of reality, particularly as this relates to Soul origination, and thus, Soul orientation. Soul orientation can be a distinguishing Soul trait, no matter what the dimension.

As we have explained, there is Soul origination and expression that is oriented towards Service-to-Others, and there is Soul orientation and expression oriented towards Service-to-Self. Human Angelics are principally aligned with Service-to-Others oriented Soul matrices. For the most part this Soul species grows in consciousness through experiences that open the individual and the group to the service and benefit of other universal Beings.

Here we are speaking of Human Angelic Souls, not to be confused with human Beings, which can carry the Soul matrices of other Soul orientations, albeit somewhat clumsily. In your sector of the galaxy, alien entities all tend to have somewhat humanoid characteristics, at least in terms of shape and particularly with respect to the unity of the mental, energetic and physical body (the true spiritual trinity of physical existence in the Third Dimension). In other words, though you might notice that one sentient Being species, for instance, has four fingers instead of five, longer or shorter arms, different facial shapes and sizes, different eyes, mouths, noses, or diverse skin textures and colors, you would consider these Beings alien but higher realities would see them as humanoid. This is a factor of lower dimensional resonance as well as the galaxy sector in which you find yourself. This also changes significantly as you move into higher dimensional frequencies, especially as you get closer to Sixth and Seventh Dimensional reality.

If we are bringing this up at all it is because it serves as background for an understanding of what the future of Terra looks like. We have said that Terrans enjoy a particularly creative and idealistic, almost utopian-like culture and society whereby those entities that incarnate on Terra incarnate into communities where their Soul's purpose and special energetic expression is nurtured and expanded for the benefit of the entity's Soul purposes. This creates a world where each is allowed to be principally occupied with and experience what is most fundamental to them. The structure of society is not one of need but one where each prospers in their ability to perform, function and grow within a specialty related to the desire of their Soul.

This would seem to present a perfect arrangement. However, as we have also detailed, the coming influx of Third Dimensional entities into Fifth Dimensional incarnation is a rather substantial influx of what we shall call "immigrant" Souls on Terra. As we have also cited, the increase in population on Terra will, potentially, no longer sustain itself and will stress communities that are aligned with sustaining its populations based on their input and the execution of their particular focus.

The future of Terra then, holds great potential for dissatisfaction from a newly minted Fifth Dimensional population of Souls that could find frustration and discontent. At the least, the current communal structures will need to find new avenues of access in order to allow all entities to experience their missions, goals and life purposes.

As an example of this, say that for instance too many Terrans incarnate into a certain region that has as its purpose food production. For those individuals whose talents are underused, (under-employed to borrow a contemporary term regarding Earth's current societal structure) for the first time in a very long time in Terran history these individuals might use free will to migrate away from those communal structures, and as a result might choose new roles and expressions, forming as a result new social structures and new communities of their wake. In this way, it is possible that someone migrating away from a communal structure specializing in his or her preference could create or join a communal structure together different than their Soul preference, or if not, a new societal structure for expressing their Soul preference. You probably recognize this as what you currently have in your societal and economic structures where a few individuals related to a specific specialty join forces with a few other individuals of a different specialty to create a new community. This then represents the social and structural evolution that has potential on Terra over the course of the coming several millennia.

There is further complication related to this potential change in that this makes it highly likely that Terrans will, through arrangement and consciousness, invite outsiders into their society as well, something new to Terrans. What we mean by this is that until the present time Terrans have been fundamentally isolated in their particular sector of the solar system, and though they do have knowledge of and contact with alien worlds, especially those of higher consciousness, they nevertheless live in somewhat isolated planetary communities that are fundamentally populated with Human Angelic Souls. Until now Terrans have remained apart from extraterrian or alien populations. Certainly Terrans are not desirous of galactic interchange or travel even though the capabilities and technologies exist, and it is uncommon to find alien Soul matrices incarnated or present on Terra.

However, over the next many thousand millennia and up until the next Ascension period approximately 260,000 years in the future, the planet

Terra has by agreement and for the purposes of Soul growth opened itself to an influx of outside Fifth Dimensional sentient Souls. This means that over the course of the coming epoch, not only is Terra to become the home of new Human Angelics coming from the Third Universal Dimension via Ascension, it will also become home to alien Souls. Up until now Terra has been exclusively the domain of Human Angelic Soul Beings.

This creates scenarios for growth over the course of the coming era and beyond. However, this potential presents an interesting difference from what such an experience would hold for Third Dimensional Earth since, as we said, Terrans have the ability to understand their life purpose, the life purpose of other Beings and the reason things transpire from the perspective of the Soul. This holds true for the incarnated entities of Human Angelic Souls as well as the incarnated entities of Alien Soul matrices.

The new potential will have vast implications for the future of Terrans concerning the creation of entirely new planetary cultural and societal structures. The logistics of how this transpires will be managed by Fifth Dimensional incarnations of The System Lords, who operate in much the same manner they do on Third Dimensional Earth. What is important is the reason the planet Terra would agree to incorporating alien Souls into its future destiny at all.

That reason is based on creating harmony in the Fifth Dimension that will have the possibility of filtering into Third Dimensional reality, lessening the impact of the current attempted infiltration and takeover of Third Dimensional Earth by alien populations (See The System Lords and the Twelve Dimensions, Chapter Ten). If Third Dimensional Earth is to have peace, prosperity and remain viable for Human Angelic Souls without becoming a prisoner-planet until the next Grand Cycle Ascension period in 265,000 Earth years, the answer may well rest in efforts exacted from a Fifth Dimensional future. If so, the successful continued evolution of Third Dimensional Earth will be based on the harmonic balancing of Service-to-Others and Service-to-Self Soul orientations. Such an effort will be undertaken on a multi-dimensional, galactic level orchestrated by the planetary Soul Beings known as Earth and Terra for the benefit of themselves and their inhabitants inter-dimensionally.

Chapter 16
The Multidimensional Karmic Influence on the Future of Terra

*An Alien Bio Invasion of Earth and the
Coming Alien Invasion of Fifth Dimensional Terra*

We have described in the past the interrelationship and inter-dimensionality of universal life. As we have explained previously, dimensions closely overlap each other and there is constant energetic give and take as well as push and pull between all the various dimensions. You tend to envision dimensions as new and different places that are not related to the specific reality where you are focused. Although this is true in the sense that there is no direct communication, the fact remains that the overlap that exists is highly relevant particularly from an energetic standpoint. There is a multiplicity of participation from one dimension to another.

In a way, one might best envision this inter-dimensionality as a whole in order to fully grasp it. In other words, there are Twelve universal dimensions and this represents the "wholeness" of All That Is (God) in the Universe. The concept of dimensional wholeness is diminished as one goes from higher to lower dimension. This occurs in much the same way that all potential exist for you in your lifetime but you choose parameters that whittle down the wholeness to create who you will be in a given lifetime for purposes of growth as desired by you and your Soul matrix.

It is thus that dimensionality is sequestered bit by bit as one recedes into lower dimensions. As we have described previously, one might also view this as a chess game being played on a floating stack of twelve different clear Lucite game boards where pieces at higher tiers of the game are not only playing in unison with the pieces on their own level but are also playing on a multitude of levels beneath them. Now add to this the imagery the idea that the ceiling of each tier in our chess game is a bit cloudy. Pieces being moved around on some levels cannot see or know the chess game moves being made above them, despite the fact that pieces on some higher levels can see (albeit with a haze) the movements of the pieces below. What happens in such a case is that you wind up playing the game full throttle on your particular level where things are clear. But you also might play on any level above or below that is visible to you, even though these levels might appear to be cloudy from your current level.

In describing this, we are also attempting to create a method for envisioning Fifth Dimensional Terra, which looking down and through its chessboard level is able to see what's happening in a hazy Fourth and Third Dimensional realm, and perhaps see down into the worlds of even the Second and First Dimensions. As such, it is not just playing its own specific game on the fifth tier of the twelve-tier chessboard, to an extent it is also playing inter-dimensionally, sometimes making moves on its own level in response to or as a result of what it sees transpiring on the levels beneath its own.

Now as we have explained already, everything is constantly in an energetic state of flux and change, and this occurs without beginning or end. Per universal law, higher can see lower, albeit in vague terms, but lower cannot always see higher. What is happening in the Third Dimensional reality can therefore be seen and has relevance in the Fifth

Dimension on Terra. So too reactions being played out on Fifth Dimensional Terra can be related to or have a basis in the field of endeavor and potentiality in the Third Dimension on Earth.

For this reason what happens with regard to the potential or probable future of Earth is often no less valid or impactful on Fifth Dimensional Terra, which is essentially a higher vibrational Earth; Same planet and universal location, different space-time dimensional wave coordinate. Of course, this must be put into context and to be clear it is understood that there is a form of isolation inherent in the time wave properties of each dimension. Thus, the internal problems of one dimension do not necessarily transcend or interfere directly with another. However, unseen energetic bonds created do in fact have impact and interplay particularly vis-à-vis the motivation behind a higher dimension's response and subsequent actions.

If Third Dimensional Earth follows its current trajectory with the probable future including a possible bio invasion by alien life forms via alien Soul incarnations into slightly genetically altered physical human bodies, this could have substantial impact with respect to the Human Angelic population. This would be true not only in the Third Dimension, but also in the Fifth Dimension as well, especially at the time of future Ascension periods. Even though the Fifth Dimension is isolated and to an extent immune from the specific consequences of lower dimensional events, it nonetheless is affected energetically as a result of the actions and events taking place within lower dimensional realities. Such an energetic event can transcend the tiers of our board game causing higher dimensions to have the need to react in order to deflect potential impact.

In essence all events serve as factors creating new opportunities for growth, especially in higher dimensional levels. Without it, there could be the tendency towards uniformity, conformity and lack of dimensional expansion or growth. In this scenario, the potential probable future described where Human Angelics leave Third Dimensional Earth incarnations en masse has significant impact on the future of Fifth Dimensional Terra. It is with that in mind that we can now examine potential future probabilities for Terra, particularly regarding Fifth Dimensional opportunities for growth that are a reflection of the alien bio invasion of Third Dimensional Earth in the coming future era.

The significant fear generated on Third Dimensional Earth found in works of fiction concerning blatant alien invasions is for the most part groundless, but has a basis in truth of a sort. Such an invasion would be unseen by most human Beings and would occur via a bio invasion of alien Souls incarnating on Earth into hybrid physical human bodies. This brings us to another timely fictionalized fear currently prevailing on Earth that partly has a basis in truth as well – human zombies and the invasion of the human form by non-human entities.

We would suggest that these popular notions have found their way into your entertainment not just as a matter of science fiction, but because these subliminal fears might in fact have potential to really exist and manifest in your world, albeit in a way not realized by you as yet. This may in fact be further based in the unconscious knowing that an alien conquest of Earth is being attempted already and will not come from outer space as expected but from within the human form itself.

As we have said in the past, the potential exists for alien Souls and Souls not related to Human Angelics to incarnate into physical human bodies through the use of emerging hybrid genetics and DNA manipulation. Though seemingly human and indistinguishable for the most part, these hybrid genetic bodies would not necessarily be suitable for housing the Human Angelic Soul. Thus, what you might see transpiring is a struggle in terms of Third Dimensional Earth's ability to house the Human Angelic Soul in a vehicle that is acceptable to the higher consciousness and energetic frequencies necessary for Human Angelics to incarnate.

We have mentioned before that Human Angelic Souls are universally considered to be the preferred and chosen Soul race of Earth. This includes all of Earth's corresponding bodies in the various higher and lower dimensions. Where then, you might ask, would such a scenario and its short-term consequences be played out both on an energetic level and in terms of actual consequence? The answer to that is already beginning to have impact as it manifests its potentiality on Fifth Dimensional Terra. The greater question here would then be this: What is the outcome of such a scenario if Fifth Dimensional Terra were to take, via our multi-dimensional chess game, actions to rectify the situation on Third Dimensional Earth with respect to the coming Alien Soul bio invasions?

As the world population becomes mesmerized by the fear of an alien invasion and take-over from space, this energy begins to have future potentiality not just with respect to Earth but also with respect to the potential future of Terra. Because of this, over the course of the coming several thousand years Terrans will most probably also experience alien invasions - of a sort. But the invasions experienced on Terra will not be those bio-based invasions being subtly orchestrated by alien Souls on Earth. Instead, they will be actual physical alien invasions that will take place on Terra itself, as well as within Terran planetary territories.

Understand that Terrans are able to empathetically know what their mission and the life goals of others are and thus they are able to understand things as opportunities for growth. Over time, these invasion events will bring Terrans into closer cooperation with other Galactic Beings, and Terra will learn to assimilate alien Beings and life forms into its world, not via hybrid forms, genetic manipulation or through bio-invasion as on Earth, but in actual form, which has not happened before now. It is important to recognize that many, if not all of the events depicted in your world's ancient mythology or modern fiction with respect to inter-Galactic battles with alien Beings or between alien Beings and humans are in fact unconscious depictions of what will ultimately transpire in the future of Terra. In many cases, those new to Terra, fresh from the Third Dimension, will be the very ones dealing with such events.

Despite these challenges, such things hold great potential for the people and future world of Fifth Dimensional Terra. Do not imagine the episodes on Terra to resemble the chaos of war and conflict as it is known to you in the Third Dimension. In a Fifth Dimensional world, battles and potential conflicts are not generally resolved in the highly violent manner they are in the Third Dimensional realm. Rather, these conflicts are fought energetically and sometimes telepathically through opportunities related to the use of a species' Will Power, Soul Alignment and Soul group choices.

The Overlap and Interplay Between the Dimensions

Let us clear up a possible misconception that might be lingering among many at this particular point. Some of you might tend to think of Fifth Dimensional Terra as separate and individual from Third Dimensional Earth. In fact, many might tend, via our descriptions, to see Fifth Dimensional Terra or any other dimension as potentially existing in its own universal location, separated by function and by physicality; in effect, a place somewhere way out in space. This, however, is not accurate and is not truly the way in which Fifth Dimensional Terra or any other dimension actually exists.

We have said many times that dimensions overlap. Therefore, it is important to envision Fifth Dimensional Terra existing simultaneously superimposed over Third Dimensional Earth, just as it is important to envision Seventh Dimensional Gaia superimposed over Fifth, Fourth and Third Dimensional Terra and Earth, and so on and so forth. This is true no matter what part of the Solar System, Galaxy or Universe you are in. Our discussions have been primarily related to the solar system you currently know and that part of time and space in which your reality currently is generated.

We have attempted to explain the structure and the make up of your Solar System within the context of its Galaxy, though we have not spoken in detail of the many galaxies and solar systems that comprise the Universe as a whole. Therefore, when we have spoken of Fifth Dimensional Terra, we have spoken of it as a separate and individualized place, as indeed it is. However, it has very close association and even closer bleed- through and interaction inter-dimensionally with all the dimensions and space-time waves in your particular Solar System. Thus, just as we can describe a Third Dimensional Mars, a Third Dimensional Saturn and a Third Dimensional Jupiter for example, all of these are also superimposed against Fifth, Sixth, Seventh, Eighth and higher dimensional versions of themselves. And each has relationship with other planetary and galactic members within their own dimensional time-space wave, just as Earth has relationship with the planets in its own Third Dimensional Solar System, which you currently know. They are all superimposed over each other in the spatial locations related to your particular region and galaxy.

If we are attempting to explain this an additional time, it is to reinforce the close association that each dimension has with the other as well as to underline how vast the Universe truly is. Not only is it vast spatially within a specific universal dimension (time-wave), when one takes into consideration the overlapping multidimensional layers, one begins to sense the enormity of the Universal structure.

For these reasons, it is in fact erroneous to think of yourself as leaving one particular location or planet and going to another location in the Universe known as Fifth Dimensional Terra. In effect, you continue to be part and parcel of your current location, but at a higher dimensional frequency in a different space-time wave. You have come to this location to incarnate and do so through the many universal dimensions therein. In general, you remain within a specific area of the Universe but operate at a multi dimensional level, if you and your Soul so desire.

As you evolve and grow, when your physical body deteriorates and is no longer viable you continue to live on in an energetic form known to your Soul matrix. While you are within one universal dimension, you migrate through what has been termed the "Astral Planes," which in your reality are the sub levels of the Third Universal Dimension. There, you are able to pass between higher sub levels depending on your Soul growth and abilities, until such time as you are prepared either to experience new physical incarnations in the First, Second or Third sublevel, or wait at higher sub level realities for the opportunity to Ascend to higher universal dimensions.

It is important to know as well that you need not be actively and physically incarnated in the Third Sub Level of the Third Universal Dimension (as you currently are) in order to Ascend but you are just as likely to Ascend from any higher sub level of the Third Dimension. Having accomplished many lifetimes in the First, Second and Third sub levels of the Third Universal Dimension, many will simply await Ascension from the Fourth through Twelfth sub levels, sub-dimensional regions that serve as the basis for the various concepts of Heaven that you know. Thus, loved ones and friends that have "passed" from physical incarnation in your particular sublevel of the Third Universal Dimension will have similar opportunity to evolve through Ascension from whatever sublevel they might find themselves inhabiting during an Ascension period.

The difference between lifetimes in all of these dimensions is related to, as we have said, genetic make up, consciousness and the ability of your Soul to transport to you sufficient light energy based on your growth, which is assimilated by your Soul matrix instantaneously as it is experienced by you. Photon light energy, as we have explained, is the universal substance that regulates vibrational (scalar) frequency and is an essential building block of the Universe and all universal structure. When you reach a certain capacity to hold light, your Soul matrix is able to accomplish incarnations at greater levels of development.

However, returning to our original theme regarding inter-dimensionality and the links between what occurs on Third Dimensional Earth and what occurs on Fifth Dimensional Terra, the close association that dimensional levels maintain is not only important, in many cases it is vital. We have described in the past how a dimension that does not reach Ascension through the crucial energy and consciousness necessary, can in fact falter and, albeit rarely, fall. This was experienced before when Fourth and Fifth Dimensional Atlantis, because of the population's inability to reach a harvestable majority due to various factors, fell back into Third Dimensional density. This period, known in your religious mythology as the "Fall of the Angels," occurred not because Atlantis existed on another planet but because Atlantis essentially existed on a higher dimensional level related to your current proximity. While it is not correct to say there is no distinct differences between the dimensions, it is possible to say that energetically one dimension is always evolving into another in perpetuity, without beginning and without end. Yet this progression is not necessarily always higher, and it has been known to occur vertically in either direction as well as horizontally.

Furthermore, we have described how there can be karmic (energetic) interplay and multi-dimensional or inter-dimensional union that results from what transpires energetically within one dimension. Close proximity means that there is an effect, however great or small that effect might prove to be. However true this may be concerning dimensions in close proximity it may not be true at a "vibrational" distance. In other words, what transpires in the Third Dimension might have minimal effect on what is transpiring at say the Tenth or Eleventh Universal Dimension. Similarly, what transpires in the Tenth or Ninth Universal Dimension, aside from the work of the System Lord Avatars who are able to return to lower dimensions for purposes of inter-dimensional growth and assistance, will usually have fairly minor impact on daily existence within the Third Dimension.

However, dimensions that are more closely aligned or similar in nature on the space-time wave tend to have more important crossover, interplay and energetic exchange. What transpires in the Fourth or Fifth Dimension has relevance and close association to what takes place in the Third Dimension, just as what happens in First and Second Dimensional reality can have far reaching impact on Third Dimensional occurrences.

A perfect example of this would be a cataclysmic geophysical experience that takes place on Earth. A volcanic eruption, earthquake or massive storm, essentially Second Dimensional phenomena happening at the elemental level, have a very clear effect energetically and, to an even greater extent, physically upon Third Dimensional life. When an earthquake or a violent storm displaces you, although the storm is a Second Dimensional occurrence your displacement in Third Dimensional density is real and becomes a challenge (or opportunity) for you to meet. Through this example you can see the correlation between what transpires in one closely linked Dimension and another.

What is less easily understood, since you are not genetically predisposed to think in such a manner and are not consciously aware of the importance, is how multi-dimensional energetic links and karmic interplay occurs between these same universal dimensions. When there is a struggle on Third Dimensional Earth, although that struggle is not immediately felt on Fifth Dimensional Terra, the resolution and energetic karmic issues inherent in that struggle can be very relevant and in a sense must be played out in all dimensional realms. Particular emphasis is placed on those dimensions and realms closest to the origination point of the specific energetic manifestation.

When there is great emotional (energetic) distress, such as the one we have described known as the "Fall" where a civilization of Beings fell from the consciousness of one vibrational state to a lesser one, karma works its way in both directions from the originating point in order to balance the energetic displacement. In this manner, karma can be viewed as a universal balancing mechanism, even inter-dimensionally. This phenomenon is exemplified in your own body's attempt to reach homeostasis when there is dis-ease or distress within it in order to keep various systems balanced and working. Through this inter-dimensional karma, Beings within various dimensions are given the opportunity to deal with new and emerging consciousness backdrops, all of which are created as opportunities for their growth.

The massive influx of population in the form of new incarnations on Fifth Dimensional Terra coincides with this, bringing as it does an influx of lower consciousness incarnates from Third Dimensional Earth. In much the same way explorers pushed forward to new worlds from the crowded, shortsighted confines of Medieval and Renaissance Europe in order to expand their horizons, the current Ascension period will deliver to Fifth Dimensional Terra new incarnates looking for growth opportunities. This metaphor of pushing into new territories becomes applicable to what will transpire not only on Third Dimensional Earth, where new incarnates will come from lower as well as parallel dimensions, but also on Fifth Dimensional Terra, where Third Dimensional Human Angelics have already begun incarnations in a new dimensional frequency.

If we are explaining this, it is as a basis for understanding that Fifth Dimensional Terra will now have inter-Galactic associations and will become truly part of the Galactic structure as it moves forward in its destiny and future. On Third Dimensional Earth, the evolution in genetics and consciousness continues to take place and many Beings incarnating into human form on Third Dimensional Earth in the future will exhibit new and evolved attributes. Some of these attributes will be expanded awareness and ability while some will be stunted and seemingly backward (to you).

Technological advances that are sustained over the course of the coming two hundred to three hundred year-period on Third Dimensional Earth will tend to push civilization into new realms. This will include a continued exploration of the Solar System that surrounds you. However, as we have said, the continued existence of Earth as it is today in the Third Dimension does remain in question. That is not to say that Third Density Earth will ever disappear but it is to say that the potential exists, as we have explained, for Human Angelics to become extinct on Third Dimensional Earth.

This will happen in part because the majority of Human Angelics in the Third Dimension are currently harvestable and ready for Ascension, but it is also based on the fact that a bio invasion of alien Souls into human form could ultimately replace Human Angelic incarnates on Earth. If this scenario is manifested fully, Third Dimensional Earth will act to rid itself of these invaders by eliminating all life upon it, beginning the cycle of creation over. This has potential to occur somewhere between the 26th and 27th Centuries on the current timeline, and if or when it takes place it will be a method for reinventing life on Earth so that it is biologically Human Angelic as well as alien Soul suitable.

The methods being used to create genetic human hybrids on Earth as well as the manipulation and transformation of Earth's environment, which is being effectuated clandestinely by alien intervention with the cooperation of unwitting government and secret government organizations who think they are fighting global warming and other planetary occurrences, will make it possible for alien Soul matrices to incarnate in human form on Earth. However, in the long term this will also render the human physical body obsolete for incarnation by Human Angelic Souls. Such a transformation will occur over several hundred years between now and the 26th Century. As a result, Earth itself will step in to restart life and, in its wake, all civilization anew. This has already occurred on Earth in the distant past, and stories based around mythological figures such as Noah and his Arc represent such episodes. Moreover, the prior bio invasion of the Draconians, who attempted to colonize Third Dimensional Earth via their genetic offspring the dinosaurs, is perhaps the best example of this.

While this occurs on Earth, Fifth Dimensional Terra will be the entity to incorporate a Galactic family that includes Human Angelics and other alien Soul Beings. Once again, much of the information you have received in the current time with respect to Earth joining its Galactic family along side the push to understand the Solar System and the Universe are for the most part a metaphor and a bleed-through of what will actually transpire successfully as the majority of Human Angelics begin Fifth Dimensional incarnations on Terra.

We have included this information in order to demonstrate that many of the challenges related to growth for Fifth Dimensional Terrans will be related to the influx of new Human Angelic Souls as well as new alien participation and interaction with Terra in the Fifth Dimension. Currently, you are unable to see these Fifth Dimensional Beings, although they are visible to you at times when and where there is a thinning of the dimensional overlap. At those times, witnesses will claim to see and interact with what has been described as UFO's and aliens.

To be clear, there is in fact interaction with some Extraterrestrial Beings on Earth, particularly at high levels of secrecy known to world governments and other multinational organizations. But for the most part, random visitations and sightings in the Third Dimension are actually Fifth Dimensional bleed-through. In fact many real participations tend to be with those Fifth Dimensional alien Beings that have the technological capability to transcend dimensional overlap, either physically or telepathically. So while unidentified flying objects and aliens do exist on a very limited basis in Third Density, these objects are generally seen up until now through the dimensional veil and are most likely Fifth Dimensionally-based.

Continuing the Discussion of Inter-Dimensional Karma

The main concept we wish to impress upon you is the idea that dimensions are integral each to the other. This is so despite the fact that you cannot completely understand, perceive or know every dimension given your current perspective. In other words, we hope we have demonstrated that what transpires in one universal dimension and its many sub levels is also responsible for energetic links that intertwine with what takes place in various other dimensions as well.

In terms of karma, which we have defined as harmonic or energetic balancing both internally within a dimension and externally throughout various universal dimensions, this remains true. In fact, as we have said individual (personal) karma, along with cultural karma, racial karma, societal karma, group karma and karma that is broadly related to associations with the planet as a whole, can all be very much linked both internally within a dimension and externally from one dimension to another.

Perhaps, it is best to see this in the same manner as you might envision your past, present and future in this current lifetime. Clearly, what happens in your past is linked to your present and probably also closely linked to future events in your life as well. Try as you might, this fact is seemingly inescapable. Karmic energy (actions if you prefer) from one part of your life can have far reaching consequences into other moments, present or future, in your life. Similarly, in other lifetimes within this dimension, a past life can be linked energetically via karma to the present life, just as a future lifetime can be linked to either of these. Energy generated in one lifetime is continually being harmonized and balanced as it occurs back and forth between other lifetimes.

Now expand this concept to include your newfound understanding of what happens in a multidimensional manner from one dimension to another. Karmic or energetic balancing is being accomplished continually at each dimensional level. Thus the energy that is created in one universal dimension is in effect being balanced out via an exchange that allows it to be met, performed, enacted or lived in another dimension.

For the purposes of our discussion here, such energetic balancing is taking place constantly between the Third, Fourth and Fifth Universal Dimension. Expressed in another way, karma generated in the Third Universal Dimension can be balanced by events, reactions and choices taking place in the Fourth and Fifth Universal Dimension. In general, this balancing is more prominent from lower to higher dimensions, with the higher dimension balancing the energy generated by the lower dimension, although the inverse can and does come into play.

Now the Fifth Universal Dimension does in fact understand and is consciously aware of these physics, just as it is acutely aware of what is happening in the Third Universal Dimension, especially in terms of this karmic interplay. In fact, you are also aware of this on an unconscious basis, and when you are in the dream state you explore the sub levels of your own universal dimension, which makes you privy to energetic knowing of just what is happening on a multidimensional level. Some individuals in your world are predisposed to such sensitivities, either genetically or through energetic opening, and they often receive information via trance or dream states coming from higher dimensional levels.

Although physical abductions by alien Beings within your own dimension have been known to occur, generally those who feel they have been "abducted" are in fact experiencing inter-dimensional communication, usually taking place through the dreamscape by entering various dimensional sub levels or astral planes in order to do so. It is important here to not conclude that "dreams" are untrue fantasy items, but can actually serve as an open line of communication with the astral state as well as higher realms and dimensions. Naturally, these communications tend to be energetic in nature, but they are no less real than if they were present in your own dimension and standing in front of you.

It is for this reason that any discussion concerning Fifth Dimensional Terra must also include a conversation regarding karmic energetic balancing on a multidimensional level. This is because unfinished business and energetic influences from the Third Universal Dimension can and will appear as situations that must be balanced in the course of Fifth Dimensional existence. As it concerns Terra, naturally these situations become opportunities for growth for Terrans. In understanding this however, bear in mind that Fifth Dimensional Terra may experience such karma differently than you might expect. This is so because, as you will recall, Terrans have a highly developed "sixth sense" and their intuitive abilities combined with the understanding they have related to Soul purpose gives them unique insight into why something is happening. More importantly, their "Super Now" that we discussed gives them the ability to experience or alter their choices immediately. This enables them to have a grasp of the learning experience being offered, which not only allows for a balancing of the karmic energy but gives them the opportunity to maximize the growth derived without the lingering stresses that might accompany a challenging growth opportunity.

In many ways, we cannot discuss the future of Fifth Dimensional Terra without discussing what is also currently transpiring on Third Dimensional Earth. This would be like discussing what is happening on Third Dimensional Earth by only talking about what is happening right now in the United States without including the history of what came before and without including what is going on in other regions of the world. You might be able to do so, but the bigger picture would remain obtuse and your conclusions would have little to no validity in demonstrating what is truly happening.

Suffice to say for now that Third Dimensional Earth, through the interplay of multi-dimensional energetic balancing and the Ascension of

Souls within it who are Ascending to Fifth Dimensional lifetimes, will bring several major opportunities for growth to Fifth Dimensional Terra over the course of the coming several thousand (Terran) years. This will include a large expansion in population and a vast potential change in the societal make up and structure of Terra. In addition, there is the potential for an influx of actual alien Beings on Terra, something that has not occurred until now. While these situations may not have direct correlation, they will combine to alter the fabric of Terran life over the future five to ten thousand Terran years.

Many metaphysical messages being received by sensitive and intuitive individuals on Earth now detail how the Earth is destined to experience a vast galactic awakening soon and at that time will take its place as a member of the galactic family, greeting extraterrestrials and joining interplanetary alliances in the future. We would suggest that such information does not necessarily apply to physical events that will take place on Earth, but rather are mass consciousness and subconscious knowing that is being disseminated within the Third Dimensional Human Angelic psyche. These suggestions act as an unconscious primer for those soon to be experiencing incarnations on Fifth Dimensional Terra.

Thus you may find yourself in a preparatory state for understanding what will transpire on Fifth Dimensional Terra as Ascension takes place and Human Angelics from Third Dimensional Earth migrate to incarnations on Fifth Dimensional Terra. Arriving there these incarnates will meet many of the challenges we are discussing. As we explained, what transpires on Third Dimensional Earth has direct consequence on the energies that will take place on Fifth Dimensional Terra. In a manner of speaking, it is completely appropriate that Souls from Earth who are incarnating on Terra for the first time are the ones destined to meet the energetic links originating from Earth that will become, quite literally, the stuff of Terra's future.

As Terra evolves through the future energetic "battles" between alien invaders and native Terrans, the culmination and outcome of those trials will prove to be harmonic. Moreover, the outcome will permit Fifth Dimensional Terra to take its rightful place in the Galactic family. Communication and alignment that is more vast and greater than anything you can imagine currently on Earth will be the result for Terra and its Human Angelic population. This will in fact enhance the evolution of Fifth Dimensional Terra, and in the Fifth Dimension at that time Human Angelics are poised to become the predominant Soul consciousness in this sector of the Galaxy.

We would like to close this discussion by returning once again to our comparison with the exploration and discovery of new worlds undertaken by Europeans on Third Dimensional Earth several centuries ago. While the native and aboriginal entities had in fact been enjoying highly civilized existences, the karmic energy generated by the ruthless attempt to annihilate the existing native culture remains in need of energetic balancing. Much of this karma will be balanced within the Third Dimension on Earth in the future. However, this karma serves as the origination point of a multi-dimensional karma that expands into the Fifth Dimension. Ultimately it will be experienced by those who originated it in the Third Dimension and who have since gone on to lifetimes in the Fifth Dimension on Terra. Energetic balancing is not as easily escaped as one might wish, neither should it be since its purpose is to harmonize and balance polar energetics that otherwise would cause chaos throughout the realms.

Although the concept of karmic energetic balancing is difficult to understand, particularly from your current view point, in meeting these growth opportunities Fifth Dimensional Terrans will learn the importance of defending and protecting their civilization without the need to violate the rights and integrity of any other culture or civilization (many having done so during lifetimes in the Third Dimension on Earth). In doing so, all participants balance their collective karmic bonds and this will assist them to rise to the vibrational level of those Fifth Dimensional Beings who themselves are ready to cycle off to higher dimensional incarnations. In its wake, these struggles also allow Terra to take its place as part of a Universal Fifth Dimensional Galactic family.

Here we are able to further explain this by providing you with a "what if" question that parallels the future scenario to befall Terra and its new incarnates coming from Earth. What if the Native Americans on Earth, recognizing and seeing the threat of the European and other settlers moving into their regions, had had sufficient consciousness and talent to meet the invaders successfully, and had been able to mingle their civilization with the civilization of the intruders? More importantly, what if the European invaders had respected the rights, cultures and civilizations of the natives, and found ways to peacefully merge the best of both worlds, encouraging and empowering each side in the process? The answer to these questions will be best answered on Terra, where many of the original participants will play out these same scenarios at a higher level of consciousness, awareness and ability within the future of the Fifth Dimension.

Dimensional Turning Points

In many ways, just as you in the Third Universal Dimension find yourselves at a turning point that will effect your world and the future of your world, Fifth Dimensional Terrans simultaneously find themselves at a similar turning point that will have far reaching consequences on their civilization and their way of life. If one were to look at this in a linear manner as we just did, one would certainly see the connection between Third Dimensional reality and reality on Fifth Dimensional Terra. One could even draw the conclusion that there is continuity and wonder if what happens in the Third Dimension always has a major influence on the future of the Fifth Dimension.

This might seem the case following our description of multi-dimensional karma except for one important fact: The Third Dimension does not suddenly vanish from existence and it continues to take place on its own timeline. Those Souls wishing to remain in Third Dimensional incarnations will do so alongside new Souls incarnating on Earth in the Third Dimension for the first time. Inhabitants of the Third Dimension that are harvestable and ready to Ascend and incarnate on Fifth Dimensional Terra, will continue in incarnations on Terra that resonate at a higher level of vibrational integrity, experiencing life lessons that are also of a higher vibrational resonance. In both instances, on Earth and on Terra, new Soul inhabitants bring with them karmic bonds, new goals and new purposes. In a certain sense, the energetic bonds that bind graduates as well.

Such moments of transition are Universal turning points based on the fact that the impetus and content of a dimension is altered substantially as its inhabitants, as well as its energetic bonds and age-old links, become altered. This holds enormous importance with respect to the direction of civilizations within those dimensions, and these are times of great upheaval that is not only related to the Ascension process itself but the fact that the very participants and fabric of the dimension have gone through an evolution and changed. Such times are, in metaphysical terms, known as being the great Universal turning points and it is for this reason that you have heard such times referred to as a "New Age."

The progression and evolution into a New Age might best be understood in much the same way one would consider the progression, as an example, of recent history on Earth. In other words, once on Earth there were tribes; tribes became communities; communities became regions; regions grew to be nations; nations expanded into new areas, colonized them, and so on and so forth. This takes place in a very linear, stable and definite manner.

Now apply this to the progression of higher consciousness, particularly as it relates to the expansion of consciousness requiring higher dimensional physics such as those available on Fifth Dimensional Terra. In this scenario, Terrans, who possess a consciousness far different than your own, suddenly after eons reach a point where a wider Universal vision is required. In its wake, social structures are stressed to their limit and new social structures must be created. The new social structures are obliged to address new incarnates who have different purposes and Soul missions. The influx of Souls and the change in the social structures open the population's field of potentiality to the possible influx of other new Beings into their world. Together with these "other" new Beings comes an array of physical Extraterrian Beings. Through the interaction with Extraterrian Beings, Terrans open to the concept of participating widely in their galaxy and in doing so become part of a galactic family of Fifth Dimensional entities. Ascension in such a case has not only served as an evolutionary powerhouse responsible for raising the vibrational frequency of a universal dimension, it has served as a vehicle for increasing the evolutionary opportunities inherent in the dimension. Those opportunities, challenging or otherwise, allow new Soul inhabitants to continue their evolution and growth as they explore lifetimes within that dimension.

Fifth Dimensional Technologies & Lifestyles

Technology on Fifth Dimensional Terra is far from lacking. However, it is not technology in a sense that you, in your current time and space, would understand or perhaps even appreciate. As an example, there is little to no need for artificial repositories of information such as the Internet and the only communication devices used are those that augment and expand innate natural telepathic abilities. In a world where telepathy is the single most important skill or sense one has, and where students are taught how to tune into energetic banks of mass consciousness and universal information, a far different notion of knowledge and wisdom is possible. On Terra, intrinsic wisdom derived from superior telepathic ability is by far the premier attribute of one's intelligence. In other words, wisdom, as the preeminent component of one's intuitive ability, begets greater intuition and foresight, which are considered the most valuable achievements a student can obtain.

In many ways, the technologies currently being discovered and used on Third Dimensional Earth serve as artificial tools fostering familiarity with technique as well as a precursor to what will be genetically inherent and strived for during incarnations on Fifth Dimensional Terra. Many reading this might assume from that technology on Fifth Dimensional Terra is more or less the same as what will ultimately exist on future Third Dimensional Earth. This is not the case, and Third Dimensional Human attributes will not suddenly be on par with inherent Fifth Dimensional genetic abilities or time-space physics. However, there is a certain significance found in the fact that those Ascended Human Angelics who have graduated to Fifth Dimensional reality will at the least have familiarity with many of the principals that are inherent in the nature of Fifth Density life as a result of the currently reemerging technologies being employed on Third Dimensional Earth.

That however, is where similarities end. As we have said, Fifth Dimensional Terra has been in existence simultaneously with Third Dimensional Earth for eons of time, and the current Terran civilization is better recognized and known throughout the Galaxy than the current Third Dimensional Earth civilization, which in the scheme of things has a very short and inconsequential existence.

Of course, we do not wish to discount the ancient technologically advanced civilizations of Earth that existed for hundreds of thousands of years before the modern era, such as those known as Atlantis, or the civilization of Lemuria on the continent of Mu, as examples. We are discussing here Earth's modern era, which most consider to have begun approximately 10,000 years ago, if not later.

Advanced technology does exist on Terra, particularly as it regards sacred geometry, dimensional physics and universal physical structure, all of which far surpass anything today's Third Dimensional Earth scholars even dream of discovering. It is the Terrans that will enable Human Angelics to enter into and cooperate with a Galactic family in ways that currently are only hinted at in limited manner in your current science fiction and metaphysical understanding.

Terrans have long understood the ways in which their world is part of a greater galaxy and Universe. They further understand that the galaxies and solar systems are all traveling through space and time in a dimensional fold, each with significant populations and Beings existing not only at different ends of the Universe but also intertwined and dimensionally overlapped. Terrans are vaguely aware of Third Dimensional Earth and its civilizations in much the same way you are vaguely aware that there are other cultures and people on different sides of the planet from you that you are not familiar with and with whom you have little to no concern. For instance, you might assume there is a small band of nomads somewhere in Mongolia, but you probably can not picture their location, their faces, their numbers, their flocks or their tents, and probably you have no real need to know more than the fact that they are out there somewhere (we are not speaking here of the scholars in certain fields who make such peoples or things the focus of their pursuit, but everyday people in your world).

The truth be told, Terrans find the limited and primitive vibrational sensations associated with lower dimensions to be dull (in the sense of muted) and uninteresting, and thanks to natural dimensional divides are not much interested in exploring these further. Think of this in the same way you might think of the life of the ant population or of a forest in some distant region not related to you. Although you might take an interest from afar and despite the fact that there are some who would seek to know more about these creatures, you probably have little or no desire to become a tree or an ant in a particular forest that is unknown to you in order to do so. More importantly it certainly is not possible for you to live among them -- as one of them -- to experience their lives.

Technologically and culturally, Terrans do not have a need for many of the things you think of as fundamental to existence in your world that you strive to achieve. A primary part of the social makeup of Third Dimensional Earth incarnations is each individual's need to meet basic requirements for survival. Originally, Source and incarnated Souls intended the survival mechanism to serve as a biological protective device as well as a means of creating additional opportunities for entity growth. This would be a natural byproduct of the need to work in relationship with others to survive, thereby creating familial, communal and other structures that would ensure interaction with each other and provide situations and scenarios for energetic exchange (karma),

Soul growth and development.

However, in your modern societies on Earth over the past 10,000 years, this biological mechanism was hijacked and placed on steroids, morphing into the solitary and difficult struggle to survive that you currently see in effect today. Such social systems become heavily skewed towards self-preservation, and the constant need to ensure that fundamental basics are met means that all other pursuits, spiritual or otherwise, must take a back seat. We would suggest that such systems were not naturally evolved but invented for this precise reason as a population and crowd control mechanism, and again would hint towards those leaders of the systems that have affiliations or are directly incarnated from alien Soul populations. Any group overly concerned with day-to-day survival, triggering a biological survival mechanism placed on highest alert, has little time or ability to pursue spiritual or other developmental exercises that are not survival oriented, socially functional or procedurally (dogma) based.

The hijacked biological system found on Third Dimensional Earth is not only unknown on Fifth Dimensional Terra, it would be ineffective and such conditioning would be frowned upon. We would go as far as to say that certain circles on Terra would laugh at or find absurd any structure, social or otherwise, that allowed want or disparity between individuals or segments of the population. Terrans do not believe in or perceive distinctions such as class, race, economic status or any social distinction other than the difference in levels of one's consciousness, ability to master emotions and thought processes and intuitive abilities. These considerations are thought to bring wisdom, peace and satisfaction, and they not only form the basis of successfully achieving personal and societal goals, they are the foundation of Terran thought and social structure.

On Terra the degree to which one masters one's psychic skills and intuitively syncs with the collective consciousness, one's guides and one's Higher Self (Soul) are by far the ideal standards for success. The accumulation of specific riches or materials that ensure survival are wholly unnecessary, and such things are not sought after in a society that makes the fundamentals of survival uniformly available through cooperation with preservation of individuality as a central departure point in doing so.

Terrans have the utmost love, respect and compassion for each other since they are privy to each individual's life (Soul) purpose. Their goal is to provide the landscape to allow the individual to explore their life purpose and excel. Such sponsorship ultimately ensures benefits for all, since Fifth Dimensional Terrans are heart centered and are incapable of emotions around issues such as envy, pride or greed, lessons chosen by many Souls that predominate in Third Dimensional lifetimes.

Thus Terrans have great admiration for each other and they make every attempt to support the endeavors, spiritually and physically, of each individual. The difference between the admiration for "celebrities" seen on Earth, including the attempt of each individual to become celebrated, and what is seen as admiration for an individual on Terra is that on Terra such admiration is not ego driven or a byproduct of a prideful lesson needing to be experienced for energetic reasons. In fact, Terran "celebrity" status, if there were such a thing, would be reserved for those who achieve great wisdom and mastery of their emotions, the time-wave Super Now experience and their intuitive skills. These are ultimately the measures by which one's life is deemed successful or one is found to be talented in Terran society.

Though technologically advanced, technology is far less intrusive in Terran society then you would expect, and technology holds no real power over Terrans. In most cases, technology on Terra is metaphysical in nature and somewhat hidden from view, so you might assume they were a primitive people if you did not realize how advanced their technology and innate talents make them. This is probably due to the fact that Terran technology is less "device" or machinery driven, and really advanced technology in the Fifth Dimension is more concerned with quantum energetics, particularly that which is inter-dimensionally based.

Terran science is based on taking advantage of universal structure by augmenting naturally existing energetics and phenomenon and merely providing links and directions for harnessing what already exists. This further gives each Terran the ability to mingle and utilize higher sciences in combination with altered states of consciousness for their highest good. As an example of this, in the Third Dimension you have an artificial repository of information you refer to as the Internet, or the World Wide Web. Information, knowledge and communication are placed thereby individuals such as you, and the knowledge is accessible via technological devices or other means.

Now what if you discovered that such a repository already existed energetically in a dimensional fold and was a natural field of consciousness? What if you knew that it contained far more than merely segments of information selectively placed and stored there, much of which is more than likely false and erroneous information or outright propaganda. What if this natural field contained all true knowledge and experience gathered from all time? In such a case, wouldn't your scientific or technological objective be to find the energetic means (a road map) to access and navigate such an existing energetic consciousness bank?

Now take this one step further remembering that Fifth Dimensional Terrans have innate abilities that allow them to access higher states of consciousness and inter-dimensional energies. In that instance, all that would be needed technologically speaking would be a method or "technique" for exploring and tapping into the system naturally using your own abilities, in a sense riding the wave and augmenting what already exists. In just such a way Terran technology, and science for that matter, is more related to exploration, discovery, augmentation and harvesting of existing natural universal systems and far less related to the invention of machinery or new technical devices as is the case on Third Density Earth.

Even so, Terrans consider themselves to be talented inter-dimensional engineers, and they excel at engineering methods to explore and exploit natural phenomenon using naturally occurring universal systems, physics and techniques. Think of this as a method or standard of reasoning that Terrans have developed very successfully over time.

Working with higher energetics is not without purpose, and at this time due to the Ascension energies being felt on Third Dimensional Earth many are seeing glimpses of what life will be like on Fifth Dimensional Terra when they begin incarnations at a higher dimensional level. Imagine what your world would be like if each decision you made truly was guided by your higher intuition for your highest Soul good. Imagine further what life would be like if it was based on providing you and your loved ones with your ultimate purpose and mission in life, not in terms of riches, accumulation or survival but in terms of situations and opportunities, even challenges, that would best assist you to meet the objectives outlined by you and your Soul for the lifetime. Life on Third Dimensional Earth would be far less confusing and probably significantly different.

Although you see pockets of this beginning to appear on Earth, at least with respect to attempts to spiritually know yourself and follow the path of least resistance to discover your ultimate purpose, it is far from what is experienced on Terra. In many cases on Earth, individuals are misled by erroneous dogma or fundamentalist belief, substituting these for the prior societal structures that obliged one to focus on surviving in the world. Such substitutions do nothing to address the real issue and most individuals will be disillusioned by their choices. In these cases dogma and strict adherence to man-made beliefs merely substitute as the main commodity needed to satisfy the basic human needs. The ego's survival instinct is no less triggered and the ego rather than the individual's "Essence" dominates the person's Life Path on Earth (See Discovering Your Essence Path, Book One and Book Two).

We caution you therefore, not to merely exchange one standard, monetary or economic, for another that measures your spirituality via adherence to a religious or spiritual dogma. Furthermore, one should approach individuals or organizations stating that they have found the new "ideal" with care. More often than not, those you consider the most caring, spiritual, compassionate and concerned about your future on Third Dimensional Earth are often the very ones that would prefer you be bound by social structures led by them, or in a system that keeps you enslaved by the very attributes, standards, riches and things you are trying to escape. Certainly, fighting to secure such things be they made of gold or a place in a golden Heaven, elicits the very survival response under discussion, and such anxiety creates distraction that will keep you from finding true inner peace through the understanding of your purpose.

In many cases the leaders that will prove the most manipulative are the very ones that call for rules to protect the collective good and this is often a disarming mask that directs individuals into misguided judgment. Of course, on Third Dimensional Earth even these situations have their place, and we have already mentioned how such things can generate challenges that serve as opportunities for individual and group growth. Individuals facing such events are forced to decipher truth from falsehood and in the process will learn to be discriminating. As we have said before however, these opportunities are approached through the negative polarity and as a result will be challenging. In addition, we would suggest that those leading you into such misguided opportunities do not have your best interest at heart, and tend to be humans incarnated from Souls that are either Service-to-Self oriented or are not Human Angelic in origin.

Planetary Electromagnetic Grids and the Infrastructure of Universal Dimensions

We have spoken many times in the past about how Ascension is an evolutionary process that occurs inter-dimensionally. This is a universal truth. In your own world you spend a great deal of time deciphering your organic origins and the origins and evolution of other species on your planet. But what you do not consider is that the most dramatic changes occur from dimension to dimension, particularly with regards to the evolution of a species as it moves into higher dimensional realms.

For example, we discussed how much of the technology you enjoy on Third Dimensional Earth is rendered obsolete on Fifth Dimensional Terra. This is because the technological devices you find so fascinating in Third Density actually become part of the genetic makeup of Human Angelics in the Fifth Dimension. It is unnecessary to utilize electronic devices to communicate with others in a world where your innate telepathic capabilities give you the same faculties. To communicate on Terra, individuals merely direct their thoughts to the individual of their choosing, energetically "tuning in" to their vibrational signature and, via thought form, energetically impress their message on a recipient's energetic field.

Where difficulties may be said to arise on Fifth Dimensional Terra is with respect to the incentive to expand one's horizons or look outside of one's immediate environment. On Terra, there is a strong adherence to familiarity and to remaining with those Souls that are known to you and to those with whom you have strong connection. Because Terrans know their life purpose and incarnate with those that can provide the means for this to be accomplished easily, there is little need to "seek" life events outside of one's own community or region. This is further complicated by the fact that through their senses, Terrans have access to all natural banks of knowledge and they can communicate or have experiences with others as if they were present, even if whomever they are corresponding with is on the other side of the planet. Moreover, this can be accomplished without ever leaving their local community, or even their home if they choose.

In Third Dimensional reality on the other hand, one is forever pursuing new horizons and pretending to oneself that the best experiences are those first-hand opportunities that exist in other parts of the world that can only be lived via personal experience with new events and new individuals. On Earth, there is an impetus that exists that causes one to seek out one's life purpose, and many individuals will travel great lengths to do so. Now in reality, almost everyone incarnated on Third Dimensional Earth has pre-contracted with and pre-arranged meetings and life events with those known to them at a Soul level. Should they meet during the lifetime, if both are still willing and use their free will to allow the opportunity to unfold, they will experience these opportunities in order to gain maximum growth potential in the lifetime. Due to the nature of incarnation in Third Density however, it is possible that the individuals with whom you have pre-arranged events may live at great distance, in other communities or even in other parts of the world. On Earth, this creates an inordinate drive to constantly move about in an effort to expand your horizons.

On Terra however, one is already aware of one's life purpose and has incarnated within the community that will provide one with the events and individuals necessary to undertake your journey. The planning of one's lifetime on Terra is done at a Soul level in close union with other Ascended Human Angelics. For the most part Terrans have no real reason to look to new horizons or far off distances. Already surrounded by the individuals and life opportunities needed to make their lives successful, Terrans would not be inspired to look any further. On Earth however, you might spend a lifetime looking far and wide to discover these same things using whatever means were at your disposal and going to the far corners of the world to do so.

Additionally, because Terrans are satisfied with their understanding of what their higher purpose is, life there is not as haphazard and disorganized as it can sometimes seem on Third Dimensional Earth. Terrans are not prone to seeking and are content to experience life standing in place. This is a fundamental difference, one that, as we have already discussed, represents a coming major turning point that will alter life on Terra. In its wake Terrans will open to new growth opportunities with respect to concepts such as dislocation, abandonment, expansion and inclusiveness.

Let us return for a moment to our discussion of technology, particularly the fact that much of the new technology you consider imperative to your daily life today is actually being experienced in the Third Dimension in order to familiarize you with inherent abilities you will have in the Fifth Dimension. As we have demonstrated, the use of such instantaneous communication techniques as texting, emailing and, to an extent, communication by voice and images across great distances are in fact all a prerequisite for learning that such possibilities for communicating exist. This is only one step away from understanding that you will have no need of a device or mechanical technique to do essentially the same thing when you are predisposed genetically to communicating via the electromagnetic and energetic grids that exist within and around each dimensional layer.

It would be helpful here if we discussed galactic and planetary electromagnetic grids, which do, in a certain sense, define and serve as boundaries for dimensional time and space. It is through these grids that electromagnetic information and light in the form of energy is transferred both within a particular dimension and inter-dimensionally. Naturally, the grid's structure, capacity and mechanism exist in concert and harmony with the physical properties inherent in a particular dimension as well as certain universal properties that may not be as apparent depending upon the dimension.

All that is existent as well as all that is possible within a dimension is contained within and relayed back and forth via electromagnetic grid systems to sublevels and to higher and lower dimensions. In a sense you could see this as the infrastructure of the Universe, and the metaphor of how a high-rise building is framed would be a good example. Imagine, if you will, that in constructing a skyscraper, one lays the groundwork by creating a steel infrastructure or skeleton upon which one is able to hang the pieces of the building. One places a roof upon the structure and defines its exterior limits. Then windows, doors and other attributes are placed within the infrastructure, and so on and so forth with the building taking shape and form continually and infinitely within the context of the infrastructure. Imagine that inhabitants are brought into the structure to function and carry on daily living within its confines. Now imagine that without much change to the infrastructure, upon which so much "hangs" and depends, the attributes, façade, interior mechanicals, partitions and decoration are constantly being renovated and altered as people come and go for generations and as time marches onward.

In a way, the Universe and its dimensions are constructed in a similar fashion, with the only difference being that each electromagnetic grid system is contained within another, each being overlapped above and below by additional invisible layers. In other words, because the grid structure does not have physical mass as you know it, a new and independent "building" is able to be constructed within the same space that overlaps the prior one, with each layer remaining completely intact and independent, but also interdependent one upon the other. It is the electromagnetic grid -- the steel skeleton in our metaphor -- that tends to serve as dimensional definition or boundary. This grid expands and enhances itself at several intersections and intersperses each dimensional level retaining integrity but having affinity and connection to other dimensional grids. This creates dimensional infrastructure that has independent time and space, but also ensures a kind of inter dimensional union. The result is a connected, ever expanding and infinite universal basis.

It is via the portals, as we have termed them, of these electromagnetic grids that energy, including the energy of the Soul, flows back and forth between multi-dimensional levels. This then becomes the starting point and key to anyone interested in passing from dimension to dimension. This is done via the inter-dimensional electromagnetic grid systems that contain the structure of the particular dimension as well as access and connection to related dimensions.

Dimensions are nested, one in side of the other and, like our building analogy, exist in unison with each other with one skeleton built around another then another and another and so on and so forth until the pinnacle is finally reached. Communicating from higher to lower dimensional grids is far easier than communicating from lower to higher dimensional levels, just as it is perhaps easier for one to jump from the second to the first floor than it is to jump from the first to the second story. The flow of energy coming from Source generally follows from higher to lower resonance, and this tends to be a fundamental of Universal structure in much the same way water flows from higher to lower points in the Third Dimension.

Note that this is despite the fact that technologies do exist to counter such natural universal flow, allowing energy, or water for that matter, to flow from lower to higher levels, at least on a limited basis. Likewise, inter-dimensional technologies do exist that allow some Fifth Dimensional Beings to physically pass back and forth unimpeded between connected or closely associated dimensions. As we have said, this is the basis of limited alien contact on Third Dimensional Earth.

It is the electromagnetic structure that allows each dimension to have access to an energetic form of mass consciousness, essentially an information bank related to that dimension. It also provides those Beings that have either understood the quantum physics or who are ready to do so to pass from one dimensional grid to the next.

As Earthlings, although you tend to be earthcentric and have few actual Third Dimensional visitors from your Galaxy, you are never truly alone. Terrans are not alone in the Galaxy either, and it is the destiny of Terra to learn that lesson after the dawn of this Ascension period. Over millennia Terrans have become isolated in terms of their learning experience via a social order that effectively shuts them off from Galactic experience.

While Terra and a lifetime there might sound perfect to you, it is nonetheless limiting in terms of opportunities for Soul growth and advancement. Thus, the alien invasion that will be occurring on Fifth Dimensional Terra in the future will not only balance inter-dimensional karma for new incarnates coming from Earth, it will generate invaluable lessons for those Terrans cycling off incarnations on Terra and Ascending to Sixth and Seventh Dimensional lifetimes. This parallels what is occurring on Second and Third Dimensional Earth, where events will serve as lessons and prerequisites for understanding what life will be like once you have Ascended to a Fifth Dimensional world.

The Originations and Developments of Human Angelic Soul Matrixes

Our discussion of Fifth Dimensional Terra, Third Dimensional Earth and even Seventh Dimensional Gaia for that matter would not be complete without an explanation related to Human Angelic Soul origination. Because you are focused within physical bodies in the third sublevel of the Third Universal Dimension it is easy to forget your inter-connectedness with your Soul matrix and the links you have energetically to other Soul cadres, your "brethren" if you will.

In most cases, as you Ascend through the universal dimensions, you arrive sooner or later at a level of consciousness that allows you to embark on the revelation that you are part of a greater entity, not only genetically in terms of your connection to a physical species but spiritually in terms of the awareness that you are an extension of your Soul, and your Soul is an extension of the Soul matrix from which it was originally cast.

We will not in this short space be able to accurately explore with you the origination of all Souls, be they Human Angelic or otherwise. In making that statement we certainly hope it is understood that we do not wish to imply any inequality in Soul origination or Universal Soul type, just as human race has no validity in terms of equality or separation, other than for those Soul matrices that derive particular satisfaction utilizing one Human Angelic race over another for growth purposes. If we have limited our discussion here and in this material to Human Angelic Soul matrices, it is because the majority of those attracted to this information and reading this book will discover that Human Anglics and Service-to-Others tend to be their true nature and Soul origin.

Suffice to say however, that all Souls originate from Source and Source is embodied, as we have said, principally in the unified dimensional trilogy known as the Tenth, Eleventh and Twelfth Universal Dimensions. Despite this statement, the true beginning of all creation in the Universe and within all universal dimensions finds its origins in the Twelfth Universal Dimension, the domain of All That Is, God if you prefer.

There is an outpouring and flow of creative energy from this higher universal dimension, which ultimately becomes the "spark" that ignites creation. The God Force or Center Source, All That Is as it is most appropriately known, gives forth of itself in the creation of Soul entities, and these are the matrices that populate the higher universal dimensions. These Soul entities existing in the highest angelic realms, many of who are considered "sons and daughters" of God, are in turn imbued or "commissioned" with the desire to create like-Beings cast into lower fields of vibrational resonance from their energetic Source.

These created offspring are holographic in as much as they are a multidimensional reflection of their Soul matrix at a lower dimensional and vibrational resonance. Yet what is cast out and created is also independent, with the ability to reflect back to their Soul matrix the essence of their experiences. Soul matrix energy originating from the highest Source is the substance that animates its creation, now incarnated physical Beings, into existence and polarity, together with electromagnetic spin, magnetizes the particles of mass into existence, attracting what you consider reality to the thoughts and desires of each Being. This is the dance of life.

Meanwhile, the unique consciousness and experience of the created Being is looped back to the originating Soul matrix, until such time as its consciousness reunites and reincorporates with the Soul and, ultimately, the God Source through all eternity. What you know as reincarnational selves are actually independent lifetimes cast out at different points on the dimensional time wave (without adherence to linear time flow) from either your Soul matrix or from you in order to balance consciousness via energetic and emotional discharge. These reincarnational selves are "you" in as much as they are formed from the same energy that animates you. Some will go on to grow in consciousness and Ascend themselves, while some are immediately incorporated into your experience prior to Ascension into a higher universal dimension.

Although each dimensional Being has life force that originates from a Soul matrix out of which it was cast, each also has independent consciousness that continues on infinitely, Ascending through the evolutionary process of the Universe until it has returned to its Soul Source. As part of this process, all experience and consciousness is constantly and instantaneously shared with the Soul matrix, which then influences new life creations necessary to balance and harmonize its energies.

Souls cast out together at the highest angelic levels form a cadre of Souls, and these cadres tend to cast out Beings into lower dimensional existence in unison. It is for this reason that you will find familiarity with some, and it is among Soul cadres that contracts and agreements are made concerning the planning of a particular lifetime. Those Beings that are in life with you and come from a Soul cadre known to your Soul matrix are considered to be your Soul Twins, Soul Mates and Soul Task Mates. In most cases, Soul cadres cooperate closely in the act of creation in order to assist the developmental and learning experiences of the many Beings they spawn, and it is not uncommon for you to experience a multitude of lifetimes with those you know well at a Soul level from dimension to dimension.

The process of dimensional Ascension complete, a Being along with its experiential consciousness reaches the level of its originating Soul matrix and is welcomed back as a Prodigal son that has endured a long journey and is now ready to once again be integrated back into the energy that is its Creator, the God Source. Once it has returned to its originator after a journey of eons, even fully integrated back into Source your consciousness has reached the point that it will remain forever eternal, as a cell in the mind of God, All That Is.

In the physical realms, procreation is a fundamental mechanism of the Universe, and in an odd sense you and others in your Soul matrix in lower dimensions become genetically responsible for creating the actual physical vehicles (bodies) that might someday house your own past or future consciousness. Cellular memory and communication, as well as the holographic nature of cellular structure, is one of the greatest unexplored sciences of your world, and it should be known that much could be said concerning the concept that there is genetic and cellular memory. For Human Angelic Souls, your great, great, great, great grandparents are as present in you now as you will be in future generations. Far from being related to just genetic predisposition, these are the real ghosts in the "machine" that is, essentially, you.

The spawning of new life therefore is a creative principle that applies to the physical body as well as the mental, spiritual and energetic body, not to mention Mass Consciousness and individual consciousness expansion. Viewed this way, procreation rather than life itself is the divine mechanism, and though it is never obligatory or even necessary for an entity to participate in or fuel this mechanism, it is nonetheless the method of expansion for whole planetary systems and galaxies as well as almost all life forms existing within those structures. This is particularly true in lower universal dimensions up to the Eighth dimension. Beginning in the Eighth dimension and particularly in the Ninth and higher dimensions, physical existence becomes ethereal in nature and a physical body is no longer required as part of a Being's life or Ascension process.

For the most part, different sectors and areas of creation and life within various universal dimensions exist in order to provide a destination point for the incarnation of Beings that are pushed forward from Source into first Soul and then physical form. In that regard the Third Universal Dimension in which you currently reside is no different than Fifth Dimensional Terra or for that matter Seventh Dimensional Gaia; all of which overlap within the same space but at a different vibrational frequency and dimensional grid.

Thus a Soul species has a specific place within each dimension, and this place generally is reserved for Soul incarnations to occur. In the case of Human Angelics that place is Earth, as well as Earth's dimensional cousins existing from the First through Eighth Dimensions. As we have said in the past, it is possible for Beings from different Soul originations to incarnate in various physical forms, with the form most closely associated with Human Angelics currently being the human physical form. However, physical form does not necessarily make one's origins Human Angelic. We have mentioned already that many physical humans currently incarnated in the Third Dimensional realm side by side with you are part of a bio-invasion of Earth via genetically modified human forms and alien Soul origins. These are not Human Angelic Beings nor are these Souls aligned with Service-to-Other orientation, as all Human Angelic Souls are apt to be. Orientation is a prerequisite and fundamental basis created when Soul matrices are first cast out and created by the God Source, All That Is.

Fifth Dimensional Terra is different from Third Dimensional Earth primarily because the sensory attributes available to individuals, combined with the higher vibrational frequency and Fifth Dimensional space-time wave, permits those born there to easily access and naturally utilize that system's electromagnetic grid. Due to this they are able to intuitively recognize and understand their Soul affiliations and the purpose of their incarnation. On Fifth Dimensional Terra, who is who and what they are all about at a Soul level is as immediate and present in your knowledge as it is unspoken.

There is no unintended masquerading or deception on Terra as there can often be on Third Dimensional Earth. It is principally because of this that Terrans have tended to isolate themselves galactically, since although still available and possible such access to Soul information outside of Human Angelic Soul matrices can be more problematic, and in some cases alien Soul matrices do have methods to deceive Terrans if they choose. At the least, they are able to prevent immediate access to their purpose and intent via their Soul information. More likely than not, in terms of their Soul purpose many alien Soul species in the Fifth Dimension do not necessarily have good intentions towards Human Angelics and others (based on their orientation and polarity), so even with the ability to intuitively access their purpose, you might simply be registering that their purpose is malevolent towards you.

This is not the case on Third Dimensional Earth where Soul origination and purpose is far from apparent. What we are attempting to show here however is that not only is there a karmic balancing from each individual entity in either the Third or Fifth Dimension, there is also balancing that is cultural, galactic and even species oriented. Do not be confused into thinking that Human Angelic is this or that physical race or even the same species when in physical incarnation. Nor is it accurate to think that Human Angelic incarnates will always look like you. Much confusion surrounds this, and it is for this reason that certain ancient religious thought erroneously states that Human Angelic Souls can reincarnate into a myriad of species, including animals and insects. This is not the case, and although Human Angelics are likely to incarnate into altered humanoid form generally, in the past and again in the future they have taken on many different genetic forms, most of which would probably be recognizable to you but certainly would be different than you from one universal level to another.

We would go as far as to state that the concept you have of "angels" does in fact correlate to Human Angelic Soul Matrices origination. In many cases, what you would describe as an Arc Angel or Seraphim is in fact a depiction of Human Angelics at the highest dimensional levels. It is also important to understand that Human Angelic Souls are not necessarily individualized in the sense of one individual Soul spread across millions and millions of incarnations and Beings in various dimensions. Instead, the Soul matrix of which you are part represents a group of Souls acting as one, pouring their creative force throughout various universal dimensions.

As a possible example, on Third Dimensional Earth, you might spend one lifetime focused at a specific point on the space-time wave for that dimension. Furthermore, you might be related to a Human Angelic Soul matrix from a higher universal dimension that provides you with your core Soul connection originating from a Soul matrix that provides you with the energetic spark that enables your physical Being to have meaning. The same Soul might be a member of a Soul matrix that provides life spark to members of your family or your community, and other members of that matrix may in turn spawn many of your relatives, community members. In addition, it should not be forgotten that the Soul from which you originate, that is a Soul in the Soul matrix of Human Angelic Souls related to you also might have several other incarnations overlapping or happening at the same time as your own within the Second, Third or perhaps the Fifth or even Seventh Dimension. Further down the line, the Matrix of which your Soul is a member is also part of a larger cadre of Souls, with cadres of Souls spawning the physical incarnates of a race, a nation, a continent or even an entire world.

Many of these lives, particularly those known to you in the lifetime, are in fact your closest relations not only in the current lifetime, but also from a Soul perspective. Often, whole families may be comprised of individuals closely related to one Soul or a Soul Matrix. On the other hand, sometimes a Soul matrix will populate different individuals a continent apart, knowing that at some point these Soul kindred spirits will have occasion to meet. This is why you might meet an individual from another community, culture or continent and feel certain that there is a connection and they are known to you. In fact they are "family," even if biologically they are not.

Once one moves into incarnations on Terra, it becomes clear that with every individual encountered, the most immediate question to consider is how this person is connected to you from a Soul perspective. The answer to this is twofold. First of all those entities, like you, are experiencing physical life for an independent growth purpose related to your own choosing. Secondly however, as a member of a Soul Matrix and family, your experiences are also intended to benefit the growth of your Soul Matrix family. What this means, as we have often said, is that you exist at a multidimensional level. You are a member of a Soul family but you are also poised to create you own Soul family in time, with ties to other Soul Matrices. Just as you have multi generations of families living and working together, so too your Soul Matrix works this way and as the creative force passes through you, you become the progenitor of your own Soul Matrix.

In other words, you have parents and grandparents, who gave you life, advised you and sheltered you until such time, having grown themselves in experience, they move on and it becomes your turn to procreate and continue the process of evolution. As we have detailed for you already, this process known to you in physical life is also quite literally a higher universal and spiritual function. Just as the highest Angelic Human Soul Matrices spawn offspring from who they learn much, they grow and ultimately Ascend to rejoin their creator. As they do, you follow in their footsteps both physically as well as metaphysically.

The Universe is aligned in this manner not only to provide for continuous expansion but also in order to insure continuity and cooperation. It is the awareness you will have in the Fifth Dimension that begins to make this process and connection relevant to you. On Terra, it is the known and felt connections to your Soul matrix, the consciousness and awareness you have developed and your genetic predispositions and continuity that provide you with the more interesting and relevant experiences Fifth Dimensional Terra has to offer.

While there will always be a Third Dimensional Earth with Human Angelic Soul incarnates, the current conflict within your realm between Human Angelics and those attempting to subvert the planet via the bio-hybrid invasion we have discussed is well underway. If you wish to call it war, you are well within your right to do so. However, from our greater perspective we see this as the basis and precursor for many of the issues that will be worked out karmically and otherwise by Human Angelics during the course of the future of Fifth Dimensional Terra.

We have attempted therefore, in the context of the story of both Third Dimensional Earth and Fifth Dimensional Terra to not only show you the connections that exist but hopefully to demonstrate that you have a future in higher dimensional realms. When Third Dimensional Earth has reached a point where Human Angelic Souls are unable to incarnate in the hybrid human physical vehicle being created, Earth itself will bring the matter to a close. Out of such calamity, reemergence is possible and a great renaissance for the Human Angelic Soul species on Earth will begin.

We would suggest that you not be overly concerned with the future fate of Universal Third Dimensional Earth. As a Human Angelic Soul, if that is what you are, your focus by that time will be on your destiny, the destiny of your family and compatriots and the destiny of Fifth Dimensional Terra. Even now in the current physical lifetime on Earth, as you gain consciousness and enlightenment you will find more and more that you have lost interest. What you see transpiring around you and happening in the News on a Third Dimensional Earth in turmoil will seem like an absurd and distant dream. This tendency will increase until at some point the myriad of events happening in your world hold no further interest for you. It is then that you will realize you are in fact poised to grow and evolve to a higher dimensional resonance through the universal process of Ascension.

Chapter 17
A Parting Word About
Possible and Probable Futures

We have taken great pains to describe what occurs on Terra in the Fifth Dimension not as an antidote to Third Dimensional Earth's future but to inspire in you the desire to raise your consciousness through intention and Ascend to incarnations in a Fifth Dimensional resonance. Many will ask if it is possible to change the events we have described on the Third Dimensional timeline. Such a possibility must always be entertained for as you have come to know by now, all time is happening simultaneously, is malleable and is changeable.

What we have provided you with in this book therefore, is the probable future based on the current trajectory of mass consciousness, mass desire and karmic need. This includes those growth opportunities needed individually and those opportunities necessary for the advancement of not only your world as a whole but in a multidimensional sense the worlds and dimensions that are interconnected with your own.

You will find that Third Dimensional Earth remains as relevant and vibrant in the future as it is now and has always been. It will continue to be relevant and vibrant even after the current culture, civilization and society, which you know and enjoy, are extinct and long forgotten. In fact, as we have described many times, extinction of other cultures and civilizations has occurred on Third Dimensional Earth many times before this. For example, as we described there were times when the Third and Fourth Dimensions were linked harmoniously with the Fourth Dimension visible within the Third Dimension. There were also times when Fourth Dimensional civilizations exerted dominance and control over Third Dimensional Earth as well as times when Higher Dimensional civilizations such as these fell to lower dimensional and vibrational status.

It could be said that in times yet to be experienced on the future timeline, some Fifth Dimensional attributes and sensory talents may emerge and become existent in Beings still incarnated on Third Dimensional Earth. Though limited in nature and available to select Human Angelics through mutations in the DNA (such as those known in Indigos), the greatest portion of these will result from the higher energies entering the Third Dimension at this time of Ascension. Having or witnessing these Fifth Dimensional sensory attributes around you affirms that you are in an evolutionary state and that you have a strong inter-dimensional connection.

The probable events that we have described and are seen on the current timeline trajectory for Third Dimensional Earth are perhaps not pleasant to hear. However, the prospect that these events will be encountered, rectified and energetically balanced on Fifth Dimensional Terra means substantial and important progress for the Human Angelic Soul species. This is not to say that Human Beings are not having lifetimes with distinct beginnings and ends, nor should it imply that they migrate miraculously while still in physical form from one dimension to the next. It simply demonstrates that Human Angelic Soul Matrices are present and continuing to evolve from dimension to dimension in this sector of the Universe.

Interestingly enough, the mass populace of Human Angelic Soul incarnates linger currently in lifetimes being experienced between the Third and Seventh Dimensions. It is therefore important to note that the current Ascension from Third to Fifth Dimensional existence is an important one for Human Angelic Soul Matrices as well as for the Universe as a whole. It is also important to understand that for the most part once a Soul casts out lifetimes into lower dimensions it tends to prefer Ascension into realms that are interconnected and related. Thus Ascension from Third Dimensional Earth to Fifth Dimensional Terra is a natural progression and evolution for an Ascending Human Angelic Soul.

You are at a pivotal time in the destiny of the Human Angelic species in a variety of dimensions, but particularly on Third Dimensional Earth and Fifth Dimensional Terra. Hopefully we have impressed upon you the fact that Earth is destined to remain the planet for incarnation by Human Angelic Souls, despite infiltration by other alien Soul Matrices with the intention of populating your region of the Galaxy. Most, if not all, of these alien Soul Matrices are diametrically opposed to the natural orientation of Human Angelics, which are almost exclusively Service-to-Others Soul Matrices.

This is an important fact for what could be surmised by these events is that the ancient Human Angelic Soul species has now Ascended, to a greater or lessor degree, to the point where ultimately Third Dimensional incarnations are no longer useful for them. That is to say that it would be easy to assume that once a certain Soul species has evolved and Ascended to the point that incarnation is not necessary in a certain dimension the dimensional level in question becomes open to colonization by other Soul Matrices and Soul Species. But this is not always the case and as we have said, specific universal regions are generally reserved as the homeland for certain Soul Species regardless of dimensional level. Your sector of the Galaxy, including other dimensional versions of Earth, is reserved for Human Angelic incarnation. Such a situation can evolve, and alien Souls can participate with you and even incarnate on the planet with you (albeit with some difficulty in the Third Dimension), but the planet itself will always remain the guardian of a specific Soul Species.

Because of universal dynamics, it is conceivable that an entire Soul Species might abandon a certain dimensional level through its Ascension into higher realms. We would suggest however, that Third Dimensional Earth is far from such an event even though in the short term there is an effort underway, through genetic and environmental manipulation, to create the inability for future Human Angelics to incarnate on Third Dimensional Earth.

If you are reading this there is a high potentiality that you are at a level of evolution that ensures your own Ascension to higher dimensional realms. It is with that in mind that we have penned this particular book assisting you to understand that the dominant timeline trajectory of Third Dimensional Earth and the events that will befall it should not concern you or your descendants. Dire though they may sound, in all likelihood you will find yourselves experiencing the Ascension process and evolving to a higher dimension at some point over the course of the coming 500-year period on Earth.

Because of this, many of you might consider Fifth Dimensional Terra to be the future of Third Dimensional Earth. This, however, is not accurate. It must be understood that each of the trajectories and events that we have described exists in a dimensional vibration that is distinctly different and removed one from the other. One is not the future of the other, and one does not suddenly turn into the other, which is currently a popular notion. Although the period heralds the evolution and Ascension of the dimension through a natural collapse and simultaneous reemergence of the space-time wave that composes it, each dimension still retains its specific frequency and continues on its own specific course and trajectory.

We have attempted to detail for you the probable timeline and events considering the current trajectory position within the space-time wave of two particular dimensions, the Third and the Fifth Universal Dimensions. Thus we have tried to detail for you the current trajectory and most dominant future timeline for Third Dimensional Earth, as well as the current trajectory and most dominant future timeline for Fifth Dimensional Terra. What we have not discussed until now is something that holds mystery and is perhaps of great difficulty to grasp given your singular and linear view of time. So let us explore for a moment the concept of possible versus probable future timelines and events.

First of all, it needs to be understood that within each current dimensional space-time wave there are many possible and potential future timelines. You may know these loosely as "parallel" timelines, and a particular dimension can proceed upon any one of these parallel timelines or trajectories. Secondly, there are points at which these parallel timelines can overlap, and because of this it is also possible that there are alterations or sub divisions in the events on a particular parallel timeline. The dominant timeline trajectory can be altered or change course at these junctures, in as much as it can merge with and become a different possible or parallel timeline. These junctions in the space-time wave are similar to sublevels of a universal dimension since they form part of the universal dimension totality but are also independent and unique.

To recap thus far then, within a universal dimension space-time wave there are various possible timelines or futures. These possible timelines are like dimensional subdivisions, even if they are not the dominant timeline that is being manifested and despite the fact that a "possible" timeline in this state is never manifested in reality. The possible timelines exist parallel and alongside the dominant timeline, and they can merge with the dominant timeline at specific junctions to modify or become the timeline that is actualized into physical reality within the dimension. As such, possible timelines could be said to be the stuff that the dominant timeline is ultimately composed from, and they hold potential but cannot be actualized until they have merged with the dominant timeline of the space-time wave continuum. Parallel timelines can, at varying points, merge with and become the dominant timeline or they can drift off and dissipate never being manifested into physical reality.

These parallel timelines, or "possible" space-time wave trajectories, which have the potential to merge with the dominant timeline and become actualized, are known as possible futures. Possible futures can be mapped out, and for the most part they are identified by their parallel trajectory position, their intensity and their potential for actual manifestation into reality. When such a possible trajectory or subdivision timeline reaches a magnetic intensity and mass that outweighs all other parallel timelines within the space-time wave, at specific junctions it can merge with the "Now" and become dominant. When this happens it becomes the lead timeline, or probable future.

Once a possible future becomes a probable future, its electromagnetic properties and dominance make it the most likely timeline to be manifested into dimensional physicality using the particular dimension's physics of creation. In accord with this, the events found on the probable future timeline trajectory become the events most likely to manifest in the future. It is the events found on the current probable timeline trajectories that we have related to you in this book in attempting to describe the future of Third Dimensional Earth and the future of Fifth Dimensional Terra.

We have discussed in the past that within the higher sublevels of the Third Universal Dimension, in what has been called the Astral Planes, an array of experimentation is constantly underway with respect to your own reality manifestation. Moreover, in the Dreamscape within the Astral Planes of your dimension, your energetic body in conjunction with your Higher Self is endlessly analyzing and reevaluating your reality experiences, experimenting with new "possible" futures. Those possible futures with the strongest thought forms, greatest emotional intensity and best connection to your growth in the lifetime, karmic and otherwise, will tend to be the ones pulled forth and magnetized to the lower dimension for physical manifestation.

In similar fashion, this occurs with mass consciousness, so that the possible futures with the strongest thought forms, greatest intensity and most power to create growth opportunities for the greatest number are pulled into reality by merging with the dominant timeline and manifesting for the benefit of the entire physical realm. Your personal possible future will coincide and intersect with the dominant future timeline for the dimension, bringing you to meet the specific probable events that are available on the timeline. This occurs both in a personal way as well as en masse.

The concept of many possible futures and a dominant probable future that is mutable according to the many possible trajectories, which can intersect with it at any point, is perhaps difficult to understand since your view of time is singular and linear. In truth, time is actually a spiral wave and not a linear phenomenon. Because the timeline transpires in an endless spiral wave and is associated with space-time dimensional definition, it has no beginning and no end. Additionally, because of its spiral nature, specific coordinates along the timeline can be closely associated with each other, past and future. This can cause the phenomenon that has been noted with regard to historical repetition, which is based principally on close proximity of different time coordinates on the spiral timeline. It is quite accurate to say that certain periods in history have close proximity to others that may not be closely related in terms of sequential time. We would suggest that these close ties facilitate the energetic bonds that are the basis of karmic balancing, which can seem to symbolically or philosophically join one "historic" period with another.

It can further be said that "Now" is truly all that exists in terms of reality, that all potentiality already exists alongside reality and the "Now" also serves as a magnet for potentiality -- nourishment for the seed that is the "Now." Prediction and prophecy then are like explaining the Now through the taste of the fruit built around it. Ultimately, it is an analysis of the timeline spiral via the dominant probable timeline, based on all the possible trajectories built around it. This assumes that the timeline with the most content and dominance will be the dominant timeline and thus the probable future, with the events it contains most likely to manifest in reality based on the dominant timeline trajectory.

Returning to our analogy, Prophesy is like predicting the taste of a fruit by understanding the core of its existence. You experience the future just as you experience a peach picked recently from a tree. You are focused on the sensation of its taste, its color and its core, but it can also have various potential or possible events alter it along the way. As an example, it can bruise, be cut up, peeled or thrown away, with each possible future becoming its probable future if enacted. But its core remains a peach, and this continues in tact until the time it regenerates itself into a new tree that yields new fruit, should that potential be realized.

In many ways the Universe is designed in similar fashion. There is a core element of reality and potentiality that grows, acquires attributes and is manifested. Things befall it along the way altering it slightly, but ultimately at its core, if the trajectory remains dominant the events intrinsic in the probability are most likely the experience that will manifest and become its future.

Unknown to you, many are at a crossroad because they are Ascending at this time. You will not float off into space physically speaking however, and as you pass from the current physical incarnation you will discover that you are no longer trapped within the reincarnational cycles of Third Dimensional Earth. Instead, you will graduate to higher sublevels of the Third Dimension, the Astral Planes, in preparation for your potential regeneration through Ascension, much as the peach we have just described. That regeneration will occur on Fifth Dimensional Terra, and once incarnated there you will become vaguely aware of your past journey as well as the journey of your Soul. This awakening will happen via your Soul connection thanks to Fifth Dimensional genetic sensory attributes.

It must be understood that potentiality is closely linked to the most probable future trajectory of a species, a culture and a world. But this does not imply necessarily that the probable trajectory must continue unaltered on its course, and because of Free Will in your sector of the Universe and a myriad of possible or parallel timelines, change is always available and dynamic. It is a conceivable that a probable event can be altered by a new possible event that is part of a timeline that has merged with the dominant timeline to become the dominant course. This can mean that the events we have described, particularly the ones that are most challenging and least desirable, may be altered. It can also mean that those same events could turn out to be far more challenging than anything we have described. Such is the nature of a dynamic, mutable timeline as it reaches various coordinates and junctures.

Again, it is to be remembered that Ascension is a key mechanism for all Dimensions, all Galaxies and all Souls in the Universe. It is primarily through Ascension that entities are able to grow and cast off the burden of entrapment within a particular dimension. With respect to the manifestation of physical reality, if what you see around you is not to your liking you have the ability to work towards altering it through your own physical endeavors, thoughts and desires, changing the possible future trajectory by investing your energy in a different one. In a similar way, you have the ability to cast off endless incarnations in one dimension by raising your consciousness, thereby finding your own personal redemption through the process of Ascension.

In many ways, the Master Jesus, who as we said originally was intended to bring forth information concerning redemption, was in fact working just as those System Lords before him and after him towards an understanding of this universal mechanism. The importance of Ascension as a universal adaption to the growth of the individual Soul, the planet, the Solar System, the Galaxy and the Dimension cannot be over stressed.

Whether or not you decide to remain in the Third Universal Dimension and experience the events that are most probable given the current timeline trajectory or you decide to Ascend to incarnations on Fifth Dimensional Terra is a matter of great personal desire and choice. This journey, as always, is orchestrated at the highest level of the Soul in conjunction with each individual incarnate.

One thing however, remains constantly true. Your ambition is to raise your consciousness and improve the quality of your vibrational signature, a factor that will invite and entice you into becoming part of the evolutionary process of Ascension. Whether you recognize it or not, your ambition will come from a pull that compels you to return to your Source and meld the unique experiences of your consciousness with "All That Is" – God. It is this phenomenon that ensures your immortality and makes you a vital contributor at the highest levels to the continual expansion of what you know as the Universe and God. Your reunion with Source is and always will be the hallmark of your personal journey through time and space.

The End

Appendix

Abbreviated Past and Future Events on the Collapsing Timeline of Third Dimensional Earth

Year	Event
Approximately 250,000 BCE	The "Fall" of Human Angelic Fourth Dimensional Civilizations to Third Dimensional Reality during the last Grand Ascension period. Founding of Lumeria in the Pacific Lands of Mu. Event to become known as the "Fall" of the Angels in later world mythologies
Approximately 240,000 BCE To 13,000 BCE	Rise and Fall of Atlantis and the Atlantean World Civilization, with three major global cataclysms over the period leading to a final collapse of the Atlantean world by 13,000 BCE
50,000 to 13,000 BCE	Age of the Anunnaki; Founding of an advanced alien-sponsored colony in lower Mesopotamia; Colony deserted by its alien founders following war with Earth's Galactic Guardians fought in the Middle East, North Africa, parts of southwestern North America, South America and India about 13,000 BCE; Hindu epics such as the Mahabharata are based on these events
13,000 BCE to 10,000 BCE	Remnants of the Atlantean Civilization continue on via former Atlantean colonies in North and South America, Egypt, Eurasia and Northern Europe in limited form; Technologies and culture ultimately forgotten and destroyed by cataclysmic events leading to a second round of vast global flooding in 10,000 BCE (The great "Flood" of the Bible); True beginning of the "Modern Era"
5,000 BCE	Rise of the Mesopotamian, Egyptian, Chinese and other civilizations, primitive off shoots founded on the remnants of former highly advanced Atlantean, Anunnaki and Lumerian civilizations; Considered by historians to be the "start" of the current modern era
Approximately 1750 CE	Start of the next Grand Ascension Period culminating in 2012 and ending in approximately 2250

ABBREVIATED PAST AND FUTURE EVENTS ON THE
COLLAPSING TIMELINE OF THIRD DIMENSIONAL EARTH

Year	Event
1350's to 1850's CE	Implementation of the Earth Free Will Zone to block destructive alien influence decreed by the higher dimensional Galactic Council charged with protecting Earth's Human Angelic population from alien interference
1880's to 2000 CE	Rise and Fall of North American/US global power and dominance
1940's CE to Present Period	Agreements of cooperation concluded between various Off World Aliens and several world powers, particularly the US and later China
Late 1960's to early 1970's CE	Global agreements creating the Petro Dollar to ensure US economic superiority and create the US Military Industrial Complex to maintain US world dominance
Early to mid 1980's CE	Technological advances began via secret agreements with clandestine factions of the US government starts the weaponization of nature and the reengineering of global weather and natural patterns
Late 1990's to Mid 2010's CE	Diminishing of US dominance via secret government factions, polarization, faltering military adventures and vast economic stresses; Military Industrial Complex undertaking efforts to hide secret factions and global money flow coming to light in the late 1990's; Determination of several global powers to no longer use Petro Dollars; US secret factions began backing of various Terrorist organizations and Fundamentalist Islamic Groups to disrupt Middle East and North African nations in order to maintain political and economic dominance; Wide scale use of scalar and secret technologies for the weaponization of natural events such as weather and earthquakes; Polarization of American political process orchestrated to maintain political inaction

Timeline Collapse & Universal Ascension

Year	Event
2011 CE	Earthquake off the coast of Japan (Fukushima) causes Tsunami that is an un-natural "natural" event meant as a warning from China to Japan to end close ties with the US and join the Chinese sphere of influence in all matters
2012 CE	Peak point of the current Ascension period; Increasing Energetic forces and photon energies responsible for transforming the vibrational patterns of the Solar System until 2012 began to decrease; Beginning of the collapse of the current Third Dimensional timeline and emergence of the next Third Dimensional timeline through the process of Ascension
Mid 2010's to 2017 CE	More nations participate in BRIC alliances (Alliances between Russia and China) to bypass the dollar and eliminate global Petro Dollar use; Escalating conflicts in the Middle East turning global
Late 2010's CE	US Economic and Dollar Collapse continues the economic turmoil that began in 2008
Late 2010's to early 2020's CE	All out war in the Middle East erupts based on turmoil that began there in 2015; All out war further exacerbates dire US and Western economic turmoil, but is used politically to distract public; Russia withdraws from major alliances to protect itself and its sphere and remains isolated and intact, only secretly involved in global conflict
2017 through 2025 CE	World War III (though not designated as such until early 2020); Worldwide conflicts; Global weather pattern shift dramatically with droughts, flooding and natural disasters caused by inter planetary and space-time wave shifts; Cataclysmic unknown electrical "lightening"

ABBREVIATED PAST AND FUTURE EVENTS ON THE
COLLAPSING TIMELINE OF THIRD DIMENSIONAL EARTH

Year	Event
2017 through 2025 CE- continues	charges emanate from the Earth as the planet attempts to rebalance the electromagnetic grid
Early 2020's CE	The great Earthquake of North Central Japan unleashes vast tectonic movement throughout the Pacific; Parts of Japan are submerged; Coastlines of Hawaii, California to Baja Mexico flooded; Earthquake is a US retaliation for Japan's new secret agreements and cooperation with China
Early to Mid 2020's CE	New Madrid fault line is triggered by combined global tectonic activity and unnatural manipulation causing major earthquake that further triggers new massive activity in the Yellow Stone Caldera; North American cataclysms ensued including the short-term reversal of the Mississippi River and substantial flooding of portions of Louisiana, Mississippi, Alabama, Texas, Florida, Arkansas, Iowa, Missouri and Illinois, among others; Police State tactics and Martial Law implemented throughout the US
Early to Mid 2020's CE	Use of Nuclear Weapons in the Middle East and North western Africa; Annihilation of the Middle East and major destruction of cities throughout the region; Nuclear incidences in European cities as well, including Paris and Rome; Annihilation of the Vatican Seat and collapse of the Catholic Church
2025 to late 2020's CE	Disintegration and continuing collapse of US Federal Authority through loss of war, political and economic collapse; American states band together loosely into regional state alliances in defiance of US Federal government; Regions form state militias, self governance and their own currencies to ensure survival

Year	Event
2025 to 2050's CE	Dramatic downturn in Solar activity due to magnetic pole wobble and prior geo reengineering of global weather patterns and the planet's atmosphere; Mini ice age begins in the Northern hemisphere leading to severe famines through 2050
Early 2030's CE	Complete US economic collapse leads to final collapse of US Federal government following the siege of Washington DC; Nuclear patriot-terrorist incidences in several major US cities; Lawlessness reigns in certain US regions leading to a new US Civil War between the "haves" and "have-nots"
2030's to 2050's CE	Increasing hostility between regional State unions and lawless ex-states; Mass relocations of US populations; Military alliances made between stronger regional unions with China and Russia; US Civil War incursions into Canada and Mexico trigger those countries to call on foreign military assistance
2050 to 2150's	Russian led Eurasian Enlightenment and Renaissance, effectively making Russia and Eurasia the leading cultural, economic and political focal point in the world for nearly a century; Russia is credited with being the "Savior" of the world through preservation and continuation of global civilization following disintegration of geo political scene after World War III
2055 to 2080's CE	Citing need for police action in lawless areas of the old US, China invades Southern and Southwestern US territories through Mexico, while Russia invades the Midwest and ex Plain States from Canada; Major regions of the US not formally regionalized and aligned are colonized by Russia in the North and China in the South of the former US

ABBREVIATED PAST AND FUTURE EVENTS ON THE
COLLAPSING TIMELINE OF THIRD DIMENSIONAL EARTH

Year	Event
2569 CE	Massive planetary cataclysm coming from off world destroys all final vestiges of the current Third Dimensional civilization, resetting the globe and returning what is left of mankind to the Stone Age to begin anew; Third Dimensional timeline is officially reset for new Human Angelic Incarnations

Other Essence Path Books

What is the relevance of 2012, is Armageddon possible and is there really an Anti-Christ?

"The 'End-Time' tales of woe and foreboding concerning 2012 that you have heard are only relevant in that they generate fear, which closes you off from the higher vibrational energies seeking to activate your DNA and cellular structure at this time. From our perspective this is far from the end, but rather a truly miraculous turning point for mankind, Earth and the entire Solar System. Your world finds itself in a state of transformation, a transition related to the collapse of your current time line and your emergence into a higher universal vibration and new dimensional reality. It is through this process, known as Ascension, that every individual Soul, Earth itself and all worlds in the universe evolve. In that regard, you are living at an extraordinary moment indeed."

This book, "The System Lords and the Twelve Dimensions: *New Revelations Concerning the Dimensional Shift of 2012-2250 and the Evolution of Human Angelics*" builds on themes began in "Discovering Your Essence Path," Book One and Book Two of the Essence Path series, providing us with a more complete analysis of coming Earth changes, the reasons an intensification of energy is coming from the Galactic core and altering our Solar System at this time, the collapse of our dimensional time line, the evolution of our DNA, the structure of the multi-dimensional universe and how the vibrational quality of our beliefs, emotions, thoughts and choices combine to raise our cellular resonance. Book Three also provides an in depth examination of Soul polarity, so-called "alien" exchanges, what to expect in the coming Golden Age and an overview of our dimension's interaction with Ninth Dimensional System Lords, Avatars who return periodically to our world and incarnate in human form to facilitate momentous leaps in consciousness like the one we are now experiencing-a time that promises to be one of the most monumental periods in the history of the planet.

a FORETHOUGHT PUBLISHING *book*

www. ESSENCE*path*.com

What do Fear and Faith have to do with your Physical Reality?...

"...And what's all this talk about a new age of peace, harmony and happiness? It is insight, and, in many cases, guidance related to the understanding that within the current synchronicity, where physical materialization of reality is sped-up, a world based on Faith (not the religious kind, but the kind that accepts that life's events have a purpose orchestrated and understood by your soul if not by your conscious waking self) will attract events and situations of a like kind. But a world based on your Fear will attract into it, faster than ever before, exactly what is feared. More and more, your predisposition for a lifetime wrought with endless challenge, or a life filled with peace, harmony and happiness, is directly related to whether you are aligned vibrationally with the frequency of Fear or Faith."

This book, "Fear, Faith and Physical Reality," Book Two from the "DISCOVERING YOUR ESSENCE PATH" series, builds on the themes began in Book One providing a more complete analysis of the coming vibrational changes, description of the coming emergence of 4th dimension attributes within the 3rd dimension, the nature of universal dimensional overlap, the polarity of belief, emotion and thought and your relationship to the manifestation of your personal reality. Book Two also examines further the reasons mastering Fear and maintaining Faith by understanding the purpose of your Higher Self during the lifetime is paramount to a successful life mission, and how your ability to carry light (en-"lighten"-ment) at the cellular level -- a component of the vibrational signature that identifies your Soul throughout the universe -- is being increased exponentially as we approach one of the most transforming periods in Earth's history.

Almost a decade of telepathic work communicating with a group of entities that collectively have identified themselves as "Samuel" has led to the breakthrough information compiled in the "DISCOVERING YOUR ESSENCE PATH" series. Book Two, "Fear, Faith and Physical Reality" continues your journey to higher levels of spiritual guidance through the understanding of your Essence.

a FORETHOUGHT PUBLISHING *book*

www. ESSENCE*path*.com

When it comes to the Dance of Life, is your path Essence driven?

"Life can truly be seen as a dance. It is your Higher Self that is leading this dance, holding you up as you guide across the ballroom floor. When you are in touch with and accepting of your Higher Self's lead, you enter into the flow of the dance and your life is smooth and seemingly effortless. But when you refuse the lead of your Higher Self, distracted by fear and your Ego, you stumble and fall out of sync...Continue to resist, and the pull will be so great as to knock you to the ground. In metaphysical or symbolic terms, this is the dance of life."

This book, "YOUR ESSENCE PATH AND OTHER QUINTESSENTIAL PHENOMENA," Book One from the "DISCOVERING YOUR ESSENCE PATH" series, builds the foundation for a unique understanding of the interaction between your Higher Self and your physically-bound self. ESSENCE PATH provides the knowledge and techniques you need to begin the discovery of your Essence, or Soul, path. In addition, Book One explores the nature of our causal reality and its relationship to thought, feeling and the fabric of life, the multi-dimensional nature of your Soul and its journey, the truth about higher guidance in the 3rd Dimensional realm, the world altering energetic changes we are facing and relevance those changes will have to our lives, how dreams and the astral state contribute to your reality, and the reasons why increasing your energetic vibration through higher consciousness is particularly important as we fast approach the monumental 2012 time period.

Almost a decade of telepathic work communicating with a group of entities that collectively have identified themselves as "Samuel" has led to the breakthrough information compiled in the "Discovering Your Essence Path" series. Book One, "Your Essence Path and Other Quintessential Phenomena" begins your journey to a new level of higher guidance and understanding of your Essence.

a FORETHOUGHT PUBLISHING *book*

www. ESSENCE*path*.com

Made in the USA
Lexington, KY
05 August 2016